Prais... ...mple

"This wonderful evocation of Dion Fortune's esoteric novels offers initiatory and practical pathways to the neophyte and reader!"
—Caitlín & John Matthews, authors of *The Lost Book of the Grail* and *Walkers Between the Worlds*

"'*The Mystical Qabalah* gives the theory,' Dion Fortune wrote, 'but my novels give the practice.' In *The Keys to the Temple*, Penny Billington and Ian Rees take her at her word, and unpack the rich treasury of practical Qabalistic magic to be found in Fortune's occult novels. It's a bravura performance, not to be missed by anyone interested in the Western Mystery Tradition."
—John Michael Greer, author of *The Celtic Golden Dawn*

"At the height of her powers as an occult teacher, Dion Fortune began to use fiction as a means of instruction.... Penny Billington and Ian Rees now take things a step further with a detailed analysis of the novels and their characters as a means of helping the reader to cross the bridge to personal experience. Highly recommended."
—Gareth Knight, author of *The Occult Fiction of Dion Fortune*, *Dion Fortune's Magical Battle of Britain*, and *Dion Fortune's Rites of Isis and of Pan*

"Not only is *The Keys to the Temple* excellent for fans of Dion Fortune's work, but it is also a necessary book for all who have an interest in uncovering the deeper aspects of the Western Mystery Tradition and its roots in Qabalah."
—Will Parfitt, author of *The Complete Guide to the Kabbalah*, *Kabbalah For Life*, and *Psychosynthesis: The Elements and Beyond*

"We shall be recommending *The Keys to the Temple* to students in the Servants of the Light School. This important book clearly demonstrates how Dion Fortune's fiction was part of her strategy to practically teach principles and initiatory magical techniques that are theoretically presented in her *Mystical Qabalah*. It is very exciting to see these teachings being so clearly made available by Penny Billington and Ian Rees. This book is *a must-read* for anyone interested in Dion Fortune's work or for those working practically in the esoteric and magical tradition she shaped."

—Steven Critchley, PhD, Assistant Director of Studies,
Servants of the Light

THE
KEYS
TO THE
TEMPLE

About the Authors

Penny Billington is a Druid speaker and author and is active in the Order of Bards, Ovates & Druids, having edited their magazine, *Touchstone*, for fifteen years. She regularly runs workshops, organises rituals, and gives lectures and has also authored a Druid Detective series of novels. She resides in Somerset, England. Visit her online at www.penny billington.co.uk. Author photo by Sue Ball.

Ian Rees is a psycho-spiritual psychotherapist practicing in Glastonbury, Somerset, United Kingdom. He has been a therapist for twenty years and spent ten years before that working in probation work and social work. He designed MA programs and taught at the Karuna Institute in Devon from 1999 to 2009. Since 2009 he has concentrated on developing and presenting workshops for the Annwn Foundation. Author photo by Alan Hudson.

THE
KEYS
TO THE
TEMPLE

Unlocking **Dion Fortune's** Mystical
Qabalah Through Her Occult Novels

PENNY BILLINGTON
IAN REES

Llewellyn Publications
Woodbury, Minnesota

First Edition
First Printing, 2017

Cover design: Kevin R. Brown
Interior art: Llewellyn Art Department

Interior art from original designs by Ian Rees©, supplied as original artwork by Arthur Billington

Llewellyn Publications is a registered trademark of Llewellyn Worldwide Ltd.

Library of Congress Cataloging-in-Publication Data (Pending)
ISBN: 978-0-7387-5066-8

Llewellyn Publications
A Division of Llewellyn Worldwide Ltd.
2143 Wooddale Drive
Woodbury, MN 55125-2989
www.llewellyn.com

Printed in the United States of America

Other Books by Penny Billington

The Wisdom of Birch, Oak, and Yew
(Llewellyn, 2015)

The Path of Druidry
(Llewellyn, 2011)

To Aly and Arthur, who also hold the keys

We live in the midst of invisible forces whose effects alone we perceive.
We move among invisible forms whose actions we very often
do not perceive at all, though we may be profoundly affected by them.
—Dion Fortune, *Psychic Self-Defence*

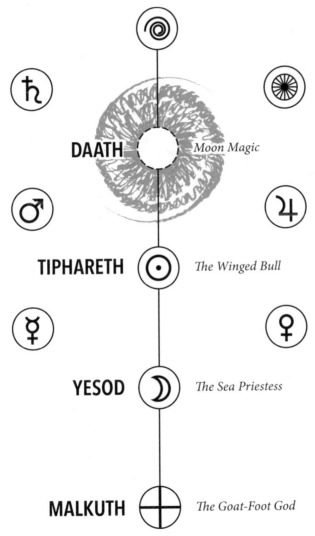

DAATH *Moon Magic*

TIPHARETH *The Winged Bull*

YESOD *The Sea Priestess*

MALKUTH *The Goat-Foot God*

Dion Fortune's Books on the Tree of Life

The authors and publishers wish to thank the Society of the Inner Light for permission to reproduce copyrighted material from the following books by Dion Fortune:

Esoteric Orders and Their Work & The Training and Work of an Initiate
Moon Magic
Psychic Self-Defence
The Goat-Foot God
The Sea Priestess
The Winged Bull

Disclaimer

Contents

List of Figures xiii

Introduction 1

Book Synopses 5

Unlocking The Mystical Qabalah *13*

SECTION 1: LEAVING HOME

1. *The Goat-Foot God:* Power of Nature 29

2. Entering Malkuth and *The Goat-Foot God* 41

3. *The Sea Priestess:* Currents and Rhythms 51

4. Yesod and *The Sea Priestess:* Making a Foundation 61

5. *The Winged Bull* and the Dance of Relationship 73

6. Tiphareth and *The Winged Bull* 85

7. *Moon Magic:* The Depths and the Heights 95

8. Daath and *Moon Magic* 107

SECTION 2: FOLLOWING

9. The Work of Change 121

10. First Steps on the Path 131

11. The Emotional Connection 141

12. Thresholds, Guardians, and Obstacles 155

13. Magical Space 165

14. The Mentor and the Threefold Way 175

SECTION 3: CROSSING THE BRIDGE

15. Magical Work: Guidelines and Boundaries 189

16. The Qabalah Applied 199

17. Working with Malkuth and *The Goat-Foot God* 209

18. Working with Yesod and *The Sea Priestess* 221

19. Working with Tiphareth and *The Winged Bull* 233

20. Working with Daath and *Moon Magic* 245

Conclusion 259

Bibliography 263

Acknowledgments 265

Figures

1. The Path from Malkuth to Yesod 16

2. The Spinning Wheel of Yesod, Hod, and Netzach 18

3. The Underworld and Alchemical Paths from Malkuth to Tiphareth 19

4. The Wheel of Stillness 21

5. The Three Paths up to Daath 22

6. The Supernal Triangle 23

7. The Completed Tree of Life 25

Introduction

Writers will put things into a novel that they daren't put in sober prose, where you have to dot the I's and cross the T's.[1]

Dion Fortune (1890–1946) was one of the most significant occultists of the twentieth century and is still considered to be a major influence on the current Western Mystery Tradition. She was one of a small band of people who brought the ancient mysteries out of obscurity and arcane ritual and made them relevant to the modern day and the issues we now face. She did this by combining an understanding of psychology with the mystical practices of the Qabalah and suggesting practices and methods that can be applied to give direct experience of inner realities.

The Qabalah is a spiritual system that has been practiced secretly in Europe since at least the twelfth century, though it draws on deep roots within Judeo-Christian tradition. In particular, it draws on the myth of Genesis, the story of Adam and Eve and their expulsion from the Garden of Eden through having eaten the fruit of the Tree of the Knowledge of Good and Evil. The Qabalah is based around the image of the other tree in that myth, the Tree of Life. This Tree is an image and diagram that enables us to explore the inner aspects of our own nature and of the world and in that process to come into communion with a fuller, deeper life.

---

1. Dion Fortune, *The Goat-Foot God* (York Beach, ME: Samuel Weiser, 1999), 33.

Dion Fortune's way of making this tradition more available to people outside her private occult group was unusual: she wrote one of the first modern accounts of the Tree of Life and the system of the Qabalah that makes ancient mythology and the mysteries behind them come to life here and now. She also wrote a series of novels that on one level can be read as slightly unusual romance novels but on a deeper level contain key images and patterns from those mysteries that speak to our subconscious and, if consciously related to, bring us into a deeper experience of our life and being.

In the beginning of the 1998 edition of her book *The Sea Priestess*, Fortune says this about the novels and the Qabalah:

> It is because my novels are packed with such things as these (symbolism directed to the subconscious) that I want my students to take them seriously. The 'Mystical Qabalah' gives the theory, but the novels give the practice. Those who read the novels without having studied the 'Qabalah' will get hints and a stimulus to their subconscious. Those who study the Qabalah without reading the novels will get an interesting intellectual jig-saw puzzle to play with; but those who study the 'Mystical Qabalah' with the help of the novels get the keys of the Temple put into their hands. As Our Lord said: "Know ye not that your body is the temple of the Holy Ghost?"[2]

This is a bold claim, and those who try to follow her formula in the search for the keys have a number of obstacles to address. They need to find a way to create relationship between

- a book of mystical theory that, while well and clearly written, can at times feel dry;
- a series of stories that are concerned with twentieth-century relationships between men and women; and
- evocative and potent ancient images.

2. Dion Fortune, *The Sea Priestess* (London: Society of the Inner Light, 1998).

Additionally there is that cryptic hint about the involvement of the body and the descent of the Holy Ghost into the body.

This book is designed to overcome these obstacles, to explain and make clear the system of the Qabalah, to show how the stories and images fit into it, and to provide a practical workbook of exercises that will work with the body and senses so that the inner realities are directly experienced.

The key novels for this study are *The Goat-Foot God, The Sea Priestess, The Winged Bull,* and *Moon Magic.* They are Qabalistic novels: not only is Fortune using images from the ancient mysteries, but the story and images of each book are aligned with an aspect of the Tree of Life, which in turn points to a pivotal process in inner development.

A particular sequence of inner development is outlined in every novel, beginning with the first step on the path of initiation: the movement from being externally directed and lost in desires and fears of past and future to gaining a direct sense of being present in the body in the world just now. This is called entering the kingdom, or entering *Malkuth,* and the first book in the sequence, *The Goat-Foot God,* is concerned with this step.

The second step arises from this anchored and present sense of being connected to both world and body; it involves exploring the pool of subjectivity and inner life that then opens up. This asks us to explore our vitality and images of self and world by mastering the art of the embodied imagination. This is called making a foundation, or *Yesod,* and the book that addresses this issue is *The Sea Priestess.*

The third step is the movement through the pool of subjective life, past a barrier, called the *veil Paroketh,* that is formed by the subliminal inner dialogue between thought, emotion, and memory. This constant dialogue acts as a spinning wheel that causes us to interpret all current experience in terms of the past and seeks to stop us from penetrating more deeply into inner life. As we pass this veil, we enter into a state of balance, feel centred, and start to be able to mediate between inner and outer worlds. This sense of heart and centre is called *Tiphareth* by the Qabalists, and the book addressing this is *The Winged Bull.*

The fourth major step that is considered in this schema is the movement from the sense of balance and centre into alignment with the deeper aspects of our nature. This opens us to capacities of clarity and love that arise from the root of our being—a dynamic stillness that is both receptive and creative. This movement into mystery is called by the Qabalists *Daath*, the knowing of unknowing, and is the place where all the opposites of self and life find rest and renewal. The book that addresses this process is *Moon Magic*.

The Tree of Life, the organising principle behind the novels, is said to be both a glyph of the soul and the inner structure of the universe: in the same way, the characters in the novels teach us both about aspects of our own nature and about the world around us.

Each novel is concerned with the relationship between a man and a woman who are guided by a mentor to find their way from experiences of deprivation and frustration into a union that is fruitful and alive, though not necessarily conventional.

They all begin with the situation of a man who simultaneously represents cultural attitudes to maleness and the rational and outer aspect of our personality, who meets a woman who is both archetypal womanhood and the feminine, or anima, aspect of the soul. These two then enter a mystery drama that enables the four steps of the Tree of Life to be taken, to arrive at a consummation that resolves the situation described at the beginning of the novel.

This book is organised in such a way as to enable you to directly discover and apply the keys of the temple to your life and circumstances. Section one describes the essentials of the formula, and then each of the four books is analysed in detail and aligned with the Tree of Life. Section two identifies the major themes running through the book, and finally section three gives a series of practices and exercises that bring the keys of the temple into operation.

Book Synopses

The Goat-Foot God

Principal Characters:

The Man	Hugh Paston, a wealthy man living in Kensington
The Woman	Mona Wilton, an artistic young woman living in bohemian poverty
The Mentor	Jelkes, an old bookseller, a failed Jesuit priest, and a student of occultism

Hugh Paston is depressed and lost, having just buried his wife. She died in a car crash with his best friend as they were on their way back from an extramarital liaison.

Hugh finds himself unable to stay in his home and district. He walks across London from the smart end of the city into the seedier and unknown places, letting his body's instincts lead him. He finds Jelkes's bookshop there, and immerses himself in novels of black magic and then more mythologically oriented books. He decides he wants to revive the cult of Pan and employs an artist, Mona Wilton, and Jelkes, the bookseller, to help him find and restore an old monastery. Having found Monks Farm, an old abbey with a bad reputation, Hugh and Mona set about renewing it. In the process, they come into psychic communion with Ambrosius, a medieval abbot who turns out to have been a previous incarnation of Hugh Paston.

Hugh and Mona start to embrace the mysteries of Pan through meditation and ritual. They address the banishing of Pan in the Christian Middle Ages, release the souls of dead monks who are earthbound in Monks Farm, and awaken the pagan aspects of their own soul. Hugh's family attempts to get him committed in order to control his money, but by integrating the figure of Ambrosius within him he prevents this.

The book concludes with Hugh and Mona marrying and performing a ritual that summons the god Pan to bless their marriage and lives.

The Sea Priestess

Principal Characters:

The Man	Wilfred Maxwell, an asthmatic estate agent living reluctantly with his mother and sister
The Woman	Vivien Le Fay Morgan, a minor adept of the Western Mystery Tradition
The Mentor	The Priest of the Moon, an inner plane teacher
Molly Coke	Wilfred's secretary

Wilfred is an estate agent who lives in a seaside town with his mother and sister and is frustrated and trapped in a provincial life. At the beginning of the book he suffers a significant asthma attack, and while recuperating begins to commune with the moon and awaken his innate psychism. He continues this communion and discovers some stables at the bottom of his garden in which he makes his home. As he installs himself in the stables, he finds a hidden river that runs down to the sea, and this deepens his contemplations.

He receives a letter from a client of his firm, Vivien Le Fay Morgan, who is looking for a property in his area. She turns out to be a glamorous and mysterious woman who has been trained in the mysteries by an inner plane teacher, the Priest of the Moon, but who needs Wilfred's help in order to take her next step (in terms of the Qabalistic schema we are working with, this is from step three to step four, from Tiphareth to Daath).

Together they find and renovate a sea fort, creating it as a temple of the sea mysteries, which are concerned with fertility at all levels and derive ultimately from the lost continent of Atlantis. Vivien teaches Wilfred the ways of these mysteries, causing him to fall in love with her, which enables her to create the magical image of her deeper nature. In the course of this, he discovers his artistic side and, by communing with the sea and the moon, paints extraordinary murals that depict aspects of the sea cult. He recovers memories of a past life in which Vivien was a sea priestess from Atlantis who came to Britain to sacrifice a young man to the sea; he recalls that he was the sacrifice that was offered to the sea gods. Their relationship concludes in a ritual in which the sea gods are invoked; Vivien embodies the Goddess while Wilfred embodies the masculine principle who gives his life energy to her. In the ritual, the Priest of the Moon overshadows him and becomes his teacher. At the height of the ritual, Vivien vanishes into the sea and is not seen again.

The book concludes with Wilfred returning to his town brokenhearted and, through a strange combination of circumstances, marrying Molly, his secretary, who we discover has always been in love with him. Vivien has left some jewellery to be given to Wilfred's wife. In the box of jewellery, Molly finds a letter that explains the work Vivien did with Wilfred and outlines a training through which Molly can become a priestess and make a true marriage with Wilfred. She does so, and the book concludes with a ritual between Wilfred and Molly in which they act as priest and priestess and find fulfilment.

The Winged Bull

Principal Characters:

The Man	Ted Murchison, an ex-army officer who fought in the Great War and cannot find his way in civilian life
The Woman	Ursula Brangwyn, a hidden priestess and initiate of the mysteries of the Winged Bull
The Mentor	Colonel Brangwyn, Ted Murchison's commander in the Great War and an occult initiate
Hugo Astley	A black magician
Frank Fouldes	Hugo's disciple

The novel begins with Ted Murchison walking in the London fog outside the British Museum. In a powerfully evocative scene, the fog rolls into the museum, blurring the boundaries between the everyday and the mysterious world, and he has an encounter with one of the winged bulls of Babylon, called the gatekeeper of the gods. The bull connects him to deeper possibilities of being, and he wanders into the museum communing with the images of the gods found there and feeling the life within them. He emerges feeling as if he is at the beginning of creation. He is inspired and shouts into the night, "Evoe, Iacchus! Io Pan, Pan! Io Pan!"[3] A voice, replying, turns out to be his old commander Colonel Brangwyn, who offers him a job to take part in an experiment involving his sister, Ursula. She was involved in an occult working that went wrong and as a result is susceptible to the manipulations of black magician Hugo Astley and his acolyte Frank Fouldes. The occult operation Brangwyn plans is the Mass of the Winged Bull, of male and female, spirit and matter, in an alchemical marriage.

Ted agrees, going with Brangwyn to his house, which is bigger and more beautiful on the inside than the outside, and enters into a secret life in which he learns to work with Ursula Brangwyn in ritual. He is

---

3. Dion Fortune, *The Winged Bull* (London: SIL Trading Ltd., 1998), 12.

both attracted to and repelled by her, and a process unfolds in which she is passive on outer levels but active on inner levels, opening up the inner ways to him. They perform solar-based rituals in which she is the green earth and he is the sun, but their relationship is characterised by ambivalence and friction.

Whilst Ursula, in a state of passivity, is taken by the black magician, who wishes to use her in a degraded version of the Mass of the Winged Bull, Ted makes contact with Hugo Astley and pretends to double-cross Brangwyn, thereby finding Ursula, who is washing Hugo's front doorstep as a spiritual discipline. Ursula challenges Ted about betraying her brother and walks off. In a moment of deep affection, he finishes her job for her, which has the effect of opening her heart.

The connection between them flowers in the midst of the black magic ritual, the Mass of the Bull, in which Ursula is cast as the woman who is the living altar and who is to be impregnated by Fouldes whilst Murchison is tied to a cross overlooking the altar. At the height of the ritual, the room is plunged into a darkness in which polarities shift. Ursula rouses herself from passivity and frees Ted from the cross, and together they go deeper into the building into a small room where they cannot be reached and they come into a deep sense of intimacy. The black magician cannot stand against their united wills and they are freed.

On returning to the outside world, their ambivalence reappears and they separate, Ursula going to Wales and Ted planning to take a job in Alexandria. He does one last job for Brangwyn, which is to find Ursula a home. This is an old farmhouse in East Anglia that had been the only place where he had felt happy as a child, renovating and creating it. In the course of his moving her in, Ursula speaks to him without reserve or ambivalence, in a sense revealing herself as the Priestess of the Winged Bull and offering to initiate him. The book ends with their intention to mate on all levels.

Moon Magic

Principal Characters:

The Man	Rupert Malcolm, a consultant physician at the top of his profession married to a sick wife who cannot bear him; he is profoundly frustrated with his life
The Woman and Mentor	Lilith Le Fay, a greater adept of the mysteries; the same figure we met in *The Sea Priestess* (called there Vivien Le Fay Morgan) but now having taken her next step of development
The Concealed Mentor	The goddess Isis

The book begins from the viewpoint of Rupert Malcolm. We meet him as he leaves a graduation ceremony at his teaching hospital, stripping off his robes to walk along London's Victoria Embankment and contemplate the River Thames. As he stands on a bridge, he considers his life and wishes it to be otherwise, fantasising that he would have been happier if he had run away to sea. He remembers a series of dreams he had in which a woman in a broad-brimmed hat and a long cloak led him through misty seascapes, and he actually spots the "dream woman" walking ahead of him. He follows her along the Embankment but loses her at a crossing, then each night afterward he visualises following her before falling asleep and finds a great sense of peace in the practice.

He encounters the dream woman again one night and follows her across the bridge to her home, a chapel directly across the river from his lodgings. He tries to enter the chapel, but she challenges him and asks him to leave. His fascination with her deepens: he visualises entering the chapel and them being together. He becomes more and more connected both to her and to his inner life. This section of the book comes to a dramatic end when the dream woman walks into his office, precipitating a crisis, and takes him back to the chapel.

The second section of the book is told from the point of view of Lilith Le Fay. We learn that she is a priestess of the cult of the Black Isis, and she describes the art and practice of magic to us. We accompany her as she finds the chapel that will be her temple, renovates it, creates the inner temple, and invites the presence of the Goddess into it.

The story catches up with Rupert as Lilith trains him to be a priest of the Black Isis. We learn that in a past life he had been a sacrificial priest as a penance for a crime he committed and that Lilith wishes him to work with her in order bring the potency of the Black Isis back into the world. They work together building the charge between them until Rupert becomes a priest who can match Lilith—there is a critical moment in his private life when his wife dies, and he is freed—not to be her lover but to be her priest. The novel ends with them experiencing a union that embraces and supersedes the unions touched on in the previous books.

Unlocking *The Mystical Qabalah*

The Tree of Life is central to understanding the work of Dion Fortune. It is the master mandala around which all her work is organised, and her book *The Mystical Qabalah* is one of the three keys to the temple. However, when most people encounter this book, they are confronted by a seemingly dense text with long lists of apparently unrelated facts: the idea that this text is linked with the vivid imagery and dynamism of the novels can be difficult to understand. We need therefore to find a way of unlocking *The Mystical Qabalah* to understand its value and potential.

The Qabalah is one of the underground mystical traditions of the West. It arose out of Jewish mysticism, appearing in Provence in the eleventh century when a book called the *Sefer Bahir*, or *Book of Light*, was studied by small groups of mystical scholars. This book is an inner commentary on the book of Genesis, focusing in particular on the myth of the Garden of Eden, which represents a state of communion between human beings and the Divine. In this myth Adam and Eve eat of the Tree of the Knowledge of Good and Evil and are cast out into the world of separation. The Tree of Life is the other Tree, planted in the midst of the Garden; if we eat of its fruit, we return to the Garden, finding our true home and restoring communion between human beings and divinity.

The Tree of Life was originally depicted in naturalistic form but later was developed into a geometric form of ten circles connected by twenty-two lines, and it became the focus of an entire spiritual tradition studied by both Jews and Christians. Dion Fortune was one of the first teachers to make it available in a form that modern people could use. She approached it through the dual lenses of Jungian psychology and the ancient mystery tradition, taking ancient mythology and applying it to the Tree to the mutual enrichment of both.

In writing about this approach, Ernest Butler, Dion Fortune's pupil, described the Tree of Life as "the mighty, all-embracing glyph of the universe and the soul of man."[4] He likened it to the Rosetta Stone, and by considering what that means, we will gain some understanding of how to approach the Tree. The Rosetta Stone is a stone tablet that contains a decree from the Pharaoh in three languages: hieroglyphs, the ancient script of Egypt; the Demotic, or everyday, script; and Greek. At the time of its discovery the understanding of hieroglyphs had been lost, but through working with the tablet and the other two languages the key was found and thus all the wisdom and beauty of ancient Egyptian culture was revealed to us. The actual text is not very important, being a purely administrative decree, but the act of bridging that it enables is essential. Ernest Butler went on to say, "It is essential to realise, however, that the Tree is not a map of the undiscovered country of either the soul of man or the universe in which he lives, but is rather a diagram of the mutual relationship of the underlying forces of both."[5]

The key point being made here is that the Tree of Life is a method and model that enables us to create relationship between the deep places of our soul and the depths of the universe. The diagram of the Tree gives us a skeleton to work with, to bring it to life within us, so that ultimately it becomes a living presence in our hearts. The practice of working with the Tree is referred to in the book of Ezekiel in the Vi-

---

4. Ernest Butler, *The Magician: His Training and Work* (London: Aquarian Press, 1963), 32.

5. Ibid., 30.

sion of the Valley of Dry Bones, when the prophet is asked to prophesy over the dry bones; as he does, breath enters the bones and they come to life. In effect, we sit with the diagram of the Tree and place our breath and vision upon it so that it comes to life.

What comes to life is the image of the Tree of Life: of a tree growing from the earth, embracing the moon, planets, sun, and stars. It holds within it an intention to bring all the elements of our inner and outer universes together so that there is an experience of a unity that is greater than the sum of its parts. The ten elements of the Tree are called *sephiroth* (singular: *sephirah*), or spheres, and represent aspects of life and consciousness.

The creation of our tree begins in the place before the Tree grows, the *Qliphoth*—the world without meaning and centre. The word means "shells," and we experience it when we find ourselves in the wasteland of ancient tradition, the dry land without water, feeling hollow and holding only a heap of broken images. To consciously experience this is very difficult, but knowing it as a *felt* experience, of aridity and the worthlessness of material achievements, is a starting point, the beginning of connection to the living Tree. This is the place at which the heroes of the four books begin, and it is our own starting position.

The longing for a deeper or more fulfilling life brings us into a condition the Qabalists called *Malkuth*, the kingdom. Malkuth is the first sephirah, or sphere, of the Tree linked to the earth and the body, a place of rooting and grounding and the anchor for all that follows. As we connect to our body and senses, we create a vessel of containment within which the rest of the work can arise. This moment-by-moment awareness of our body and its relationship with the outer world creates the beginnings of a sense of inner sovereignty and capacity to take possession of both our inner kingdom and our place in the world.

As we start to create this sense of being anchored, grounded, and rooted, we discover things about the internal and external worlds and the relationship between them. We begin to relate to interiority, to dream and memory, to image, and to the flow of our life force and sexuality. We start to connect to the sphere of the moon called in Hebrew

Yesod, the foundation of life. This sephirah represents our unconscious and preconscious self; it is also called the "treasure house of images" and is the storehouse of all our memories. Yesod contains the image of our self and the image of the world we live in and is often imagined as a pool that can be still or turbulent, clear or filled with imagery.

The journey into this place is described as the descent into the underworld (figure 1).

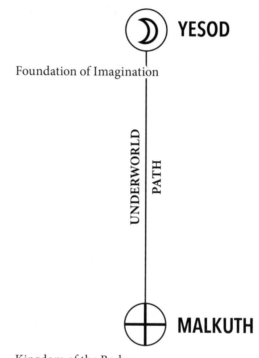

Figure 1: The Path from Malkuth to Yesod

As we become more proficient in relating to these aspects of life and being, we start to become aware of their interplay in the world. We gradually notice when there is a feeling of being grounded or anchored in the world around us, and the flow of life energy, sexuality, and the power of images. We notice the power of ideas and emotions.

As we do this inwardly and outwardly, we create paths of connection between these aspects of our nature and start to grow our tree.

Until we do that, however, these energies of Mercury, Venus, and the Moon—or thought, emotion, and unconscious memory—form a spinning wheel that keeps our attention trapped in the past: in a place of need, resentment, and future fear (figure 2). These entangled energies develop considerable momentum over the course of a life. They are a major barrier to the process of transformation and constitute the matter that needs to be transformed. In each of the heroes of the books, we see these energies built deeply into the structure of their personalities.

As we work later with the exercises of section three, the sense of anchoring into the body and of becoming aware of the spinning wheel will act to reduce and stop its spin. As this slows, we will find that mind, emotion, memory, and body can find new ways of relating together.

As we become more proficient in feeling the interplay of these archetypes and their patterns, we discover a subjective sense of depth and connection between our different states and our perception of the world.

At times we will touch a sense of stillness or presence behind the flow of feeling, thought, image, and body sensation. We touch on the archetype of the Sun, *Tiphareth*, the beauty of presence whose quality of stillness starts to interact with the whirl of energy we are becoming used to. Tiphareth is positioned in the central line above Hod and Netzach (figure 3). Experiencing this sphere is sometimes called "the Knowledge and Conversation of the Holy Guardian Angel." This is a deepening sense of immersion in stillness and a dialogue with a presence both intimate with us and yet standing behind our everyday self.

The path that leads to this place is called the *alchemical* path. It calls upon us to transform the tangled matter of our life, to cooperate with the sense of presence and guidance emanating from the part of us that is the angel of Tiphareth.

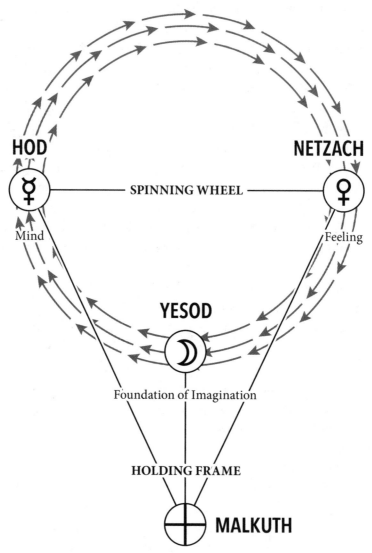

Figure 2: The Spinning Wheel of Yesod, Hod, and Netzach

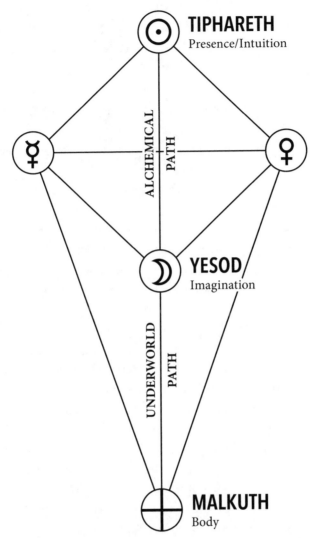

Figure 3: The Underworld and Alchemical Paths
from Malkuth to Tiphareth

As we become more centred in Tiphareth, we start to become aware of greater depth and capacity in both thought and feeling. This is the inclusion of the deeper archetypes of Geburah (Mars) and Chesed (Jupiter), representing, respectively, the energies of discipline, clarity, and will and the energies of love, compassion, and expansive growth. Our mind becomes more focused and our emotional nature more loving and compassionate. This creates a new wheel of stillness, acceptance, and clarity that deepens our connection to our interior life. These spheres are positioned on either side of the central line above Tiphareth, so that Geburah is above Hod and Chesed above Netzach (figure 4).

As this new triumvirate of archetypes comes into play, there is a much greater sense of depth and possibility. Through this we sense the mysterious aspect of ourselves and the greater universe called the sphere of *Daath*, mystical knowledge, or the knowing of not knowing. It is the gateway to the deepest parts of our being.

Daath is also called the bridge across the Abyss, as it asks us to relinquish our old ways of thinking, feeling, and doing in favour of a surrender to the unknown. It is placed on the central line above Geburah and Chesed and is depicted as a dotted circle to indicate the sense of mystery it conveys (figure 5). As we deepen, we become increasingly responsive to the deeper aspects of our being and more focused on this oddly tangible but unknown ground. This path is called the *desert* path and represents the leaving or stripping away of all we have previously known as we cross or bridge the Abyss. It is the main transition point of the inner process, though it is prefigured in the movement from the Qliphoth to Malkuth and the journey between Yesod and Tiphareth.

As we pass the gate of Daath, we enter the deepest places of the Tree: a pair of spheres called *Binah* (understanding) and *Chokmah* (wisdom), or Saturn and the stars, respectively (figure 6).

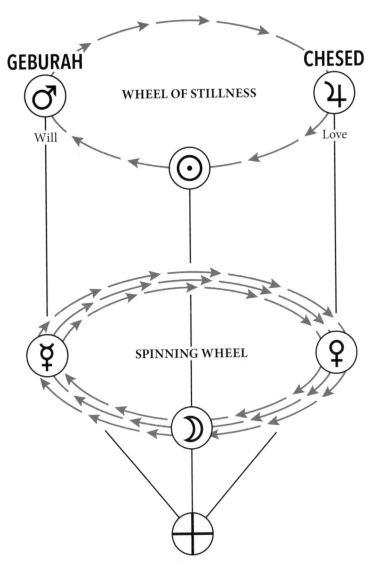

GEBURAH

CHESED

WHEEL OF STILLNESS

Will

Love

SPINNING WHEEL

Figure 4: The Wheel of Stillness

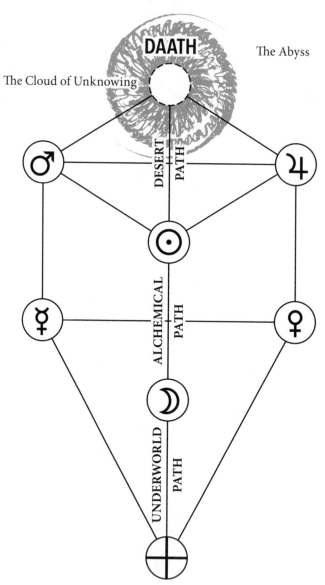

Figure 5: The Three Paths up to Daath

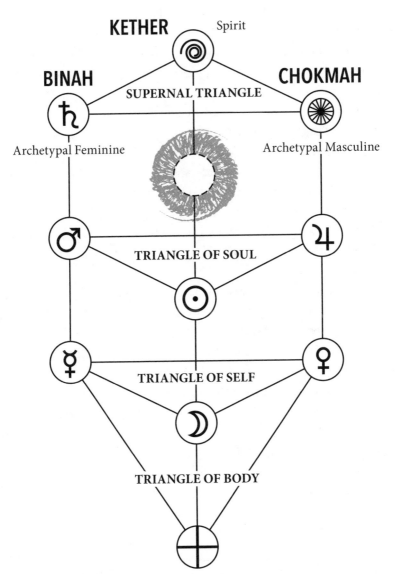

KETHER   Spirit

BINAH   CHOKMAH

SUPERNAL TRIANGLE

Archetypal Feminine   Archetypal Masculine

TRIANGLE OF SOUL

TRIANGLE OF SELF

TRIANGLE OF BODY

Figure 6: The Supernal Triangle

At the time when the Tree was developed, Saturn was the outer-most planet, the container of all the inner planets; and here it represents the archetypal mother and the womb of space, while the sphere of the stars, as the great fertilising principle, is the archetypal father. These spheres arise from Kether, the crown of the Tree, called the *primum mobile*—the first movement. These three sephiroth are depicted in a triangle at the top of the Tree and represent our deepest connection to Spirit and the energies of creation. Kether is our own deepest self, Chokmah the deep will that arises from it, and Binah the deep imagination that births the image of that will through the rest of the sephiroth of the Tree of Life.

In figure 7 we see the complete Tree of Life that we have built through the process of inner work. It is not, nor was ever intended to be, a cognitive diagram on a page.

Each one of these spheres (each sephirah) is a focus point or cluster of meaning that enables us to investigate the relationship between the inner aspect of our souls and the inner aspect of the universe. We have given some basic meanings of the sephiroth here, but many more can be found in Dion Fortune's *The Mystical Qabalah*.

Until we begin our explorations, the deeper aspects of the Tree and the paths that connect them are latent or asleep, or they awake only occasionally and the relationship between the lower sephiroth is often unbalanced and confused. Our personal tree will have grown in accordance with our life circumstances, unconsciously, unless we have worked on ourselves to deepen our awareness. The side sephiroth need to be balanced in order for the central sephiroth, the balance and transition points, to operate correctly.

SUMMARISING THE PROCESS OF EXPLORING THE TREE

In approaching Malkuth, we move from the kingdom of the shells into the living kingdom of the body and the ensouled earth.

As we step from Malkuth to Yesod, we walk the path that leads from the body and senses into the underworld of the unconscious, with its potent life energy and store of images and instincts.

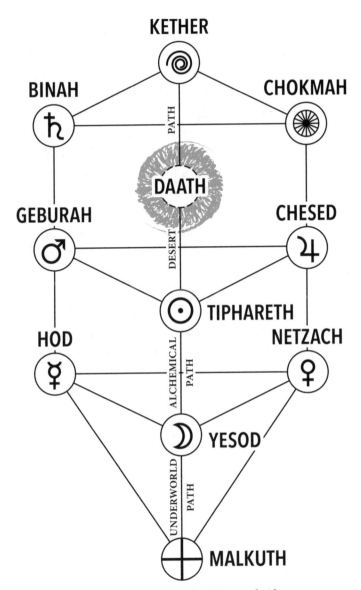

Figure 7: The Completed Tree of Life

As we take the further step from Yesod to Tiphareth, we walk the path of the deep unconscious. In passing through, we balance the spheres of the mind and feelings, connecting them to the body and the subconscious mind. We find a way to pass through the veil maintained by the tangle of our habitual thought processes in order to make contact with the intuitive presence of the watcher within us.

As we do this, there is a profound reorientation that opens our mind, heart, and body to a much deeper sense of ourselves. Having established ourselves in this still presence, there is an even deeper path that leads us to the root place of our own being, moving beyond the opposites and to a direct experience of the Divine. Here we follow the desert path of surrender, stripping away of all we know and think so as to become most truly ourselves.

It is this process that we find Dion Fortune exploring in her fiction, and if we engage with it in the way she suggests, we will find that we have indeed been given the keys to the mysteries.

SECTION 1
LEAVING HOME

As we now follow each story in turn, we open further to the reality behind the reality and to the development of a deep embodied understanding of the Tree of Life.

In this section, two chapters are devoted to each book, evolved from the process of "close reading." This technique involves focusing on short passages and scrutinising them for meaning—the reader might already have read the books in this way, intuitively picking passages that drew them and reading slowly and deeply.

An alchemical process occurs as we use this technique consciously. Through our close attention, our experience and wisdom are added to the mix, and new connections can emerge that the author could not have predicted. When we read thoughtfully, we start to own the texts, and their meaning finds expression through us. Like the fluid interconnections of the paths and sephiroth of the Tree of Life, our conscious, subconscious, and superconscious minds are beginning to find the pathways to relationship.

This section visits and then revisits the same ground from two viewpoints—a technique Dion Fortune used so effectively in *Moon Magic*. First we view the action from the psychological context, and then we place it firmly on the support of the Tree. Through this, each sphere makes valuable pathways and multilayered connections to the others. The reader is asked to deliberately disengage from each chapter after reading in order to view the similar content in the next afresh. In this way, we enable the two interpretations to meld and fuse deep within, ready for the work of sections two and three.

—————1—————
The Goat-Foot God:
Power of Nature

What I want is that something vital which I feel to be somewhere
in the universe, which I know I need, and which I can't lay my
hand on. . . . Now I call that 'something' the Great God Pan. [6]

In *The Goat-Foot God,* the subtle realms are singing from the earth as
the breath of the god Pan and the reincarnation theme reinforce the
"joining up" of the characters' inner and outer worlds. As Pan gives
life in fullness, so the book is about abundant, natural relationships
of all kinds; first in the intimate family permutations between "Uncle"
Jelkes, Mona, and Hugh, then between the hero and the local community, and, by inference, out to the widest reaches of possibility. It is
a long journey for a man noted by Mona to be far more in sympathy
with his car than with human beings.

It is clear that Hugh and Mona have complementary qualities.
Mona, as priestess in waiting, has the spiritual understanding necessary for the expanded life and to facilitate Hugh's development, as she
needs Hugh to make her progression possible, from a practical and
an esoteric point of view. In *The Goat-Foot God,* the priestess teaches
overtly, whilst Hugh, the achiever, makes all possible in the mundane
world. A base is found, and the derelict Abbey is soon transformed

---

6. Fortune, *The Goat-Foot God,* 63.

into a working temple and living space that is thoroughly embedded into its surroundings.

Relationships

The development of the relationships in each of the books reminds us first that we all share the frailties of human nature and cannot discount real life, and second that every character is also a facet of our essential nature and that we hold many warring relationships inside us.

The relationships grow naturally and include the minor characters: the enchanting but infuriating Bill and Lizzie, with their own lives and needs, are very much built in to the structure of the hugger-mugger, idiosyncratic household. It is a believable and organic development of small-community living. Dion Fortune possibly experienced communal living early in life at boarding school: she certainly "lived in" as a horticultural college student and shared living space at the teaching retreats of her first teacher, Moriarty. Later in her occult career, she lived communally at 3 Queensborough Terrace, the original headquarters of the Society of the Inner Light.

Hugh is lucky: his talent is for gathering precisely the people who will support him best. There is mutual fellow feeling between the two of them and the local solicitor, shopkeeper, and landlady at the local pub, who are sufficiently embroiled in local politics to enjoy upsetting the local "gentry," Miss Pumphrey. Hugh shows himself to be a "man's man" in dealing with the locals, who recognise his sincerity and are able to discount the veneer of class. And the influence of Pan, to bestow life in abundance to his followers, spreads out from Mona and Hugh's work to influence their servants and others in the vicinity.

A House of the Mysteries

We find many similarities between the temple properties in all the books.

All the temples are disguised or overlooked buildings. They are old and well made and have suffered the depredations of time and unkind ownership before being rescued for esoteric work.

In *The Goat-Foot God,* Fortune puts into practice all her tenets for the preparation of magical space, starting with the conscious courting of Otherworldly influence through setting up a house dedicated to the mysteries. Hugh and Mona embark as servants of the gods in this, the most down-to-earth of the books. Monks Farm is placed where the ancient gods are accustomed to being worshipped and is quickly transformed by the first of the author's old-fashioned craftsmen, who appreciate the opportunity to restore the timeless beauty of the ecclesiastical buildings.

Making a home is one of the most resonant themes in fiction, and even the most prosaic story can have a profound effect on the reader. Stripping out the cheap fittings and getting back to bedrock is a good analogy for the spiritual work of the characters: we are drawn to care deeply, to be intrigued by the homemaking that is a reflection of the characters' individual development and their relationship, and the gradual uncovering of the beauty of the building echoes Hugh's journey of discovering Ambrosius.

Monks Farm was originally built for a sacred purpose. Far from starting from scratch, they are, as Mona explains earlier, awakening old energies first invoked by the Pagan monks in the places where they are accustomed to being worshipped.

We can see the juxtaposition of Christian and Pagan practice as echoing the tenets of the Western Mystery Tradition, which does not deny Christianity but celebrates it in an expanded form, fused with an understanding of earth mysteries and ritual magic.

Mona gives the argument for a fusion of Christian/Pagan beliefs, both of which are the spiritual heritage of the West and the heritage of Ambrosius's house.

On the outer level and the inner planes, the characters are "coming home" to a harmonious acceptance of all their cultural influences, just as we can.

The Tone of the Book

The subtle emanations of magic respond immediately to Hugh in the bookshop's nurturing environment; he starts to forge an authentic way of being in the world. Immersion in ideas of the wider life of many dimensions coupled with his need and the empathy it provokes effectively change his direction.

Away from Mayfair, Hugh, for the first time, sees how people should and do behave in supportive relationships, as Jelkes and Mona treat him as an intimate. The habitual attitude of his former life—that his only use is as a cash cow—gradually diminishes, and later he is indignant at the family expectation that he will continue in this role. He is amazed by the way that Jelkes handles Mona when she is ill, and quickly develops an understanding with all the key members of the rural community. There is a joy and a deft touch in these small scenes of rural domesticity and the characterization of those who people them. After a lifetime of being disregarded by the servants, Hugh is helped immeasurably by the subsidiary characters, who assert his correct status and respond to him sympathetically. They provide a background of everyday life to contrast with the high drama of the spiritual journey. Dion Fortune's skilful alternation between lyrical prose and the colloquial—for which she says she was criticized at the time—keeps her books fresh and accessible.

The magic in this earth-mystery story is of growing and integration, delving into a deep relationship with ancestry, with the soil, and with the psyche. It is a story of rooting and coming home through work and service and is both grounded and grounding. The dance of relationship is whimsical and gentle as Hugh and Mona come into synchronicity on the higher planes: they develop beyond the belief of the medieval period that the spirit must be elevated by the mortification of the flesh. By the conclusion of *The Goat-Foot God*, we understand the esoteric concept of honoring the spirit *through* the body, in the sacred marriage.

Adding to this expansion is a youthful, guilt-free relationship with the god Pan. This ancient being, who brought joy to the Olympian gods, brings them to an understanding relevant for the modern world. One concrete result is the ditching of their earlier plans for "medieval" gothic furniture in favour of streamlined, modern décor that relates better to ancient Greece.

Mona

Mona, a little brown rabbit disguised in her drab coat with its worn coney collar, is a far cry from the glamorous heroines Ursula, Vivien, and Lilith of the other books. The twitching, nervous, self-deprecating Hugh is an unlikely hero, with stooped, jerky movements and nervous energy but no stamina. Both are lacking "It"—then a current term for sex appeal. But insignificant Mona is the embodiment of the "pal"— the helpmate who was the ideal for soldiers returning from the First World War, who had lost so many pals at the front. She is the antithesis of the Mayfair "type," being generous and capable of selfless love; a chum, a fellow quester, and an intimate. She is Hugh's perfect complement, supplying the quality of earthed energy that he lacks.

Her circumstances are the realities of life in Britain before the welfare state, showing the very real dangers of poverty between the wars and the lack of opportunity—the ability of a poor craft worker to network successfully being necessarily limited. Mona is ready for the role of priestess, but Jelkes fears for her virtue and so presents her simply as an artist. He is a fiercely protective mentor to them both.

This can all be viewed as rather workaday, a business relationship chaperoned by an elderly bookseller, yet there is an important pointer early on. Considering the possible outcome of Hugh and Mona's meeting, Jelkes compares Hugh's quest to Arthur's foray into the Otherworld. This reference, taken from the ancient Welsh poem *Preiddeu Annwn*, has a great mythic resonance. It describes King Arthur's raid to steal a magical cauldron, which Dion Fortune equates to the quest for Cerridwen's cauldron. To her this is the grail of the earth goddess, the ultimate symbol of the spiritual made manifest, and Jelkes hints that it might be achieved. Hugh does not understand, but the reference to Arthur, the once and future king, the hero of the primary myth of the British, tells us—even if we are not versed in the earliest Celtic literature—that great things are afoot.

Hugh

Hugh is the man of action. Whilst Jelkes is content to philosophize, Hugh's instinct is to wind up his previous life, get a car, and go and *do* something. But, post-trauma, it must be something real, not the thrill-seeking that has distracted him from the shallowness of life in the past. His new quest to contact the gods comes from the critical urge to find a meaning in life, to put down roots and have a fulfilling home life. His deep self pursues what is needed for his spiritual welfare, going quickly beyond the fascination of the Black Mass to the larger, invisible reality that informs the physical world. He invokes and is answered at every stage, for as Mona says, sincere commitment is an invocation. His esoteric reading is a tool that urges him to the quest; he is compelled to experiment, to get on the trail. He is a student thirsty for knowledge that he can put to a practical application.

Their Relationship

Reciprocity is an important theme: Mona points the way and supports Hugh, both practically and esoterically, as he in turn begins to free her, from poverty and insignificance. Together they blossom, and deep calls to deep. The business relationship Mona tries to establish is useless for this purpose. Hugh resolves to humanize her, and fortunately his bereavement activates Mona's maternal instincts: she feels a responsibility first of all to mother him—to care in a way that is new to him.

Hugh buys her a jade-green coat—a lovely analogy for their relationship; it protects and warms her, cutting through her disguise, so that, wearing it, her striking and elfin nature is apparent. With Hugh's car and clothes, they stand out as exotic figures in a street scene where Jelkes blends in. It is the first intimation that the breath of Pan has already imbued them with a vitality out of the ordinary, and they go straight to the village where they will find Monks Farm and the Ambrosius contact.

Hugh's noticing Mona's discomfort in the car and acting on it is a tangible indication that the bubble separating him from the world is cracking. And as Mona sees his "Ambrosius" nature when driving, she wants ardently to protect him from exploitation. This she does, teaching him about human nature during the process of house buying and setting up his home. The many small instances of care between them throughout provide a contrast to the high drama of Ambrosius's contacts with his succubus.

Establishing themselves in the farm, Hugh and Mona become hypersensitive to the beauty surrounding them; they are like people recovering from illness—in this case the illness of over-civilization. Pan is referenced in subtle ways: through the untamed landscape echoing Arcadia and in the smell of the herb goat's rue. Living in Pan's natural landscape gradually transforms Mona from her London persona of priestess-in-disguise into a representation of the active aspect of the Goddess. The change is lyrically noted: "Mona, whose neutral-tinted clothes looked so drab in London, looked here as if she had risen from the grey winter pasture like Aphrodite from the wave of the sea."[7] The change alerts us to Mona's increasingly active role in Hugh's own transformation. And Pan works within through the extremes of emotion expressed by the emerging Ambrosius, as well as Mona's responses, which become deeper through shared experience. The last change, into active priest/priestess of the gods, will be the culmination of their story.

The Quest

The quest allows Hugh to put his money and his organisational skills to his own creative use for the first time in his life. Through regressions into Ambrosius's life, reenacting his final moments, Hugh integrates the experiences into his psyche. These scenes in the medieval buildings show Hugh's development; they are an absorbing study in psychological process. As he comes into his rightful place, things move fast, and with synchronicity. And through it all, Hugh and Mona's heart-searchings and explorations constitute the lessons of the spiritual mating.

---

7. Fortune, *The Goat-Foot God*, 211.

We know of Mona's limited Christian upbringing and its denial of her creativity. By opening up to the wider morality with Jelkes's help, her worldview and spirit have expanded. Hugh's similarly deep exploration and integration is laid out before us. Ambrosius, who could only dream of a fulfilment denied him by society, has been reborn in this life as Hugh the supplicant, coming into the presence of the God to be made whole. Gradually, his spontaneous and frightening experiences come under control as he deliberately works with them towards a synthesis of the two personalities: the medieval and the modern. The culmination comes when, donning the monk's robe made by Mona, Hugh consciously brings Ambrosius back into himself, secure that he will not get lost in the past. Despite Mona's constant support, it is a journey he must take alone.

Jelkes has taken a back seat: the Pan current is directing the action, and by now his mentoring role is purely practical. He realises that Mona is essential to hold the reins of the household and his concerns are for her safety and morals, as Ambrosius's charisma becomes apparent in Hugh, who for the first time becomes capable of dominating other people, a heady and a testing experience. When Hugh steps back from the opportunity to force his will on Mona, he passes a test of integrity: coming down to bedrock, Hugh is sound. He is comfortable enough with his Ambrosius persona to tease Mona, and elicits her unguarded response to him in a startlingly modern phrase: "This is the Ambrosius that won't get no for an answer."[8] From the moment Mona asks Hugh to give Ambrosius her love, she is giving him a clear signal, and the courtship progresses with tenderness, concern, and subtle flirting as a counterpart to the tension of the spiritual work. These are journeys of personal development, but with a shared history, causing them to orbit as the God directs their dance of discovery.

The old church is very much Hugh's own space, as the garden is Mona's: she tends the shrine of the earth goddess. Here, with the scent of the aromatic herbs in her nostrils, she meets Hugh's crisis with a spontaneous deep vision of her own. As Hugh reenacts the death of

8. Fortune, *The Goat-Foot God*, 289.

Ambrosius in the cellar, the monk's original death cell, Mona's vision is of the ship. She steers them both into harbour under the auspices of Pan, the guardian of outcasts who have no place in cities and towns, describing exactly what is happening on the inner planes: she sinks back into a surrender to nature and the cosmic life, which is the true invocation of Pan. It is magically potent, directed by the woman who, drab and starving in London, has come into her own through Hugh's largesse.

After this, Mona enacts the scene that should have occurred in medieval times, consciously taking on the persona of the succubus and leading Hugh from the cellar of Ambrosius's death to call his faithful acolytes. Coming fresh from her Pan meditation, she is gradually glamoured and dominated by Hugh/Ambrosius and feels the stirrings of the great love. It is Hugh who, after fulfilling Ambrosius's ambition to embrace her, sends Mona back to the house to conclude the process. As he tracks back and rearranges the things in this life and the past, he realises that the invocation of Pan has produced the appropriate composition of place—the reverse of what he set out to do. The scene is set for the last acts of their magical journey.

The ritual in the church starts under the auspices of Jelkes. Through his methods of applied psychology, Hugh and Mona reveal themselves to each other and Hugh finally sheds the last vestiges of his old life: the guilt over his wife's death. Mona takes charge then, leading the ritual from the psychological into magical realms, using her priestess persona to dominate the men. She leads them from the church to witness the magical dance of the moon that magnetizes and draws Hugh to her. Mona has held the direct spiritual connection through her quiet work of service as earth priestess combined with the qualities of Aphrodite, and this is a practical demonstration of the call of Isis that will be fully explored in its sexual aspect in *The Sea Priestess*. Here, it is necessary to complete the "Ambrosius" cycle. Mona is the Priestess of the Earth enacting the moon rites, in a reflection of *The Winged Bull*'s Ursula, Priestess of the Moon, who takes the part of the Earth in spring.

The Christian Jelkes, whom Mona suspects of mentally making the sign of the cross throughout, is helpless as she draws Hugh's soul to her. He is the witness of Hugh/Ambrosius's breaking free, as Hugh's etheric body emerges from the shadow of the church to stand in the moonlight. He is helpless as the renegade priest holds Mona and the unseen world of sentient nature partly manifests in the dance of Pan around them. This is the result of Ambrosius's experiments, and for its duration, the fabric of the world becomes fluid. Not until the rite is over is Jelkes released to earth the two with light, warmth, and food.

Later that night we look at the crossover between psychological and magical explanation, and its implications. Mona suffers a severe reaction. Ambrosius has had a marked effect on her, and she is shocked by her behavior. She is left to her aspirin and tears, whilst Hugh, also sleepless, is thrilled that Mona has been carried away; it opens up new possibilities for the future. Ambrosius is now fully integrated, and Hugh considers how he has achieved this and the use of magical fantasy that goes beyond psychological practice.

The vital truth he recognises is that Mona is not his problem—she is already a priestess—but that he is Mona's. To proceed, he must become the priest, to mate and worship with her in the right way. It is the final realisation, and is of sufficient power to set the process working.

Becoming the Priest

Morning brings a change in the dynamic: an embarrassed Mona is reassured by the newly confident Hugh, released from stiff tweeds to the freedom of shorts and sandals. Although she has led the way throughout, it is his role to instigate this last change, the first stage of which is their marriage. The broad humour verges on slapstick: love among the moderns that scandalizes Jelkes. But as their clothes are the modern equivalent of the Greeks' freedom of dress, so their horseplay represents their entry into the innocence and gaiety of Arcady, with the nymphs and satyrs.

Being free to lead is part and parcel of Hugh's realisation that he has magically laid Ambrosius to rest by fulfilling his ambitions. He has become capable of leading his priestess with confidence because her subconscious has spoken. Mona, for her part, fulfilled Pan's promise to Ambrosius when she took Hugh from the cellar death reenactment. In return, Pan gifts her the priest she needs for his worship.

The expression of the Pan within allows Hugh to experience life in abundance, which alters him irrevocably: he notes a simple happiness akin to inebriation. He goes at once to find a magical space for the marriage rite—connecting with Mona's goat's rue on the way, and becoming irresistible to nanny goats. He finds a gift from Ambrosius—the grove of yew planted in the Middle Ages, in order to celebrate just such rites as are proposed.

Becoming the priest is an act of mystery and faith. As Hugh and Mona's relationship started with him admitting that he didn't know how to achieve his objective, so it finishes this cycle with a ritual into the unknown, led solely by intuition. Hugh is like us: a seeker gradually making sense of his world and realising where fulfilment comes from. Hugh and Mona's marriage rite will be a connection to the cosmic life, against which he will measure the rest of his life. Mona's words have been proven true: they have gained the greater life by proving that they will work with the mysteries, and they are married in the sight of Pan.

The Challenge of Continuing Life

The fact that Hugh and Mona are from different worlds becomes irrelevant to their future life together: they will engage with the wider world only on their own terms. Hugh tells us how it will work out in the real world in the future: they will have an idiosyncratic, creative life in London and at the farm that will attract only those in sympathy with them. Their ongoing worship of the Pan principle will be in safeguarding a shared life that has transformed the mundane into the life of connection. It is the spirit behind what they—and we—do that counts, not the show that people put on for the world to see.

Committing to the spirit of Pan in the world gives them an understanding that fuses the everyday and the wider life in a seamless flow between practical and highly spiritual living. Their marriage is an initiation, a beginning: their invitation to the dance of life played on the pipes of Pan, in their Arcadia in Hertfordshire.

2

Entering Malkuth and *The Goat-Foot God*

Malkuth is the gateway to the Tree of Life. It is the anchor and connection point and marks a transition as we move from the world of the Qliphoth, or world of shells—a world of fragmentation and broken boundaries, without containment and safety. We come to Malkuth, which by contrast is called the kingdom—it represents a place where there is a sense of connection to a living world and is accessed by bringing awareness into our body and senses.

The experience of Malkuth begins with a sense of presence and feeling anchored in the body and bodily sensation; at the same time there is a connection to a deeper, more inward life, which offers possibilities that the merely outward-looking life does not. In a way we feel rooted, a part of the Tree of Life, and this sense of connection grows as we deepen our experience of this sphere and follow the journey of Hugh Paston.

Like all the spheres of the Tree of Life, there are four levels to Malkuth, which we can align with the middle-pillar spheres of the Tree:

- The world of the body and action; Malkuth of Malkuth
- The world of energy and subtle formation; Yesod of Malkuth
- The world of creation, of generating and balancing opposites; Tiphareth of Malkuth

• The world of the divine non-dual experience of the supernal triangle; Daath of Malkuth

These four levels in effect create a miniature Tree within that sphere that acts as a three-dimensional mandala, which enables the reader to incorporate the energies of Malkuth within them. Dion Fortune denotes these four levels in her books by describing four locations in which the action takes place. In *The Goat-Foot God*:

• **Malkuth of Malkuth** is Hugh's house.
• **Yesod of Malkuth** is Jelkes's shop.
• **Tiphareth of Malkuth** is Monks Farm.
• **Daath of Malkuth** is the yew grove.

Qabalistically the characters in the novels represent different aspects of the psyche as well as being people we might recognise from Dion Fortune's time or indeed from our own. Hugh Paston is what we might call the "point of view" character; he shows us the process of becoming a full initiate of Malkuth, in effect a priest of Pan. He moves from the experience of dissociation and disempowerment through rage and bitterness into fullness of new life and must claim and transform the archetype of the devil within him.

There are two principal figures who help him: Jelkes, the intellectual bookseller, and Mona, the creative artist. These two represent the twin pillars of the Tree of Life and the spheres Hod and Netzach helping him to step more deeply into the inner worlds.

Malkuth of Malkuth: Hugh's House

This is Hugh's house in Mayfair, where we find him sitting in front of a dead fire having just come from his wife's funeral. Here we are shown Hugh sitting at home in the ashes of his old life. He is in the world of the Qliphoth in that moment, awake to its futility and needing to leave it.

His only way of doing this is to let his restless body carry him on a rambling walk out of Mayfair. In this process he starts to enter Malkuth, at first just surrendering into bodily experience by letting one footstep follow another and letting the body lead him deeper into the experience of the unknown.

The Path into the Underworld: Malkuth to Yesod

As he lets his body lead him, Hugh finds himself leaving the known environment of Mayfair, exploring areas that are less salubrious and known to him. This is the descent into the underworld—the movement from our conscious self into the unconscious.

Yesod of Malkuth: Jelkes's Shop

The underworld path takes us to the sphere of Yesod, the pool of subjective life. It is sometimes called the treasure house of images and is said to hold both our image of ourselves and our image of the world. The treasure house of images is Jelkes's shop. And whilst any bookshop is a good image for the sphere of Yesod, a secondhand bookshop with books from many different ages and many stories is a particularly good image of the subconscious mind. Hugh finds in this shop the key image: the myth of Pan, the goat-foot god.

He encounters the shop at sunset and roots through the twopenny book bin, finding a copy of A. E. W. Mason's *The Prisoner in the Opal*. This proves to be a magical book for him. "'The Prisoner in the Opal'———. It raised visions.... 'The affair gave me quite a new vision of the world,' he read. 'I saw it as a vast opal inside which I stood. An opal luminously opaque, so that I was dimly aware of another world outside mine.'"[9]

Hugh buys the book, goes to a hotel to read it, and is immediately fascinated by the Black Mass and the image of the devil. Here is the shadow of the goat-foot Pan, the key archetype of the whole book. For Hugh, *The Prisoner in the Opal* speaks to his rage and sense of futility.

---

9. Fortune, *The Goat-Foot God*, 5.

Two things in particular stand out:

- The image of the prisoner in the opal itself conveys both the sense of a deeper world and the experience of imprisonment.
- The idea of the Black Mass aligns him with the image of the devil and of a certain kind of hidden priesthood.

The central image of the Black Mass is the priest placing the wine and bread on the naked body of a woman, witnessed by the horned devil.

Hugh's Progress

Hugh identifies with the figure of the priest: he feels that his way to freedom and that deeper world he can just sense will be to perform the Black Mass. As he makes this commitment, he moves more deeply into the experience of Yesod; he has chosen a myth pattern to work with. He remembers Jelkes mentioning a book on the Black Mass by Huysmans called *Là-Bas*—literally *Down There*, although more commonly translated as *The Damned*. Mythically he moves in and down, literally going "down there" as he returns to the bookshop, is shown into the inner room, and begins his apprenticeship with Jelkes's bookseller and failed Catholic priest.

The succession of the books he is given to read and contemplate—Huysmans's *Là-Bas* and then *The Devil's Mistress* by J. W. Brodie-Innes and *The Corn King and the Spring Queen* by Naomi Mitchison [10]—show the transformation of the images that Hugh is focusing on. They move from the out-and-out Satanism of Huysmans, to the introduction of the witch Isobel Gowdie and her encounters with the world of faerie in Brodie-Innes's novel, to the sacred marriage of the God and Goddess in ancient Greece described by Naomi Mitchison. Hugh's reading and meditation come together in a key moment in which

---

10. Fiction books commonly available since the 1920s. See the bibliography for details.

he suggests to Jelkes that he put together Huysmans,[11] Ignatius of Loyola,[12] and Iamblichos [sic].[13] Hugh decides that he should furnish a temple as Iamblichos suggests, live in it night and day, and put his imagination behind it like a priest saying mass, as Loyola and Huysmans indicate. He feels that if he did so, the old gods would manifest.

Here is Hugh engaging with image and story under Jelkes's tutelage and starting to understand the method of invoking the old gods in just the way that Dion Fortune taught. This experience opens the way for the appearance of Mona Wilton, who represents the quality of Soul and the feminine principle. In a way she is Hugh's anima or muse, guiding him onwards.

Hugh meets Mona in the shop and, having decided to buy and furnish his temple, engages her to help him select it.

The Alchemical Way: Yesod to Tiphareth

The movement from Yesod to Tiphareth involves not just a sense of deepening but also an awakening of opposites and the resolution of old dilemmas. It is a more active process than the contemplative process pursued so far. Mona as Hugh's anima figure represents that energy of excitement and disturbance that draws him onwards. Very swiftly we see him searching out and finding a property; just as swiftly we find him relating to Mona and his emotions and sexuality coming into play. The fiery energies of Netzach are acting as the awakener and bringing heat and energy into the inner process.

---

11. J. K. Huysmans (1848–1907). His hero in *Là-Bas* sets out to recreate the Black Mass as an antidote to his empty life.

12. Ignatius of Loyola was the founder of the Jesuits (1491–1556). Hugh intends to use his theory of using the focused imagination in what Loyola called "the composition of place."

13. Iamblichus (c. 250–325 CE). Similar ideas to those of Loyola from Iamblichus's treatise *On the Mysteries of Egypt* give Hugh a key to the technique of the higher consciousness.

Tiphareth of Malkuth: Monks Farm

Monks Farm, built by an infamous medieval abbot called Ambrosius as a place of retreat and meditation, has a sinister history. As a result of the abbot and monks being indicted for heresy, it became a penal house in which the monks were locked up in their cells and Ambrosius in his priory.

As we discover that the medieval illumination of Ambrosius looks remarkably like Hugh, and that he was engaged in the summoning of Pan, we see the emergence of personal myth and what might be described as the magical personality as the work deepens. Hugh is invited to commune with the image of a heretical priest who has bought Greek manuscripts and is summoning the real presence of the old gods. We move here from the generic images found in the books to something that is arising from the deep places of Tiphareth—an aspect of Hugh that understands these mysteries.

Simultaneously we are presented with a detailed image of the monastery: a cloister with a large house on one side, entered through a large church door, bringing us in front of a spiral staircase up to the abbot's room and the cells of the monks. On the ground floor on the left side we find a chapel, and on the right side we find the old quarters, where Mona and Hugh will live.

The chapel has an unusual arrangement: an old, faded picture of the Tree of Life painted on the east wall where there would normally be a window, a zodiac circle on the floor, and a waist-high stone pedestal for an altar.

This is the temple place in the story, a step on the way to final transformation. It is also the place of healing where we see Hugh rebuilding the temple and dealing with the experience of his past life as Ambrosius and his attempt to restore the mysteries.

As well as restoring the temple that is both an inward and outward act, Hugh has to confront Ambrosius, who sits in his psyche as an image offering both possibilities and problems. Various processes of healing are carried out in this part of the book as Hugh and Mona learn to work together. Hugh has to commune with Ambrosius and draw him out of the depths of his psyche. Mona, through her inner working, must draw on her life in ancient Greece as a bacchante, or priestess of the god.

These tasks are stimulated by challenges to the work—the Qliphothic energies in the shape of Hugh's mother and sisters and the society doctor who are all trying to get Hugh committed as insane so that they can control his money. Dion Fortune tells us clearly, "Into their Eden the Serpent erupted and his name was practically legion."[14]

This provokes an important moment in which Hugh and Ambrosius merge, with (for this phase) Ambrosius dominant, and the resulting self is aware of the goat-foot god as protector and guide. Hugh leaves the family: he walks to the chapel, kneels, lays his hands on the stone altar, and surrenders himself to the energies of the universe. This is the beginning of the desert way for him, which involves also resolving the life of Ambrosius.

At this moment, stimulated by the challenge of the Qliphoth, the priest and temple start to come into operation. There is a practical arrangement that protects Hugh's outer affairs, but from our point of view the key process is the inner process in which both Hugh and Mona connect to their own deeper selves. They do this through the art of what Dion Fortune refers to as *phantasy*, which leads them both back through the Middle Ages to Arcady and the mysteries of Eleusis.

As these first steps are taken, we feel the clarity and liberating energy of Geburah and the active compassion and acceptance of Chesed. These increasingly inform the work that addresses the problems both of this life and of the Middle Ages in the personal and the collective. Hugh and Mona work both personally and for us all; any work of this kind addresses both dimensions. In both cases they must trust the images that arise for them: they must embody them, live them out in meditation and ritual, and ground them in their personal relationship.

As these energies build, we find Hugh walking around Monks Farm contemplating the road ahead. He remembers the experience of being the prisoner in the opal and all the things that have happened since he

---

14. Fortune, *The Goat-Foot God*, 221.

broke out of its opacity. He contemplates the rising of Ambrosius within him and the coming of Mona. He realises that it is the resolve to break out of the opal and serve the powers of life that invokes not just the inner Pan but also the Great God Pan without him. In this moment of realisation he returns to the chapel and consciously draws Ambrosius into himself, absorbing all the energies, abilities, and struggles of that past life and owning them as his own.

As he is doing this, Mona is similarly contemplating her own life and her childhood fantasies based on her book of Greek legends. As a child she had visualised herself running in Arcady with a boy companion, which later became the pursuit of a lover, and later still an adoring maenad following Dionysus over the mountains.

As she contemplates her situation, Mona is given a vision of the god Pan amidst the sea and stars, guiding her home to the wild green world, helping her and Hugh to find the unshakable bedrock of their souls and of the world.

The Desert Path: Tiphareth to Daath

As Hugh and Mona receive the blessing of Pan, they step out on the path to Daath—the mysterious place of the knowing of union. They come together first in the cellar, in a deep place that is the beginning of entering Daath. This sphere of the Tree has the quality of entering into the mystery but also dealing with the lost and broken energies of the past. It is the doorway into the Divine and the Abyss of lost souls. Mona's entrance into the cellar, where she finds Hugh meditating on the life of Ambrosius, is the culmination of his old dream in which a spirit woman comes to him and opens the gates of Pan's kingdom to him. She leads him up from the cellar and he processes through the old cells, freeing the spirits of the old monks who had been imprisoned with him. He ascends to the abbot's chapel in the attic and there contemplates his life backwards. This is a very potent inner practice; it is one of the first exercises given, but reaches its apogee here in the contemplations of Daath.

Hugh, Mona, and Jelkes meet in the chapel for the ritual in which Hugh and Mona bring together their dreaming. Mona draws Hugh outside, dancing the moon dance for him and awakening his deeper self. It is a moment of high polarity magic in which the priestess, through will and imagination, summons the Pan within from the deep places of Hugh's soul and draws it into relationship with her. In a sense their dreaming bodies come together in union. This is a moment also of the coming together of body, heart, and mind in an act of exploration and surrender. Significantly, mind, in the shape of Jelkes, is left behind here, because the will and creative imagination represented by Hugh and Mona are pressing forward into regions it cannot enter; Jelkes must wait humbly in the chapel to hear news of the deeper mystery.

All this is the preamble for the culmination of the book in the Rite of Pan worked in the deep wood. This is the true entry into Daath—the doorway into mystery and the full manifestation of Pan between Mona and Hugh.

Daath of Malkuth: The Yew Grove

The experience of Daath is concerned with the process of union—the sacred marriage that brings new life. Moving beyond the wounds of the Middle Ages, Hugh remembers that he was once a hierophant of the Eleusinian Mysteries. He creates a new temple, finding a lozenge-shaped yew grove in the centre of the wood with a fallen standing stone at its centre, which he erects. The shape of the temple is worth noting; the grove is the shape of a vesica piscis, formed by the overlapping of two circles—the ancient symbol of both union and the divine feminine—with the phallic standing stone at the centre, and Mona and Hugh deciding to marry underscores the theme of union.

They prepare themselves for the inner marriage, with Mona dressed in green and Hugh in the fawn-skin. He leads her into the pinewood to the grove of yews that has had an opening cut in it, filled by a medieval oak door. He leads her into the grove, placing her at one end and himself at the other, with the waist-high standing stone between them.

At this point there is a very classic Daath experience of complete unknowing: they stand there not knowing what to do. Hugh then traces in vision the route by which he has come, recapitulating the entire journey; he visualises himself in the fawn-skin following the dream where he pursues a mystery woman. As he enters the deeper wood, he feels the pang of fear and Mona also shudders as they both feel the presence of the God. A golden light then manifests between them and they experience the earth aura and its place in the cosmos.

The Crowning Experience: Daath to Kether

The culmination of the rite comes with the experience of the sun at midnight, for Hugh is overshadowed by the titanic figure of Helios, the ancient sun. He brings the fire and life of the sun to Mona, placing his hand between her breasts and blessing her as she steps towards him. The book ends with the ancient cry of the Eleusinian Mysteries, "Be ye far from us, O ye profane," and we are left to conjecture that they make love.

This is a powerful description of the movement through the levels of the Tree, and its culmination has Hugh and Mona as priest and priestess of the mysteries of Malkuth—that is, of the living earth. In effect, they are a modern example of the corn king and spring maiden referred to in Naomi Mitchison's novel. This is the crowning experience of the book.

3

The Sea Priestess: Currents and Rhythms

Then I noticed a thing I have noticed before when listening to waves breaking on rocks—the sound of the bells in the water. [15]

The Goat-Foot God delves deep into the ancestry of person and place identified with the worship of the old Gods long before the building of Monks Farm. The earth contact is key, and is honoured throughout. With *The Sea Priestess*, Dion Fortune ranges far and wide into the cosmos, the great spiritual currents of the past that have formed us, and the rhythms of the sea.

Here, the magical work of individuals is linked to the evolutionary current in a far more overt way than in the earlier books: it is the link between them and the magnificent culmination of *Moon Magic*.

In *The Sea Priestess*, Wilfred's first vision of the cosmos and his place in it takes us into uncharted territory; it is the intimation that great things are afoot. The potent combination of moon and sea provides the tidal rhythms reflected in Wilfred's journeys through the liminal lands of the salt marshes from his everyday world to the sea temple. This deep feeling of the current of cosmic life evokes a response that makes us yearn to do magical work.

---

15. Dion Fortune, *The Sea Priestess*, 51.

For the first time, we have a priestess wholly dedicated to the mysteries. Where Ursula is withdrawn and Mona is disguised, Vivien has led a full life in the world. She has even been on the stage, a reminder that *The Winged Bull's* Ursula, according to Astley, is divided between her instincts for stained-glass sainthood and a bohemian life on the stage. Vivien has integrated the two. Her story of occult experiments during her early life of poverty reminds us that Mona, despite her own spiritual work, had to wait for her priest before she could achieve contacted priestesshood, her true form. Vivien has done the groundwork of dedication and making her inner contacts. She has confidence in dealing with the outside world on her own terms. She doesn't need a man of action to lead her to initiation, but the passive, potent Wilfred, who will enable her magic to arc up from the personal to the cosmological. Everyday concerns are totally subservient to the work of the sea priestess, which is for the evolutionary current to bring the world into harmony with cosmic principles. Her bloodline connects her back to Atlantis, and she has recovered her own deep memories of that civilization.

Appropriately for one who has been a priestess for millennia, the magical partnership is completed this time by a discarnate entity, the Priest of the Moon. The human limitations of earthly mentors are no longer a concern—we are in the realm of direct contacts. In this book, Fortune unequivocally owns her allegiance to the divine feminine, the Deep Mother, in all her complexity and her aspects of dark and light, from whom all life comes and to whom we return to have the wellsprings of our souls refreshed.

It is a theme that will be developed in *Moon Magic*. And, in case it should become too worthy and indigestible, it is contrasted and complemented by the delicious bathos of Wilfred's everyday life—reminiscent of most readers' experiences. Each moment of lyrical beauty and magic is balanced by trivial and ridiculous family squabbles and the minutiae of small-town life with all its irritations.

The Cosmic Theme

The vision of the beginnings of the cosmos sets the tone of the book, and Wilfred swiftly moves from restriction into liminal space and wide horizons. The tip of the headland on which the sea temple stands [16] looks straight across the North Atlantic to the New World. It is a pristine seascape, its movement controlled only by the winds and the magnetic pull of the moon. There, Wilfred can look out on a sea world with no indication of the earth.

His first vision came spontaneously, introducing the themes of the harmony of interstellar space and the machinery of the universe that are at the root of Wilfred's being: "I preferred that God should geometrise." [17] It is the beginning of his communication with the moon as mistress of tides and growth. The cosmic theme is constant throughout his visions, and we note that Vivien, who advanced her own psychism with the planchette, [18] uses a variety of tools to aid Wilfred's deep memory.

Wilfred's meeting with Vivien occurs in the spring, immediately after a dangerous bout of asthma and his vision of the arrival of the sea priestess to the area in ancient times. Already we have been introduced to the Atlantis connection and the theme of sacrifice. Disclosing this vision is a formative moment for Wilfred; with Vivien's crystal as amplifier, he accesses his deep connection to the landscape of the past, which changes his world paradigm forever and is the beginning of his movement forward.

The next tool is the Fire of Azrael. This takes him back to the high places of the earth and the birth of spirituality, ranging over the ancient world to arrive at the great days of Atlantis and the escape of the sea priestess from its destruction. After building her image, Wilfred's visions become deeper, and through the next Fire of Azrael he envisions his life and death as the sacrifice to the sea. This helps him to

---

16. Based on Brean Down, a promontory off the coast of Somerset, England, extending into the Bristol Channel.

17. Fortune, *The Sea Priestess*, 4.

18. A tool for automatic writing, popular at the time.

understand Vivien's precept that the priest and priestess should not be personalities but should represent all men and all women. The vision ends in a blissful union that leads to a severe asthma attack and resumes as he meets the sea gods in a storm that imperils the temple.

This work represents their breaking the trail for society, reintroducing the understanding of the subtle, magnetic relationship between man and woman that should be behind the attractions felt on the physical plane.

In the next vision, prompted by the blazing fire surrounded by seawater, and continuing late into the night, Wilfred sees the beginnings of the formation of the land and the first life proceeding from the sea. The nature of man and woman and the forgotten knowledge of the rhythms of their relationship prepares Wilfred for the final ritual. In the sea cave, Wilfred experiences the machinery of the universe, yet, vitally, it operates with the sensitivity of a living system. When he returns to the temple, the space appears even more liminal, impregnated by a strange sea world; in it Vivien becomes the living embodiment of the Goddess before disappearing, and Wilfred communes with the Priest of the Moon. There are lessons here of respect for the integrity of ritual and trust in the process, which we are wise to heed. These visions and their progression should be visited again and again.

After Vivien's disappearance, Wilfred shares his experiences with his new wife, Molly. They feel the direct contact themselves as the Priest of the Moon takes on Molly's education so that she and Wilfred can ground in physical marriage the magical current set in play by Wilfred and Vivien.

In order to experience the tides of nature, the action of the book takes another full year, after the year of Wilfred's solitary training. As in her other books, Fortune uses the correspondences of the seasons to add emphasis to the action. From the idyllic "secret" summer out at the fort through Wilfred's winter period of bereavement after Vivien's disappearance, we come to the spring, with the flourishing of the young vines and sun-warmed herbs to symbolise Molly's and his new life together.

The Roots of Spirituality

The beginnings of civilizations and their spiritual lineage underpin the story. Through visions, the characters reach far back into the roots of the ancient spiritual and religious systems that have informed those in the world today.

As we've seen, Wilfred examines biblical texts in his earliest searches —the first of our four heroes willing to do so, and to use them as a valuable resource. In terms of following the way of the Western Mystery Tradition, it is a major breakthrough that many modern readers have still to make.

Wilfred's vision of Vivien's history shows us the death of Atlantis—information that formed part of Dion Fortune's actual recovered memories in her early childhood. Buying the sandalwood for the Fire of Azrael, Wilfred speculates on the very birthplace of the human race, where people connect back to their ancient lineage and might understand better than civilized people the mind of God. Appreciating the evolutionary nature of the work, Wilfred is pleased to be linked to the place of the gods that made the gods. This echoes an actual vision of Dion Fortune, of the two spiritual beings that first set her on her own spiritual path. By using this association, one speculates that she is finally taking the leap of faith fully to fuse her own journey with a fictional subject. It is a generous imbuing of the story with her inner wisdom and deep understanding.

The Essential Nature of the Sea

The paradox throughout the book is the life-giving and life-taking nature of the sea, and the ethics of magic historically and today: the wonders, the possibilities, and the costs.

The site of the temple is liminal land, on the end of a small peninsula: the elemental contacts are essential for magical work, and Fortune never lets us forget our vulnerability in the face of that power —a lesson vital for our safety. The sea is a constant threat to the old fort, accurately reflecting the situation in the far past when the depredations into the land of the mighty ocean caused the first visit of the sea priestess from Atlantis to these shores. That which gives life can also kill.

Vivien draws on Wilfred's vitality to recover these mutual deep memories through the Fire of Azrael—again a reference to danger, as Azrael is the angel of death; in Judaic tradition, the separator of the soul from the body. Wilfred has in part experienced these during his asthma attacks, so we can see the archangel as a constant presence as psychopomp throughout the book.

There is much about the dark latter days of Atlantis, inviting us to think deeply about the ethics of magic through hints of the perverse forms of the black magical arts that caused the destruction of Atlantis. The vision showing us the escape of the sea priestess whose blood would later inform Vivien's fey Breton ancestry reminds us of the conversation in *The Winged Bull* about human "stud books." It is not a pleasant idea and is part of a dynamic state of attraction/repulsion that emerges frequently through the book as Wilfred is glamoured and yet periodically repulsed by Vivien's aloof attitude and lack of empathy. Coming to terms with her priorities and surrendering into being the willing sacrifice to her work enables him to relax into a relationship that, in turn, activates her more human reactions. And he also has to make an accommodation with the ruthless sea, understanding its nature through his frescoes and putting himself totally in its power.

Vivien is a human of the present era as well as a priestess, with a genuine affection for Wilfred. Referencing the human sacrifice of the Atlantean era, the book shows how significant ritual can be enacted in the current era. We see how sacrifice must become appropriate to the present, though the ruthless nature of the elements is highlighted by the death of the builder's son, which so disturbs Wilfred. Dion Fortune flags his role as sacrifice first by calling him a "moon-calf"—dedicated to the work of the moon current—and by the old superstition that a holy building always demands blood in its building. Nevertheless, in our more sensitized times, his sacrifice is an even more uncomfortable and unacceptable idea for us than it is for Wilfred.

Happy as the eventual outcomes are, they result from the characters' deep commitment. In our modern times, we interpret sacrifice as a personal matter, subsuming everything else we legitimately and ethically can to the demands of the work. We take responsibility every time we act magically, bearing in mind that evolutionary work can make ultimate demands.

Psychological Journey

Whilst Hugh and Ted escape from their relatives by moving, for Wilfred, his mother and sister are a constant presence in the town, his business, and his house. He makes daily accommodations with these mundane relationships and gradually transforms them as he journeys into true manhood.

The physically slight and ailing man gains self-respect and confidence, gradually abjuring his sly digs at society, behaving in a more straightforward and practical way, and cutting through the emotional blackmail of his sister. Slowly he becomes the man of the house. If some of his actions are reprehensible, he has a lot of ground to make up; we must remember that his actions would not have jarred the readership of the 1930s to the same extent. Secure in his sanctuary and in his frequent visits to the temple, Wilfred starts to assert himself in his house and eventually faces down his future father-in-law's physical bullying and his sister's manipulation.

Vivien's effect on him and his achievements in the inner and outer worlds add to his self-belief, but only when he moves from Dickford to Dickmouth does he realise just how debilitating the atmosphere of antagonism and disapproval has been. Wilfred's family's view of him is as more or less half-witted—a distinction he shares with heroes and heroines of Fortune's short stories. He respects the tough core that resists this influence and he realises how detrimental "psychologising people backwards" can be. By this, he means the common habit of making assumptions about people and treating these as truth, resulting in the unfortunate subject fulfilling them through their lives. It is an important process that has probably happened to us all in some form or other during our formative years.

The Building of the Temple

As with Monks Farm in *The Goat-Foot God*, we become deeply involved with the careful construction of the temple. Once again, there is an old craftsman, connected to past ways of working and to the natural materials of the earth. With the shoring up of the building we are reminded of the perilous position of a building so close to the ocean. Again we have a sturdy building that has fallen into disrepair: this time it is brought to life and beauty by the skill of the hero and the craftsman working together, in service to the priestess, trusting her whilst not knowing what the outcome may be.

Relationship

So far in Fortune's fiction, the worship of the divine feminine is through ritual. This novel also shows it in day-to-day relationships and discusses temptations for both sexes.

With Ted in *The Winged Bull* and Hugh in *The Goat-Foot God*, both know what is available sexually to their varying social positions and have eschewed affairs. Wilfred, intuitive and open, is more susceptible: his grief over Vivien's disappearance leaves him very vulnerable to the various temptations of the flesh. He has gradually taken to drink and is shocked at the hold it has on him, only realising it when he honours his promise to Molly's dying mother. More importantly, he is sliding into an affair. It is a gradual process, which is halted and then resolved as the seasons of grief turn. Wilfred finds that he can cope with reading Vivien's papers, and by also giving Molly access to them, he sets in train her education into priesthood. As she grows in vitality and power, she becomes a fit partner for him, so that petty temptations then become irrelevant.

Molly needs Vivien's training: her father deserted his modest wife and family for another woman, and Molly has not had a grounding in erotic literacy—an instinctive understanding of her sex appeal—

which badly brought-up girls whom Fortune called "Aphrodites" have learnt from an early age. Tongue very slightly in cheek, Fortune praises the pictures (movies) for having raised the standard of feminine immorality.

Vivien's instruction is that it is the woman's responsibility to take the emotional initiative. It comes at just the right time, as Molly's family history nearly replicates itself and the bereaved Wilfred, Molly's husband, is tempted by a predatory sweetshop assistant, who has obvious sex appeal in abundance.

The emotional climate changes after Wilfred and Molly's move to Dickmouth. As Wilfred emerges from grief and shares his ideas, the vital spiritual element of their marital relationship ignites. This happens at the farm at the landward end of the promontory, a place more of the earth than the sea, yet of the cosmic earth, which is also ruled by Isis.

The atmosphere there becomes ever more otherworldly, a fitting setting for the teaching that will awaken and incorporate the primordial woman within Molly. The sound of the sea, the smell of incense, smoke, and moonlight all combine to herald the manifestation of the Priest of the Moon. There is a flowing and mingling of energy between Wilfred and Molly as they embrace, exchanging the love they feel but which hitherto has had no channel.

For the first time, we are privy to the physical progression of the sacred marriage and its natural consummation as the couple make love.

The changes in Molly and Wilfred in this period deserve very close attention. Following the teaching of the Priest of the Moon, Wilfred feels a subtle connection has been made between them that will set their marriage alight. He realises that they will be used for the Sacred Marriage, and when Molly begins viewing herself as the impersonal representative of the principle of woman and conversing with the Priest of the Moon, she transforms into a dynamic, vital woman. This is the final part of the rite started by Wilfred and Vivien: a human man and woman earthing the magical current by enacting for a whole generation the Sacred Marriage that connects humanity to the greater life of the universe. It coincides with the turning of the cosmic tide to a new aeon, from the Age of Pisces to the Age of Aquarius; we are left with no doubt that it is their mating that has helped effect a change in consciousness. Succeeding generations will be enabled to understand human and natural life as holy: "For God is made manifest in Nature, and Nature is the self-expression of God." [19]

The practical end to their story is that Wilfred and Molly are happily married, living in the liminal lands. Whilst they operate fully in the everyday world, their farmhouse on the salt marsh, on the landward end of the peninsula, has become, like Hugh and Mona's farm, a place of magic and enchantment.

The book's message is of large vision, and of work, creative and selfless service, and reciprocity. Dion Fortune tells us that the greater laws of the world do not operate on a tit-for-tat basis. We do not give to one person in order to receive from them in turn. The greater harmony of the cosmos ensures that what we do in love and service for the gods, as an act of faith and trust for the evolutionary current, will be rewarded in ways that we cannot predict. It will be entirely right for our enjoyment of life in all fullness. We, like Molly and Wilfred, will be supported by the unseen, fluidly interacting mechanisms of the universe as we harmoniously align our lives with the tides of the time.

---

19. Fortune, *The Sea Priestess*, 220.

— 4 —
Yesod and
The Sea Priestess:
Making a Foundation

There was the pyramidal pyre of burning drift, blue-flamed from the salt. And the slow waves licked towards it ... till at last the high fiery crest fell sparkling into the water, and all was still save for the slow quiet wash of the dark waves on the rocks again. [20]

The Sea Priestess is the novel focused on the sephirah Yesod, a word that means "foundation": it is aligned with the energies of the moon, and one of its titles is "the machinery of the universe." In this book, Dion Fortune looks deeply into the mechanisms of inner work and the construction of magical images.

The experience of Yesod is a complex one; it is an encounter with deeper life and energy—and it is also the foundation stone of our sense of identity, of our images of self and the world we live in. Its planetary archetype is the moon and all that is moonlike; indeed, we see that the moon itself is a powerful player in the book.

As with the other novels, there are four levels to this work of Yesod:

---

20. Fortune, *The Sea Priestess*, 17.

- **Malkuth of Yesod** is the ground or matter that needs transforming, here represented by Wilfred's family home.
- **Yesod of Yesod** is the entrance into the subterranean kingdom of life and dreams, here the cottage at the bottom of the garden.
- **Tiphareth of Yesod** is the place of healing and transformation; the sea fort.
- **Daath of Yesod** is the rock in the sea and the sea cave.

Malkuth of Yesod: Wilfred's House and Home

The basis in Malkuth is the situation in which Wilfred, the asthmatic estate agent (surely the least romantic leading man in a romance novel), finds himself. He has inherited the run-down family business and has had to nurture it for years: he is responsible for his widowed mother and unmarried sister, who constantly criticize and dominate him. The book begins with Wilfred unwell as a result of his efforts. He has restored the business to health and is made a good offer by a rival firm of estate agents. His plan to invest in a publishing business in London, creating a new, more exciting life for himself, falls through when his sister and mother refuse to allow him to sell the family home to the new firm. Wilfred is apparently resigned to the situation, but shortly afterwards he has an unusual argument with mother and sister, loses his temper, and has a dramatic asthma attack that confines him to his bed. It is while recuperating that he starts to commune with the moon. The asthma attack is his descent into the body and his entrance into the direct sense of Malkuth.

The Underworld Path

The underworld path begins with the life-and-death experience of the asthma attack and continues with his lying in bed letting the moon take him inward. As Wilfred lies there, suspended between life and death, he wonders about the dark side of the moon: he contemplates the stars and interstellar space, seeing there the origin of all life. The connection with the energy of life and indeed his own life is linked to the understanding of Yesod, whose name, "foundation," relates to the foundation of life and whose god name, Shaddai El Chai, means the almighty power of life.

In these opening scenes the Malkuth problem is revealed to us— the absence of life and living in a dull and contracted way—in effect a living death. We also see a profound distortion in male and female relationships: the emasculated masculine and the suppressed and emasculating feminine. It is this situation in Wilfred and in us all that the sea priestess addresses; and in this stage in the book Wilfred receives an important insight that we can contemplate as a seed sentence out of which the rest of the work grows:

> I let my mind range beyond time to the beginning. I saw the vast sea of infinite space, indigo-dark in the Night of the Gods; and it seemed to me that in that darkness and silence must be the seed of all being. And as in the seed is infolded the future flower with its seed, and again, the flower in the seed, so must all creation be infolded in infinite space, and I along with it. [21]

Here Wilfred is opening up to a deeper sense of the universe and his own soul more than ever before in words that are reminiscent of Dion Fortune's *The Cosmic Doctrine*. Fortune develops Wilfred's experience by quoting from Robert Browning:

> God be thanked, the meanest of His mortals,
> Has two soul-sides, one to face the world with;
> One to show a woman when he loves her. [22]

In this quote we see the prefiguring of the appearance of the sea priestess, and it is this side of his soul that Wilfred touches in his communion with the moon.

---

21. Fortune, *The Sea Priestess*, 4.
22. Ibid.

We see an inner progression as he moves from contemplating the moon, to encountering the sea priestess, to contemplating the depths of the sea and stars.

Following on from this profound experience, we follow Wilfred's further steps into the deeper places of the underworld path as he moves out of his house to an old stable block at the bottom of the garden. In order to find this, he has to follow a "long-lost path," coming to a brick wall and in it a locked door with a pointed arch, like a church door, that he has to force open. He finds there some small stables, and going up to the hayloft he opens the shutters to find the stables are set on the banks of a hidden river that runs through the town to the sea. As he renovates the place, he comes across an old woman called Sally whom he employs to live downstairs and to look after him and the stables.

This is classic symbolism of the underworld path: we go down to the bottom of the garden or turn down a road that we have never seen before and go through an unknown door. In practice this is the inner road we follow in dream and vision that takes us to the Door without a Key. As we pass through that door, we find a new place to live in and are guarded and fed by the old woman of dreams.

Yesod of Yesod: The Stables

Wilfred arrives in Yesod and discovers the hidden river, twenty feet broad: it is in a way underneath his current life and will take him to the sea. Yesod and Daath are both transition points on the Tree and they are often reflected in each other. It is a reflection of the river that begins *Moon Magic*, though here the emphasis is on connections to the secret life of water and the idea of the hidden rivers that run through the world. As Wilfred establishes himself here, we see also his changing relationship to the feminine in the person of Sally, who feeds him better than his mother and sister ever did. In a sense he puts himself beyond their reach, and we also see a change in his relationship to the divine masculine in his appointment of Scottie, a very grounded working-class man, as a partner in the firm.

On inner levels Wilfred embarks on a deeper communion with the moon, Fortune teaching us about the power of the moon and the practice of dreaming with open eyes. Yesod is preeminently the sphere about fantasy and dream life. Ernest Butler, the great twentieth-century Qabalist and Fortune's student, would often say, "Fantasy is the ass that carries the ark."[23] That is to say, fantasy applied in the right way brings us into the place of spiritual growth and transformation. Wilfred is beginning to master the art of the directed daydream, or dreaming true, referencing the then-popular book *Peter Ibbetson*,[24] whose eponymous character "dreams true" from his prison cell, so that he and his love experience a spiritual reunion in each other's dreams.

We also see Wilfred, under the influence of Theosophical literature, imagining past incarnations for himself. He is starting to make connection with his deeper soul, and he notices but does not really understand the process of reversing one's awareness and going backwards through the day. When he tries to do so, he can form no connection to the deeper parts of himself, unlike Hugh Paston in *The Goat-Foot God*, for whom this exercise is fundamental. Hugh represents the training of the will, while Wilfred represents the training of the magical imagination; his path is not through will and action, but rather through the capacity to dwell on images and give them life.

As he deepens his capacity to flow with the image, Wilfred reads and immerses himself in story. There is an important moment when he reads the Bible imaginatively, connecting with Melchizedek in a way that he cannot quite understand. Melchizedek of Salem (Jerusalem) is a key figure in Dion Fortune's world. The priest of priests is the wellspring of her work, so Wilfred's connection through the story and image makes a tangible energetic link between himself and the inner tradition.

As this appears, Wilfred has an uncomfortable realisation during a Theosophical Society meeting that many of his past incarnations

---

23. W. E. Butler, *Apprenticed to Magic* (1962; reprint, London: Aquarian Press, 1990), 52.

24. See bibliography.

are probably fantasy, so he returns to communing with the moon, the river, and the sea.

These contemplations are deeper, grounded in body and land, and bring to mind the legend of drowned Ys.[25] Wilfred's imagination moves to the interplay of sea and land and brings him to the Fire of Azrael, the sea fire extinguished by the rising tide that is the gate of vision and the bringing together of opposites. This leads to a further image of the sea priestess arriving from lost Atlantis to make peace between the sea and the land.

The Alchemical Path

The sea priestess now appears on the outer levels in the person of Vivien Le Fay Morgan—anima, soul-woman, and femme fatale—who scandalizes Scottie and fascinates Wilfred. Here we find resonances of Fortune's approach to the Arthurian legends and in particular to Morgan Le Fay, who in Geoffrey of Monmouth's version is a great healer and teacher, the real Lady of Avalon. Vivien Le Fay Morgan is the teacher/fantasy lover who draws Wilfred onwards to the Tiphareth centre of our book, the sea fort on Brean Down. Her biological age would place her late in life, but when Scottie visits her she is seen to be a beautiful woman in mid life.

There is a very interesting small detail in their first meeting: Vivien has her collar turned up and hat pulled down in such a way that Wilfred cannot see her face. This is a reference to the Goddess, whose face cannot be seen save by those who have pierced the veil of the mysteries, and Wilfred has not done so. But as he shows her properties, they get caught by the rain and there is a moment in which she unveils and shows him her face.

Wilfred is fascinated and repelled by her—a conflict that provokes another asthma attack that leads to her visiting him in his stables. In this dream place of Yesod they exchange their experiences of their inner lives. He learns that she and the first Miss Morgan made contact

---

25. A Breton version of the "drowned land" myth. Others are the Cornish story of Lyonesse and the Welsh story of Cantre'r Gwaelod.

with the Priest of the Moon through a Ouija board, and she describes the area in terms of sacred geography. The river beneath his home called the Narrow Dick is really the Naradek, named after the sacred river of Atlantis, and Bell Knowle, a local hill, was a sacred mountain containing a sea cave. In an echo of *The Goat-Foot God*, we learn that local monks were seeking to summon the sea gods when something went wrong and their monastery was drowned.

In the mutual exchange between Wilfred and Vivien that begins with her revealing her face, we see the activation of the alchemical path. The polarity working here has two fundamental aspects: for Wilfred, the waking up of his dynamism and passion through falling in love with Vivien, and for her, the establishment within her of the image of the sea priestess seen through his eyes. This inner process depends on the alchemy of longing—it is the way of the troubadours, and Wilfred gradually embodies it as he follows the path. One of the crucial aspects of this path is the destruction of the current house of life, and we see this in Wilfred as he determines to pursue her even though it means his death.

Tiphareth of Yesod: The Sea Fort/Temple

This process begins as Wilfred brings Vivien to the sea fort for the first time. The vivid description of the journey across the salt marshes to Bell Head with Bell Knowle behind it gives us a general sense of the sacral landscape they are entering and of the sea fort. Vivien draws him down to the sea, where he goes into a trancelike state and nearly falls in. There is a powerful moment when she tells him she has no ulterior motive in befriending him and he flees. At this point the path takes us to the establishment of the temple of Tiphareth: Wilfred awakes as an artist and master of images as he creates the temple of the sea priestess.

The temple itself consists of a whole landscape centred on Bell Head, land shaped like a lion with its tail facing to the sea. Inland is Bell Knowle, with its sea cave linked to the area around Bell Head by a river: on the land side at the base of the head is a small farm, on the sea side is a ruined Napoleonic fort, and further out again is a slab of stone in the sea which is the altar stone and base of the Fire of Azrael.

The fort is square in outline, with a flat roof and set around a central courtyard. The windows are converted into Gothic arches, and the tunnel leading into the courtyard is sealed by two great oak doors. On the sea side Wilfred builds a stone pergola carved with sea beasts and sea plants. Inside there is one great room alongside the bedrooms with a vast window that looks out on the sea and is in effect the temple room. Beyond it is a stairway decorated with sea horses, leading down to the half-submerged sea altar.

As Wilfred is showing Vivien the temple, the son of the old builder who created it falls into the sea and is drowned—a curious episode depicted without feeling; and just after it Wilfred has a major asthma attack and has to stay at the fort. We need to consider the consecration of the temple and the necessity for sacrifice—very often sacrifices were buried in the foundations of sacred buildings to guard and protect them. We must remember that in the larger view this book is all about the foundation of life, and Wilfred is the willing sacrifice.

In this part of the book this sacrifice is being explored and made clear to all, for this principle is key to the experience of Tiphareth—in its simplest form the surrender of some aspect of life and ourselves given in the service of a deeper truth or greater need of life. The death of the builder's son and the link with Wilfred's willing sacrifice is significant—the son is a skilled craftsman with stone and in a way represents the gift of Wilfred's skill and life dedicated to the task of enabling the magical image of the sea priestess to come into being. In the same way that the builder's son is given to the deeps, Wilfred gives himself to Vivien.

The Desert Path

The next movement begins with Vivien describing the deeper topology of the land and the soul. Sitting on the landward side of the head and noticing the sea cave, she demonstrates that it is aligned with Bell

Knowle and its sea cave, so that anyone sitting there on the longest day would see the sun rise over the Knowle.

Simultaneously she teaches Wilfred the art of the Fire of Azrael, an important key to this book that is referenced a number of times. Azrael is the angel of death and portals in Jewish tradition, and the Fire of Azrael is described here as the fire arising out of the sea. The myth structure underneath this book is the loss of Atlantis, the great continent of wisdom and magic, at the heart of which in Dion Fortune's cosmology is the island of Ruta, at the centre of which is an eternal flame coming from the centre of the earth. The sea flame represents the inspired or empowered imagination, the fiery water or the watery fire that connects us to both an ancient place and a cataclysm that needs to be put right. Azrael is the angelic figure that teaches us this art and thus enables us to move through worlds. The sea priestess comes in the wake of this vision out of the drowned world—in a way, out of the deep unconscious—to bring something back that has been lost in the cataclysm. We do not see the fullness of this return until *Moon Magic*, but this is the foundation of that work.

The practice of the Fire of Azrael is described as laying wood out in the shape of a cross, and the wood of three trees is needed: Lebanon cedar, sandalwood, and juniper. Wilfred's ways of finding them are worthy of contemplation. He finds a cedar in his hometown that was brought from Lebanon, sandalwood he buys from a Tibetan in the port of Bristol, while the juniper is supplied by gypsies, one of whom reads the tarot for him, giving him the High Priestess card and the Hanged Man and telling him that a woman is preparing to sacrifice him.

The practice of finding vision in the Fire of Azrael links them with the deep spiritual traditions of the world, beginning with the Himalayas, the highest place on earth, leading to the Middle East and the roots of Sumeria and the Fertile Crescent before turning westwards to the water and soil of Britain, and all leading back to drowned Atlantis—the deepest and most ancient place. This connection with the deep roots of the tradition leads to the establishment of the temple and the creation of the Fire of Azrael at the point at which the sea meets the land. We see also the coming of the Priest of the Moon, Vivien's inner teacher, who takes charge of the work and draws them deeper into Atlantis. In the process we see Wilfred communing with the deep archetypes and the primordial energies of life: there is a profound moment in which he is taken in vision to the part of the Atlantic where Atlantis once stood and is received by vast angelic figures. There he is consecrated in such a way that forever afterwards he perceives the sacredness of life and death.

Daath of Yesod: The Rite of Isis, the Rock in the Sea, and the Sea Cave

The experience of Daath of Yesod is the culminating work in which both participants undergo the experience of death and rebirth. It begins with Wilfred sitting in the sea cave waiting for moonrise and sinking into trance in which he connects with the beginning of the universe. As the moon rises he feels the call of the Goddess and slowly walks to the temple, where she is waiting for him. Vivien is to him as the Goddess: in a key moment in the rite she presents herself as the veiled Black Isis, telling him that those who part her veil must die. Assenting, he feels his life flowing to her, consecrating her as the Goddess, giving himself entirely to her. He finds himself journeying into death until the energy changes and Vivien arises as the fertile mother and returns his life to him. At this point she walks out into the rock in the sea, becoming one with the sea: he never sees her again. He is taught by the Priest of the Moon, who takes him into the mysteries and implants images and thoughts in him that will later come to fruition. The vigil cave is dynamited and we do not know if Vivien is within the cave or within the deeps of the sea.

This is a powerful magical image, for it suggests that if we wish to seek the sea priestess, we must find her within the deep earth or the deep sea. There is a great storm after Wilfred leaves and the sea fort collapses, the temple having fulfilled its purpose.

Crowning: Daath to Kether

The crowning experience of this book is the partnership between Molly and Wilfred; she becomes a priestess, the pair become magical partners, and we are then shown a meditation regime whereby the sea and moon mysteries become grounded in their lives. They live in the farm at the base of the Down, and the book culminates in the Rite of Isis performed in their home.

5

The Winged Bull and the Dance of Relationship

She was looking at him as if she had never seen him before; in the same way that he had looked at her when he saw her in her leaf-green robe, and Brangwyn, watching them, nodded to himself with inward satisfaction. The experiment had begun to move. [26]

Although *The Winged Bull* is a story of magical transformation, its plot takes centre stage. The most potent magical connection between Murchison and the winged bull is spontaneous, and within the first few pages. After that and the sun ritual, overt magic, in theory or practice, is absent until much later, when Astley's black magic ritual provokes a transformative response in both Ted and Ursula.

After the earthiness of *The Goat-Foot God*, *The Winged Bull* is airy in its nature—in the withdrawn intellectualism of Brangwyn, in the air element's traditional correspondence to intellect and clarity, and in Ursula's association with the moon. The story is not embedded in earth but moves back and forth between London and North Wales, between lands with historic associations that suit either the hero or the heroine. The two main dwellings direct our attention upwards— the roof garden with its view of St. Paul's Cathedral in London, and Ursula's sanctum in the high and rarefied places of Snowdonia, on top

---

26. Fortune, *The Winged Bull*, 53.

of the world, with clear air and long vistas. It is only at the end that Ted earths the current in his ancestral lands, in a farm that seems to have been grown organically over time.

This was the first book to be published in the Qabalah tetralogy. It is Dion Fortune's toe in the magical pool, seeing just what truths she can express in fiction, and how; her way is through the psychology of the characters. Knowing the importance Dion Fortune accorded the "head" and "heart" centre of the land, working always with balance, the central axis of the middle pillar is the obvious place to start. But it is not the easiest place, for polarity issues were, by the standards of her time, very risqué subject matter. It is a delicate balance for an author relatively inexperienced in the genre, who also feels the weight of responsibility as an occult teacher.

We have made such a shibboleth of equality of the sexes that viewing past attitudes from a distance of over seventy years is a challenge. Our job is to interpret ideas in a way that is relevant today. We recognise first our physical gender and how we express it in a world full of choices, and then our inner reality that contains both male and female components, to be utilized for our health in all the realms—which include the physical, mental, emotional, spiritual, and magical. Externalizing "male" and "female" characteristics in the stories, Dion Fortune interprets magic in the light of psychology and interprets psychology with a magical perspective and understanding. The magic is there in the story, but we have to read carefully to access it—and much of it comes, surprisingly, through the character of Ursula.

Ursula's Outward Appearance

Ursula is presented as passive and infantilised in the mundane world, a pawn in the magicians' game. Brangwyn, Murchison, Fouldes, and Astley control her movements and her fate: both magicians repeatedly refer to her as "child."

The writing is informed by the dominant patriarchal attitudes of the time, so that Ted, the novice, is consulted about Ursula's treatment, whereas she, the "high grade pythoness," is not, although Brangwyn acknowledges that, when not under hypnotic/magical control, she has psychological self-awareness. Ursula as a fully consulted partner, rather than a reactive cypher, could have contributed to a magical working of two partners and a mentor that we see in various forms in the other books.

Murchison's Psychology

The infantilisation of Ursula, so uncomfortable to our thinking, is an important key to Murchison's essential psychology. He is resentful of women in general and the cultivated Ursula in particular. But it is only through her child aspect that his compassionate, protective nature— the noblest attribute of the warrior—can open in service and giving. This is the only state in which he feels comfortable in their relationship, until the end of the story. Then, with Fouldes's hold broken, Ursula comes into her power. For the first time she takes the initiative actively in the outer world as priestess, beginning to teach Ted the magical truths that support and inform adult intimacy.

Ursula's customary stance, as a true priestess, is withdrawal and stillness; she appears suddenly in the flat and disappears to her own quarters silently after each scene. Even her domestic duties, such as making coffee, remind us more of Vivien/Lilith's cooking alchemy than the unwholesome efforts of Ted's sister-in-law or the flamboyant artistry of Luigi, Brangwyn's chef. Her sanctum in Wales is isolated, supremely private: even after Fouldes's attack, she refuses to leave it for the companionable farmhouse.

This space is necessary to one so active on the inner: it is through the mix of psychological/magical wisdom that she has imbibed from Brangwyn that we are kept keyed in to the inner reality. With this in mind, we can view Brangwyn's ordering her from place to place as a device, to rationalise the habit of appearing and fading that is a necessity of her inner nature: each time she appears, she provokes change in Murchison.

Re-viewing the Story

When we start to view Ursula as an active priestess throughout, we can reassess the story. Overtly, the magician and apprentice save the maiden, but beneath the surface, the story is about the active saving of Murchison, who is truly helpless in the real world, unable to support himself or progress in life in any way. Ted's active role makes it easy to overlook his limitations, but recognising them makes the story far richer and more evenly balanced.

It is the journey of two souls who must develop a relationship in order to become fully realised individuals. On the rocky road of coming to terms with each other's true nature, learning to value and accept each other, they reflect our own foolish mistakes. They are like the figures in an old-fashioned weather house: one comes out for fine weather and one for stormy, but they are never in the same place together. In this story of misunderstandings, we notice how often it is Murchison's complexes and insecurities that short-circuit what should, after the first magical ritual, be a seamless flow of magnetism.

The Dynamic

The couple's misunderstandings, advances, and withdrawals form the dynamic of their relationship. Murchison activates the magnetic flow very early on through an emotional dance with Ursula, then his protective instinct takes the brunt of a magical strafing and opens a channel which embarrassment—made worse by Brangwyn's comment "you little vamp"—makes Ursula reluctant to feed. She can only re-magnetise him when she remembers the war and recognises the nobility of the warrior. Then, she compares Ted to the pacifist Fouldes, and instinctively she responds to the fighting man. From our current place of privilege and safety, we should read the text with respect for the fact that the author had lived through the First World War and was married to a former soldier. Our twentieth-century views can be barriers to the deeper meanings that Fortune intends. She was, after all, brought up in the heyday of the British Empire. To balance this aspect of the story, we need only refer to Fortune's *The Magical Battle of Brit-*

ain (letters to students during the Second World War) to be impressed by her forward-thinking, global, and humanitarian stance.

Effects of Ritual

The effect of a full magical ritual on Murchison is initiatory: he is re-born, with every part of him changed. From clumsy, he becomes light-footed and agile, a Norseman. Murchison's was the active role as the sun, yet Ursula was not passive but a complementary nature force: she actively draws from him what she needs. After this, Ted has a liberating dream of riding the black horse: his transformation makes Brangwyn regret that Ursula cannot witness it. By sending her away immediately after the ritual, he has artificially cut their physical contact, yet pro-gressing with that might have earthed the connection forged by the ritual too soon. He—surprised by the success of the ritual—has to train Murchison before they go further, lest he fail through inexperi-ence; and Murchison, coming into his power and feeling the change of balance, resents Ursula's removal. His relationship with Brangwyn is becoming mature, as opposed to the hero-worshipping stance of the young soldier.

The Work of the Book

The subsequent story shows how Ted and Ursula undergo diametri-cally opposed changes in order to bring them into magnetic flow.

Ted's work is to integrate his inner and outer selves: to come into his magical personality and bring it through consistently into the world, in a way that happens naturally when his finest instincts are aroused. He will learn to generate a controlled power to make him effective in the everyday, and he must come to understand the magi-cal component behind successful intimate human relationships. His habitual gaucheness and lack of confidence are overridden at mo-ments of high drama—taking the blast meant for Ursula; carrying her off twice, the second time in spite of having just given grave offence. For all of these he fears he will never be forgiven—a view we might share—yet they are necessary actions in an unbalanced situation: it is a book of balancing polarities, and Ursula acknowledges his right to take control.

Ursula has only lived in a convent and as a withdrawn pythoness.[27] Her only male contact has been on a magical level; she undergoes a process of gradually integrating and applying this knowledge. Through the first ritual, she embarks for the first time upon what will become a normal adult relationship. Murchison's flashes of crude misogyny during the ritual show the worst side of the dominant male out-of-balance. As the ritual takes hold, the goatish instinct is replaced by his real nature, and it is contemplating the winged bull that pulls him back on track. His instinct is accurate that Ursula needs rolling in Mother Earth to become a saner, more normal person. But far from that happening from his satyr-like instinct to "learn her," the opportunities to teach her the ways of the world—ironically by saving her from danger—are activated by his true nature. She comes to recognise the nobility and self-sacrifice of the male instinct behind his actions, and her authentic response is to accept them.

Ted, the bull, symbolises strength and endurance; an earthy creature but with a fiery, solar strength; and Fouldes, the stag, carries the connections—shared with the greyhound and racehorse—of lightness and speed.

The latter's quick, supple nature reflects Ursula's own, and in her we see it as the liberating black horse, or the cat, an elegant symbol of supreme individuality. Fouldes and Ursula are too similar, with not enough complementary earth in their makeup, and she recognises this, comparing Ted's tough nature to Fouldes's brittle intellectual who snapped under the pressure of the magical work.

What she also realises after Fouldes's attack is the unhealthy nature of his attraction for her. Fouldes's magnetism is "epicene"—having characteristics of both sexes—which allows her to be dominant, an irresistible attraction in a world that had such strict expectations of the place of women. With Fouldes she has felt the heady freedom of intel-

---

27. A *pythoness* was originally a prophetic priestess of Apollo at Delphi who mediated messages from the god to his petitioners.

lectual equality. She has contrasted the two men to Ted's detriment, yet later realises that she can talk to him "man-to-man"—as Lilith and Rupert will talk in *Moon Magic*. Then, it hurts Ursula's pride; but she ultimately returns to that feeling of unfettered communication, in a totally feminine and intimate way.

Ursula decides to open to Ted completely, explaining all; but, as in real life, it all goes wrong. From that time there is a series of misunderstandings and unfortunate synchronicities. Their reactions dictate the action, which eventually allow each to move deeper and deeper into an understanding of the underlying principles of harmonious relationship. And, as is the way of us all, whether neophyte or magus, they suffer in the process.

The Effects of the Bull

The bull, after its first magical appearance, is strangely and subtlety present: absent from, yet active in, the plot development. Having set the esoteric wheels in motion, it is effortlessly hovering, until the successful conclusion. Murchison recognises that the bull image will "keep him straight," for it is his particular doorkeeper to the mysteries, as Brangwyn is in the physical world. Significantly, when Ted first relaxes in Brangwyn's flat, his host's face and the bull's face become interchangeable, as does his arm in its scarlet silk with the rose-granite arm of power. And we are given an early hint of Ursula's role as mentor—her first appearance overwhelms Ted as if he witnesses the bull walking off its pedestal.

It is when the winged bull—on Ursula's necklace—first appears to them simultaneously that she starts to explain the magical experiment to Murchison; the bull is their mutual friend. As the bull is guardian of the mysteries, it is not long before Ted realises that whenever it turns up, something extraordinary starts to happen.

Studying the bookplate starts his journey into an exploration of society and Christianity and all its attendant ills, followed by his first "tutorial" with Brangwyn. Whenever Ted has demeaning thoughts, the image of the bull brings him back to his proper state. He is glamoured by the hope that the bull will take wing, and speculates as to what sort of adventure it will bring. It is the thought of losing the glorious uprush of power, the sense of possibility and the feeling of being a baited bull, that makes him charge and rescue Ursula in the café in Wales and pursue Fouldes like a berserker in their final fight.

The situations that Murchison most fears—the "goatish" aspects of losing control, awakening the lowest passions—are transmuted by the influence of the winged bull: although Astley tries to arouse his base instincts with a pornographic retelling of the Minotaur myth, Murchison finds when he walks a labyrinth in fear of the minotaur that he finds instead the virgin. Fearing passion, he finds supreme peace, which is Brangwyn's guide to a true spiritual mating.

A deep part of him recognises this—even before the Ritual of the Sun, when, plodding like the bull breaking new ground, he uses Ursula's Christian name and communicates through touch, holding her hand. The peace that he experiences then foreshadows the final mating at the end of the book. Yet even as he forms the magical personality gradually throughout the book, his position of servant in the household constantly inhibits his initiative, so he keeps responding in the old accustomed way.

With our understanding of an underlying reciprocal, symbiotic, and, most importantly, equal exchange between Ursula and Murchison, their journey is a fluctuating wave of magnetism, constantly moving and changing. It carries the protagonists across countries that support their own energies, allowing the human protagonists to respond not only to events but to the deep energies of place.

Wales

Murchison is acutely aware of Wales as a foreign country. It has another language; it is primitive and the heights of the mountain are the place of gods strange to him. Here, where he is most disadvantaged, it is Gwennie the sheep dog, a guardian wedded to the soil, who protects Ursula. Murchison is disempowered, far from his native soil. It is Ursula's role, in her sanctum of warmth and dim light, to make him welcome after his dash to her side. Instead he overhears a conversation that sounds the death knell of his hopes, turning him to stone. From thence, in Wales, his reactions all come from his ingrained insecurities.

But in Wales, the Celtic Ursula's natural homeland, she comes to terms with the magical experiment and recognises Ted's worth. Her deep introspection tells us what has been happening beneath the surface: her revealing self-analysis explains much of the modus operandi of the magic of relationship. Astley accurately explains the virginal warring with the bohemian in Ursula's psychology, but in Wales she faces up to her fate, with the maturity to excuse Murchison's worst excesses of behaviour. She has reached a level of understanding and is ready to progress to a physical level—unlike Ted, whose fear of intimacy still needs to be addressed.

His lack of desire, or inability to acknowledge and express it, will stop the circuit between them, for the impartial kindness of the warrior is not enough. Ted's early vision of coming home to a wife and children shows the conclusion he desires, but it is beyond his power to initiate the process leading to that end.

From this point, Ursula will make the running, trying to be friends, and determining that the next kiss will be returned, so the rite can begin. Unfortunately Ted feels that his behaviour will never be forgiven and withdraws from all communication, until Ursula is kidnapped.

London

Back in London and the Scandinavian-settled East of the country, Ted comes into his own. He supports Brangwyn's magical tussle with Astley and enjoys the seeming double-dealing, although it eventually results in Ursula falling into Astley's clutches. It is one of the descents into comedic observational writing that punctuate Dion Fortune's works, but the danger of the situation that develops allows Ted to respond from his depths once more. Ironically, the taste of the realities of life that Brangwyn and Ted agreed earlier would be good for Ursula is supplied not by high drama or "sheiking" but at Astley's house, where Ursula is scrubbing the front steps.

Murchison's selflessness in swabbing the steps after Ursula has dismissed him is pivotal: he is the only man she knows who would have considered such an action. They have a highly significant conversation on that doorstep. For the first time in the book, she is given a choice, and Murchison is the man who gives it to her. It is a reflection of the medieval story of the Loathly Lady,[28] where Gawain discovers that what women want is sovereignty, the right to make their own decisions. Murchison offers to help, but never to overwhelm her again. He acknowledges her rights: "If you will take one step, I will take you the rest of the way, but you have got to do that, this time."[29]

She sees his depth of kindness and self-sacrifice again in the black magic ritual that is a parody of Brangwyn's working of empowered and equal energies.

Astley's house symbolizes Dion Fortune's view that black magic is at the rearguard of the evolution of humanity, for his home has literally been overtaken by evolution. The building of the railway embankment has swamped the two lower floors. The cellar is tawdry, smelly, garish, and vulgar, a gimcrack venue for a prurient audience. It is an unwholesome setting within which Murchison touches the heights of abnegation.

For the first time since the ritual that caused the bond between him and Ursula, Ted touches the mystery of "the reality behind the reality." Suspended as if crucified, he takes on the role of the God sacrificed for another who despises and rejects him. Yet after this revelation, he, who has always been the man of action, is helpless on the cross.

It is Ursula who unties him and supports him to a space from where they can plan their escape; she shares her cloak and apologies handsomely. Their closeness in the dark is followed by the high comedy of the standoff that culminates in Fouldes's hold over Ursula being broken forever, as she sees him run like a frightened hen from Ted's

---

28. A medieval Arthurian story of a lady enchanted into a hag who is freed by being given the choice over her own fate by the knight Gawain.

29. Fortune, *The Winged Bull*, 204.

beating. During this, Murchison damages the pillars of the cellar, significantly undermining the house itself.

After heartfelt thanks, Ursula is once again removed, hopefully leaving Murchison to reach the conclusion that she has already drawn, that the experiment has succeeded. She writes frequently, keeping open a line of communication to which he is unable to respond.

Finding a house for the Brangwyns is medicine to Ted's soul, but he breaks down at the deserted farmhouse. It is when the evening sun shines on the old farm, as it does on the church in *Moon Magic*, that he realises he is literally "at home" in a house of his childhood and the land of his ancestors.

The therapeutic work of restoring a home for Ursula is a period of forgetfulness, an enchanted time. Ted is totally absorbed in the here and now, and the expression of his feelings spills out into the planting of the garden. Whether or not Dion Fortune had a working knowledge of the Victorian language of flowers, those that Ted chooses are remarkably apposite. Lad's Love was the plant used by inarticulate men to initiate courtship, and was dedicated to Artemis, a goddess of the bringing together of opposites—virgins and childbirth, the moon and nature. It is the plant both of Ted's nature and of Ursula in her power. The primroses lining the path symbolise silent love, and the roses bring the promise of their future life together; purity, thankfulness, and grace from the pink and white; voluptuous love from the moss rose, and the sweetbriar carrying the message of the relationship we have been following: "I wound to heal."

The last chapter is the culmination of their love story, and more to our point, it shows Ursula taking up the reins, initiating a conversation about the sexual aspect to relationship that inducts Ted into the deeper aspects of marriage. She starts by, in the parlance of the time, "making love," as the only way to cut through his defences, declaring herself openly to him and demanding a response. The style is both tender and joking as they draw ever closer: "Put more water with it. Brangwyn's given you an overdose." [30] This is a real relationship, not one that is idealised. And again, Murchison acclaims her right to lead

---

30. Fortune, *The Winged Bull*, 238.

when he tells her to set the pace—and he is not just referring to the physical level. Their conversation ranges from charting the course of their relationship, as all lovers do, to the beginning of Ursula's teaching.

She explains fully the principles behind the Ritual of the Winged Bull, the esoteric interpretation of sex, and the worship of God made manifest in nature. The "naturalness of the physical and the tremendous importance of the subtle and magnetic aspect"[31] behind it is what will make their marriage a true spiritual mating, blessed by the gods, and Ted's agreement allows peace to fall between them. Ursula has come into her own as the bringer of the gifts of the divine feminine to the male. The winged bull, with his sexual aspect, human intelligence and spiritual aspirations, flies effortlessly: the rite is successful and its blessings inform their reverie.

---

31. Fortune, *The Winged Bull*, 240.

6

Tiphareth and
The Winged Bull

*I am Horus, god of the morning; I mount the sky on eagle's wings.
I am Ra in mid-heaven; I am the sun in splendour. I am Toum
of the downsetting. I am also Kephra at midnight. Thus spake the
priest with the mask of Osiris.* [32]

The Winged Bull is concerned with Tiphareth on the Tree: the middle
sphere that balances the pillars and the inner and outer. It is the pre-
eminent sphere of healing, redemption, teaching, and guidance. Unusually for a Dion Fortune book, however, we can see a clear link here
between this novel and that of another writer—namely *The Rainbow*
by D. H. Lawrence. One of the key figures in Lawrence's book, published in 1915, is Ursula Brangwen. The book is based on relationships
between men and women and concludes with a powerful description
of Ursula envisaging a new creation as a rainbow manifests over the
grim landscape of urban Britain.

This image of a new world and a new relationship between men
and women is key to much of Dion Fortune's work. At the centre of
The Winged Bull are a brother and sister, Alick Brangwyn and Ursula. Brangwyn is the overt teacher figure in the book, but behind the

---

32. Fortune, *The Winged Bull*, 12.

scenes Ursula is the hidden teacher. She is in a way the rainbow bridge into the new world.

There are four levels to this work of Tiphareth:

- **Malkuth of Tiphareth** is Murchison wandering around London, homeless and directionless.
- **Yesod of Tiphareth** is the British Museum.
- **Tiphareth of Tiphareth** is Brangwyn's house.
- **Daath of Tiphareth** is Hugo Astley's house.

Malkuth of Tiphareth

The point-of-view character in this book is Ted Murchison, an ex-army officer who has not been able to find his way after being discharged. He is unemployed, living with his brother and sister-in-law in Acton. There is a sense of despair and purposelessness about him; he has just failed to get a job.

Ted's situation is the matter of Malkuth—he can be seen as the wingless bull with nowhere to place his energy. We meet him walking restlessly.

The Underworld Path

Ted is on the underworld path, walking through a fogbound London; like Hugh Paston, letting his body and instinct dictate his way. His feet guide him to the entrance of the British Museum. As the major focus of this book is Tiphareth, the underworld way is not dwelt on, yet its key feature is presented—the journey by night into the unknown parts of the psyche.

Yesod of Tiphareth: The British Museum

The British Museum is Yesod, the treasure house of images—in a strange way open to the outdoors, with mist filling the galleries; and Ted, walking into the museum in the mist and being confronted by the figure of the winged bull, communes with him. This is an initiation moment for him: he walks into the inner and is given access to the treasure house of images, contemplating the healing and salvic images and the images of disturbance. Later we learn that he has a capacity for ecstatic trance and during his war years drew on the collective energy of the Race to keep himself and his men safe in very dangerous situations. In a sense the war gave him a purpose, and he was able to surrender himself to those deeper energies behind him. In this moment he goes into this realm with the permission of the winged bull as gatekeeper, and meets the images on their own ground.

The winged bull is a central symbol and doorway into the mysteries expressed by this book. Babylon's ancient name is the Gateway of the Gods, and the human-headed winged bull a clear image of the illumined initiate of Tiphareth—the human, animal, and the spiritual at one and the capacity to mediate between the depth and the height.

The Alchemical Path

As Ted emerges from the museum into the mists, we find him on the alchemical path and seeking to penetrate the veil. Behind him is the energy of the bull and the raw power of creation that Ted used to draw on in the war. He finds himself in silence and total blackness and opens himself to the potential of life. At the moment of making the invocation "Evoe, Iacchus! Io Pan, Pan! Io Pan!"[33] he penetrates the veil and encounters Brangwyn, the first of his teaching figures.

Tiphareth of Tiphareth: Brangwyn's House

Brangwyn, Ted's old colonel, leads him through a series of alleys to his house: these are the deeper reaches of the alchemical path and the entrance into Tiphareth. It is a feature of this path that as you deepen into it you have to pierce the veil Paroketh[34] and work with the experience of opposites.

---

33. Fortune, *The Winged Bull*, 12.

34. The "veil" between the middle triangle of the soul (Tiphareth, Geburah, and Chesed) and the lower triangle of the personality (Yesod, Hod, and Netzach).

This sense of opposites and mystery is held in Alick Brangwyn's house, which from the outside fits into a slum street but, once you penetrate through two locked doors, is revealed to be a palatial house that, Tardis-like, is bigger on the inside. Once admitted into the sanctum, Ted is given a warming, sandalwood-tasting cocktail and asked to remove his outer clothes and don a robe. This is the beginning of the teaching process: he steps forward a little into what we might call his magical personality, reflecting that it would now be easy to invoke Pan in a green/blue robe. He is being shown the path of the chameleon, the use of colour, smell, and taste as entrances into deeper parts of ourselves.

There is an important moment when, drowsing in his armchair, Ted feels as if the face of the winged bull is superimposed upon that of Alick Brangwyn. He experiences the two becoming one, his arm in its red robe as the arm of power of an Egyptian god he had been attracted to in the British Museum. The episode concludes with his accepting a job as chauffeur and being offered a bed in Ursula Brangwyn's part of the house.

Here the inner teaching begins, for as Ted looks at one of her books, Jung on the psychology of the unconscious, he comes across the image of the winged bull again on a bookplate bearing Ursula Brangwyn's name. This is followed by a dream of the war with celestial music and coloured searchlights. It comes together in a moment of clarity in which he sees a small woman's head floating at the foot of his bed focusing intently on him.

This is the beginning of a whole process of development and interaction between him and Ursula in which she leads him deeper into the inner worlds while needing his energy and power on outer levels. When he returns to the house to take up his position, it is she who receives him, leads him upstairs to his room, and shows him the rooftop garden and the dome of St. Paul's Cathedral. He also spots that she is wearing a winged bull pendant, and his reaction to it leads him to tell her the whole story, up to and including her appearance in his dreams the previous night. In response she hints about the work that is to come. The emotional tonality of both relationships is interesting to note. Ted and Brangwyn are comfortable with each other, but Ted and Ursula are uncomfortable—a meeting of opposites in which antipathy plays as much a part as sympathy.

The teaching then shifts back: Alick points out that he needs a different robe for the morning, in earth colours, and explains more concretely what he needs Murchison to do: he will work with Ursula and honestly recount his dreams and experiences. Ted recalls a dream of chasing a black kitten around his room, which Alick recognises as an image of Ursula and asks him to read and contemplate various works on mythology and Jungian psychology. He brings Ted back to the image of the winged bull, inviting him to consider what being the winged bull might be like: Ted remembers the feeling when he invoked Pan.

The work moves on as Brangwyn dresses Ted and Ursula in green to dance together and then shows Murchison watercolours of ancient Egypt and Amazonian temples, introducing the idea of Atlantis and the concept of sacramental mating. This leads to Ursula encountering Frank Fouldes, her previous lover but now a black acolyte, and Ted rescues her and defends her from him and Hugo Astley, Frank's master and black magician, when they try to force entrance into the flat. Ted learns then that the magical operation he is engaging in with Ursula had been tried once before by Ursula and Frank with disastrous results.

There are various levels at which we can understand the story. On its simplest levels it is a story of recovery from loss—Ursula from the trauma of the failed magical working and Ted from the loss of purpose and direction following the war. On an interpersonal level it teaches about how men and women can work together magically, but perhaps at its deepest it reveals the relationship between different levels of our psyche.

The sphere of Tiphareth is the bridging sphere of the Tree—it mediates between the crown and the kingdom and it balances the pillars. Ted represents the outer aspect of ourselves, with our energy and dynamism like a maimed bull, with no direction. Brangwyn and Ursula are aspects of the deeper self acting as bridges and mediators—Alick is the more formed cognitive aspect of that bridging who teaches us about the nature of the personality senses and about the deep images that lead us onwards, who shows us the inner tradition and its roots in Egypt and Atlantis. Ursula is the hidden priestess, a Beatrice-figure[35] who constantly leads us onwards through hint and vision and longing. She bridges between opposites, between the white adept Brangwyn and the black adept Hugo; between the man of fire and earth, Ted, and the man of air and water, Frank. Her apparent passivity is part of the teaching—she is the still, small voice of mystery, sparing in her activity but potent when roused.

As Ted steps into being Ursula's protector, we see a potency coming into him, replacing the depression and resentment that has so far been a strong part of his personality. Brangwyn teaches him about connecting with the group soul of the race and the idea of divine inebriation. The next phase of the work commences when Hugo Astley calls Ursula to him telepathically. She responds, only to be held by Murchison, who counters by projecting psychic force back to Astley in a berserker rage, freeing her from his influence for the time. Murchison is drained of energy and the following day is visited by Ursula, who places her palms against his and restores him.

At the next teaching session, Alick explains what he is asking of him, to Murchison's disquiet; and he agrees to be a gigolo but not a bridegroom. We see his rage and resentment rising to the surface again; at deeper levels he recounts a dream of a zoo and a black panther being released, which can be interpreted as his deeper engagement with Ursula and feeling of fear of her power.

In a powerful ritual enacted in the deepest part of the house, the inner basement—a golden temple—is lit by six great candles (Tiphareth is the sixth sphere on the Tree). Ursula stands for the earth at springtime and Murchison for the returning sun, with Alick as the priest who joins them. Murchison experiences himself as the sun and

---

35. Beatrice di Folco Portinari (1266–1290), the principal inspiration for Dante Alighieri's work, who leads Dante deep into the world of vision.

they perform the Mass of the Sun, which has considerable resonance with the Rite of Pan found in *The Goat-Foot God*. That night Murchison dreams of riding a black horse across sand dunes and experiences a profound sense of freedom. On being questioned, he says that the blackness reminds him of Ursula's hair—showing us again that while externally it seems to be Ted protecting Ursula, in reality she is carrying him.

The Desert Path

The desert path first manifests in Ursula returning to Wales and Ted longing for her, though not able to admit it to himself (Dion Fortune makes reference here to Achilles sulking in his tent). It continues with an attempt by Fouldes to get Ursula to go with him from the cottage in Wales that is foiled by a farm dog, and Murchison driving across country to Wales with Brangwyn to get her. In the process that follows between Ted and Ursula, both experience their darker sides and enact them with each other. Here we see the stripping away that is such a feature of the desert path and a swapping back and fore of polarities—attraction and repulsion, love and hate, depth and surface. This process concludes with Ursula going into the House of Darkness, Hugo Astley's temple, and Ted following her there. Ursula here is a kind of Sophia excluding nothing: in her apparent passivity is a great mystery. There is a powerful interchange between her and Murchison, who finds her cleaning Astley's doorway. In that moment he acknowledges that she must go her own way and that he cannot simply carry her off. He surrenders his will to the will of the Lady, in acceptance of which he swabs the step in her place.

Daath of Tiphareth: Hugo Astley's House

Here the place of Daath and of profound transformation is in the experience of the Black Mass in Astley's house. We are now in the Abyss in which a ritual is conducted with Ted as the crucified saviour and Ursula the living altar. There is an interesting echo here into the beginning of *The Goat-Foot God* when Hugh Paston wants to perform the Black Mass. In the way that *The Sea Priestess* and *Moon Magic* are a pair, the same can be said of *The Goat-Foot God* and *The Winged Bull*. *The Winged Bull* takes the themes of *The Goat-Foot God* deeper.

We are confronted with a strange and powerful tableau: Murchison as the crucified sun on the black cross of sacrifice, Ursula hooded in a white cloak over a silver robe and lying at his feet. Only he can see her face (there is an echo here of the meeting of Wilfred and Vivien). As the Black Mass of the Bull proceeds, Ted has a surreal and powerfully redemptive experience of surrender and sanctity, as he hangs on the cross looking at Ursula's face. There is a moment when all light is extinguished, and in that moment Ursula frees him from the cross and, in a small but significant detail, they go backstage and find their way into a small room underneath the coal hole. There is no escape from the place, and in order to keep warm they shelter together under Murchison's cloak. There is then an experience of great intimacy between them, in the course of which it becomes obvious that Astley and his minions cannot touch them—they have gone beyond the Abyss by embracing it.

Crowning: Daath to Kether

The desert path has not yet finished with them, however, as on returning Ursula goes to a nursing home, withdrawing once again, leaving Murchison to complete his part of the path. We see a resurgence of his resentment and anger and a desire to leave her and Brangwyn for a job in Alexandria. It is possible that Dion Fortune is indicating here that at a certain point there is no escape from the mysteries, Alexandria being the great ancient mystery centre.

Murchison does one last job for Brangwyn: finding Ursula a new home on the east coast of Yorkshire, his homeland. He finds a ruined farm that had been one of his primary refuges when he was a child. In the despairing moment of finding it ruined, he is touched by the sun's rays and sees that it is the place that Ursula must live in. In an echo of Hugh Paston, he restores it, though here he is working not for himself but simply for her, expecting nothing. Not only does he restore it, but he arranges her furniture and clothes and makes the place ready for her. There is more than an echo here of the path of courtly love, and in this process his resentment finally subsides. Ursula comes to him and reveals herself as priestess by telling him she wanted to be a nun, and she starts teaching him the path of the winged bull. The book ends as the rite is going to be outwardly performed, in a way setting the stage for *Moon Magic.*

—7—
Moon Magic:
The Depths and the Heights

And even as she watched, the mirror seemed to open and another world appeared. She and the priest working opposite her were vast forms of light, their feet in the dark chaotic deeps, their heads in starry space, between them the earth as an altar and their hands linked across it. [36]

Moon Magic is an extraordinary achievement. Together, the story and the changes of perspective within it produce a pure vehicle for initiatory experience—Rupert's and the reader's. We will examine how the deep themes are relevant to our magical study.

As we progress in magical practice, we notice the resonance of flux and reflux in the organic nature of our work. Dion Fortune establishes the main character and his situation, then loops back for a master class from Lilith in the creation of the magical personality, via the techniques of psychology. But this is psychology informed from a higher source—the tools to break the chains of society's mores, to allow transformation into the wider life.

We move from the linear time of the first three novels into a sinuous, spiralling, touching, and receding of past, present, and future. We visit and revisit scenes from differing viewpoints, and the action

---

36. Dion Fortune, *Moon Magic* (York Beach, ME: Red Wheel/Weiser LLC, 2003), 223.

waxes and wanes like the moon; it ebbs and flows like the tidal River Thames, and the sea in *The Sea Priestess.*

Rupert Malcolm

With Rupert Malcolm, Dion Fortune's early psychological training has culminated in the creation of a conflicted personality whose journey to full expression is mesmerising. Within *Moon Magic*, the resentments of Ted, Hugh's search for intimate connection, and Wilfred's need to subsume himself in service to the divine feminine are deepened excruciatingly, in a way that makes us feel, as Lilith says, as if we are looking "into a man's soul." Rupert's psychology is dominated by his most significant previous life: he is the only character whose past incarnation came through at puberty as ghastly stories, and he carries the horror of blood with him from a past aeon. He also has a legacy: although a renegade, he had a priestly role and so comes to his present incarnation equipped with that training. The work he does with Lilith allows him to fully remember his past-life memories.

The theme of death by torture is not new in the books. In *The Goat-Foot God*, Hugh works through it by entering imaginatively into his past incarnation, but his visionary experience of Ambrosius's suffocation soon gives way to the freedom of ancient Greece. In *The Sea Priestess*, death is part of Wilfred's reincarnation experience; his past-life death by drowning is dreamlike, the culmination of an ecstatic spiritual experience that transcends its horror. It is after the vision that the resultant asthma attack becomes his gateway to his vision of the sea gods. In *Moon Magic*, however, Rupert's past death is not left to the elements— water and air. As a deliberate desecrator, his death is protracted and agonising, at the hands of men. During it he is confronted by the shade of the violated priestess; this is deliberately equated with Lilith's forensic probing during their first meeting in the consulting rooms. Later, she makes important points about the modern interpretation of "sacrifice" through this juxtaposition.

Rupert's past-life agonies are reflected through his continuing humiliations, which are exacerbated by being witnessed by Lilith. For the first time in Fortune's fiction we have an awareness of a genuinely dangerous man. Rupert has been pushed to the brink; he could easily take revenge on the world, and on womankind through Lilith, for the wrongs he has experienced.

Every emotional response—the fuel of magical workings—is powerful, because Rupert is mentally, ethically, and physically stronger than the earlier characters. He has a huge reservoir of energy and is more frustrated, and therefore is more dangerous. Ultimately, far more hangs upon the outcome of the Lilith/Rupert rituals, as the magical focus of the book is consciously to align to, and inject new energy into, the group-soul of humanity.

The story externalises the techniques of magic. Rupert achieves astral travel over water; he infiltrates the depths of Lilith's magically guarded inner temple, and he achieves a partial manifestation. Safely within her temple, his trained mind quickly takes him out into the astral deeps and the magical mirror allows him direct communion with the goddess Isis.

Our emotional involvement with Rupert encourages us to ponder which parts of our own personality have been bent out of shape in their growth. There will be many incremental steps that have taken us away from the path of our soul's calling. Most will be made up of our "Hugh" passivity, taking the line of least resistance and fulfilling other's expectations; or of Ted's lack of opportunities and subsequent resentments; or Wilfred's having to shoulder unfair responsibilities early in life; and some might be owing to the cruelty of our fellow humans. But we can hold all this knowledge gently, for we also have within us the Priestess of the Dark Mother, who can support us throughout the process of re-expressing these energies creatively. With discipline and distance, we will not identify personally with our past in a way that revisits despair; rather, the part of us that is Lilith will hold us until we emerge, as Rupert does, into magical transformation.

Ethics and Ways of Practice

Working for the evolutionary current, we are not concerned with the vivid psychic phenomena that endanger Rupert's sanity. As Hugh in *The Goat-Foot God* says, "One expects psychic phenomena to be reasonably tangible and to have something of the miraculous about them.... We've had nothing you could call evidential... But all the same we've had—or at any rate, I've had, some pretty drastic experiences. I couldn't prove them to anybody else, and I'm not such a fool as to try to; but I'm quite satisfied about them in my own mind."[37]

There is the guideline, learnt way back in the place of Malkuth, the earth. To wish and work for "effects," and to regard them as some sort of proof when they appear, is to miss the point. They will come, as genuine experiences, and we will hold them lightly on their own plane—in the imaginal realms that are both subjective and a link to a wider, invisible reality. We learn to live with, and respect, paradox. When we are truly home in our internal space, this becomes part of our deep understanding, an acceptance of and release into mystery that cannot be comprehended rationally. The intense emotion in the story indicates the depths of experience that we can achieve on the inner planes, and Rupert's mental state symbolises our profound yearning for connection. The corollary is, as Rupert finds, that the result of working will be an experience of the peace that passes all understanding. We step into our rightful place as valid and valuable connectors to the wider workings of the universe. Living with this knowledge is our place of ultimate rest.

Past Lives

Rupert's journey is rooted in a seminal past life—so is our own history of past lives relevant? Feeling that we need to investigate them might equate to Rupert's interfering with his process by consulting the New-Age thinker: it is unhelpful and might hold up the process for us. The whole thrust of this work is to loosen the tentacles of a self-obsessed

---

37. Fortune, *The Goat-Foot God*, 366.

culture from our psyche, to place ourselves in a wider arena; delving in this way can prove a personality-centred distraction that can easily glamorise us.

Our present reality is that for some reason we have been born with an instinct to consciously try to join with the higher processes of the universe, to advance our spiritual development and benefit humanity. It seems grandiose written down, but it is a sincere instinct that we need to satisfy to feel complete. We will do that to the best of our abilities developed in this, and perhaps other, lives. Maybe we're fortunate "old souls" who have been here many times before, or maybe very young ones. Just writing that invites speculation—but it would be into areas where no one can know the truth. Whatever that should be, our only concern should be in taking our rightful place. And if any information should become relevant from other lives, from the higher planes or some other mysterious source, we can be assured that we will get the message. The clearest hotline is disciplined practice, focusing not on our personal line but on the greater good. When we pursue the work, the tools we need become available.

The Magical Dwelling

Lilith's description of making the temple shows us how to prepare a magical space, as much in intent and attitude as in the very specific picture—pillars, furniture, mirror, lamp, altar, planetary symbols, and so on. She tells us this is a stripped-down magical lodge template, and it is far simpler than the Golden Dawn temples Dion Fortune would have experienced in her early occult career.

To each generation its own requirements: with limited incomes and small houses, most of us compromise, and without formal training from a magical lodge, the traditional accoutrements may not seem relevant. But *Moon Magic* is always there for us as a reference tool for many kinds of magical work.

We don't need a reserved space to use the psychology of colour and scent to transforming effect: and however simple the tools at our disposal, like Brangwyn, Wilfred, and Mona, we choose and create with discrimination. Like Lilith, we go slowly, preferring the clarity and sparseness of the classical ideal until we find the perfect implements. Once they are chosen, we can keep our temple artefacts in a box or cupboard except when working. Without the inestimable Mr. Meatyard to wait on us, we are responsible for the essential physical and symbolic cleaning of the space before we start, and for returning it to the everyday on finishing. And we will keep our own temple gear—a lantern, an altar cloth, accoutrements—pristine.

To establish a temple space, we look at the bedroom, study, and space under the stairs with fresh eyes. The changes we make, even if temporary, will establish it as "in the world yet not of it." Like the temple in *Moon Magic*, it will be completely camouflaged from the world of the everyday, a sanctum in which to connect when, like Lilith, we are waiting in faith for the next stage of the work to present itself. The book advises us on riding this uncertainty by grounding ourselves in practical action: as Lilith sews and cooks, walks and collects, so can we—or garden, walk in nature, and earth, sky and moon watch.

Tidal Nature of the River

Vital to *Moon Magic* are the deeps of the sea (represented by the tidal Thames) making us increasingly aware of the essential nature of elemental connections. The Thames floodwater and Lilith's near-fall into the river exhilarates, reminding us of similar rushes of feeling—gusting wind on a hilltop, swamping waves on the shore, a deep cave-embrace, and the ecstatic response of every pore to a dazzling summer sun. In *Moon Magic* the elemental link is of water and the deep earth, but to us, the four elements are all equally available. Engaging emotionally to them not only empowers us but also reflects our understanding of the tidal, organic nature of our work: the deep currents of earth, sea, and sky and the movements of the cosmos.

Contracts and Relationships

Part of Rupert's work is to slough off the past relationships that sap him. His loyalty to Lilith amazes her—whilst taking account of present responsibilities, he offers himself to her unconditionally. But because that is a trait of his nature, he has also offered it to his wife. It was a foolish choice, and, looking in hindsight at our own contracts, we find how often we have done it ourselves. We have to gently disentangle our early expectations of relationship on the human level and make sure that our present loyalties are still appropriate and feed our growth.

For Rupert, there are three stages to unclenching this primary tie from his soul. The first instruction comes from the outside world when the doctor gives him permission to stay away from his wife. This freedom, ironically, sets him adrift, for even an unhelpful tie gives our lives a structure. But as we begin to prioritise occult work over unsympathetic relationships, we use the discipline of Lilith to stop the drifting. Second, Rupert finally realises his irrelevance to his wife's life and the waste of their long suffering, which allows him to reassess his rigid code. The third release is when he saves her life, in his own mind, repaying any residual debt to her. That final repayment is swiftly followed by her death and his release from the contract. But typically, bereavement leads to the looping back to past attitudes and stances. If we experience similar circumstances, responses, and reactions, we must simply be patient, allowing and observing the process. We remain aware that the time will come when a sharp jolt or a gentle nudge will take us back to the discipline of the path—and keep our senses alert for that message.

Through our work, we develop a productive relationship with our inner selves, our inner priest and priestess, to join with the work of the greater humanity and evolution. These are relationships that do not take us away from the world, but rather allow us to return from meditative states refreshed and ready for the wonderful challenges of life. Incrementally, we are opening connections that will result in the everyday being informed by the greater consciousness. It sounds so simple, but it is work for a lifetime.

Isis and Osiris

In the earlier books, the characters are under the auspices of gods and goddesses. In *Moon Magic*, the myth of Osiris informs the action and explains Rupert's redemption. Here, the high king Osiris is killed by his brother, the red-haired Set, and then resurrected by the work of his sister-wife goddess Isis.

In his past life, red-headed Rupert is the butchering priest. He has, through his defilement and murder of the priestess, taken on some elements of the stealthy and jealous god Set, the bringer of destruction. Rupert in that ancient incarnation took what he had not the training to understand or appreciate, and the sacrilege was in his working from selfish human desire and not from a higher priestly function.

In this present incarnation, however, his main correspondence is to the murdered Osiris, torn and scattered by the vicissitudes of life. Rupert's early Calvinist training, the lost profession of sea captain, a loveless marriage, and his uneasy relationship to the medical work he pursued as reparation for his mistakes have all caused a complete fragmentation of his psyche.

Early in the book Lilith reflects the ceaseless search of the goddess Isis for her lost partner through the worlds, and the shadowy fellow priestess who visits her periodically provides the help given by the goddess's sister Nepthys. During that period of waiting and sewing, the flashing of Lilith's black diamond and black pearl remind her of the two goddesses: it is then that she first experiences Rupert's presence through astral projection. Once found, she emulates her divine sponsor, gently gathering the disparate parts of Rupert's psyche and teaching him the art of magical connection.

Rupert, like Osiris, has been emasculated, through his non-marriage and his puritanical morality: his natural urge to sexual fulfilment cannot be realised. Yet Lilith, again following Isis, fashions a substitute virile function for him—in this case, the rituals of the higher evolutionary magic. These advanced rituals allow him to connect directly to the essence that is contacted during sex, resulting in a spiritual union. As in the other books, the proof of its success is in the perfect peace it brings to its exponents.

The lack of a physical marriage allows us to investigate the mythic strain so seamlessly interwoven, taking us beyond the give and take of human relationship in the other books. Fortune tells us through Lilith that the sexual act is no longer appropriate between priest and priestess: "That epoch has passed away. Evolution has moved on. We are in the airy sign of Aquarius today. The workings are astral. . . . That is why you get the ideal of celibacy in religious life instead of the old ideal of fecundity. The priestess is installed on the astral."[38] And she also tells us about current practice, that "the use of the actual woman as the goddess is high Tantric magic, and rare."[39] She is referring specifically to the ritual where Rupert naturally conflates Lilith and Isis at the beginning of the mirror working, but there has been no separation between the two from his earliest thoughts, just a gradual understanding of her qualities and potential.

There is a subtle dimensional shifting back and forth throughout the book that insists on Lilith both as Isis and as her ancient priestess. In a reflection of the forms of Isis—the unveiled Goddess of Nature and the veiled Deep Mother of the starry heavens—Rupert continually sees her afresh, from the shadowy form who turns into the invisible challenger to the regenerating spirit of life.

We see the adept's journey and how her mythic status has grown, from the impoverished Vivien becoming the magical adept of *The Sea Priestess* to her present revisioning as Lilith. In *The Sea Priestess* Wilfred talks of the potency of sharing thought silently to give it power in a different dimension; in *Moon Magic* the living experience of that, the "experiment in telepathy," is the motif.

The Thames is also the Nile; the chase along the Embankment is also a pursuit by a renegade priest. Lilith's long wait for her priest is the search of Isis for Osiris, and Rupert is the despoiling priest of the past with his jealous Set-nature. When he, the impotent male, tries

---

38. Fortune, *Moon Magic*, 127.
39. Ibid., 175.

to dominate a ritual, Lilith controls it by arcing the power back up from the personal to the higher levels. In *The Winged Bull* the danger of Hugh's subconscious urges cause Jelkes's concern for Mona's safety. Hugh learns to integrate them through his solitary work in the chapel at Monks Farm, but Rupert's primitive archetypal levels come to the surface in ritual, and his civilised processes are in abeyance. Lilith knew that "the levels of consciousness were coalescing—the subliminal and the superliminal."[40] It is tense, but with Lilith steadying the power, the levels come together in Rupert's understanding.

At last Rupert is able to enter into the ritual as of right—as an acknowledged priest, not as a thief in the night. His role is spelled out: he has to descend into Hell to unleash the elemental forces for the priestess. Here we have the only past-life scene of the actual sacrifice of another human being, immediately moving to Rupert's agonising death and the scene of his breakdown in the consulting room—disquieting scenes that are placed together deliberately. They show the progression of magical and ethical thought into the present day: that the only relevant sacrifice is of the self. This can come in a variety of forms, most frequently of time, effort, and commitment. But Lilith is unequivocal about responsibility in occult work: "I have passed out by the path of fear so often. ... I do not mind [the danger] when I am alone. But I am the sacrifice! It is to that thought I cling. If anything goes wrong, I am first in the line of fire."[41]

There is in the scene of Rupert's torture and death one priest who is more farsighted and wiser than the others. This we may equate to the deep voice of our authentic self, not bounded by the mores and laws of time and space but only by those of cosmic evolution: it promises that the time will arrive for those who have acted too soon and suffered because of it. Through his ritualised ordeal, Rupert's very pulse becomes one with that of the primordial force, and it leads to the cosmic marriage.

---

40. Fortune, *Moon Magic*, 220.
41. Ibid., 143.

Rupert undergoes a symbolic death; Lilith composes his limbs as if for burial, waiting over the body like Isis over Osiris and feeling the life flowing back into him. After the vigil, he compares her to her own mummy, which transforms into the likeness of a beautiful young girl, magically revivifying before his eyes. In Dion Fortune's interpretation of the myth, the mummified Isis did so to her worshippers—making the point that the Goddess is in stasis until the time is right for her worship to return. Rupert says that they have paid the price to bring something new into the world. Like Isis and Osiris, having birthed the new aeon, their relationship will change yet still be a magical partnership.

Lilith promises that as the ritual has brought him peace—the peace that passeth all understanding—the next ritual will give him strength, as he will "learn to love as those love who are free from the Wheel of Birth and Death,"[42] which is the next phase. It leads to his truly understanding himself as a part of nature, with a level that has never been disconnected from the earth soul. It brings freedom from the personality and an acceptance of what is true connection with the whole cosmos. It gives him knowledge in a flash—not channelled through the rational mind but as a deep understanding beyond words. It equates to the mythic journey whereby Osiris moves into the depths to rule the underworld after his resurrection and magical mating.

Whilst Isis, and Lilith, continue to help orchestrate a changing world, both Osiris and Rupert will provide the power from the depths. As Isis and Osiris together brought nourishment to the ancient world—barley and corn, vines and grapes and the knowledge of how to farm along the fertile Nile—so Lilith and Rupert, working their magic on the bank of the tidal Thames, will continue to nourish the sterile society in which they live. From the union of Isis and Osiris comes Horus, the ruler of a new aeon; whilst Lilith and Rupert continue the ongoing work of bringing to birth a new paradigm for the coming age.

---

42. Fortune, *Moon Magic,* 228.

— 8 —
Daath and *Moon Magic*

He knew that, deep in him, was a level that had never been sepa-rated from the earth soul, ... and he knew that he too, at the spi-nal level, belonged to Nature, and that through the channel of that hollow rod Nature would use him. [43]

Moon Magic is the culminating book and takes up the themes of the other three in a deeper way. Here secrets are revealed and we learn about the mystery of the priesthood: what it is to be an adept and the path that leads to this place. There is much more in this book than is immediately apparent, so repeated and close reading will bear fruit. Here Dion Fortune reprises the themes of the other three books. We see Rupert introduced to the mysteries out of a loveless marriage; we see him learn the art of working with inner images and participating in a ritual of renewal. The difference in this book is that the mysteries are revealed, and we are taken forward into the depths. This book is said to have been finished mediumistically after Fortune's death, and in a way this is the book that is concerned with the mysteries of death. The story congregates around the spheres thus:

- **Malkuth** is Rupert Malcolm having gone as far as he can in his unhappy marriage with his disabled wife and frustrated life, and Lilith Le Fay seeking to manifest the greater mysteries.

---

43. Fortune, *Moon Magic*, 223.

- **Yesod** is the embankment and the river that is both the Thames and the Nile.
- **Tiphareth** is Lilith's house—the converted church.
- **Daath** is the upper room of the church in which the mysteries are celebrated.

The key process considered in this book is the consecration of a man and woman as priest and priestess and their coming together in an act of union and blessing. This is the sacred marriage of *The Goat-Foot God* on a much higher arc, the fulfilment of the images of *The Sea Priestess*, and the healing of *The Winged Bull*. Step by step we are shown the whole process, and as each of the figures in it represent aspects of ourselves, so we must carefully consider even the small details.

The sephirah Daath represents the fusion of opposites, the fall into the Abyss—the experience of being lost in the labyrinth of discursive reasoning and simultaneously the transforming movement into the non-dual. The whole of the work is reprised, explained, and taken into powerful new depths. Daath in some ways holds the mystery of the embodied creative imagination, and as we follow the story of the novel we are shown how to work with it, how to develop it, and finally the mystery of death, union, and resurrection.

The book is set in London but perhaps not the London we know. This is the archetypical London of Arthur Machen and Charles Williams:[44] the polis (city-state) as the Byzantines would have known it—that is, as the emblem and container of the greater universe. We begin in the centre of the city on the Embankment just down river from Cleopatra's Needle, and unusually this book has two point-of-view characters: Dr. Rupert Malcolm, a consultant physician, expert in the nervous system, and Lilith Le Fay, a magical adept seeking to work with the greater mysteries. In *The Sea Priestess* she works with Wilfred in order to embody her magical self, and in *Moon Magic* we meet this self in expression and pursuing her work in the world.

---

44. Influential fantasy novelists of the early twentieth century, whose works deal with the melding of the everyday with a mythic reality.

She is significantly renamed from *The Sea Priestess* as Lilith, Adam's dark and shadowy first wife. Therefore in the background of the book are the intertwined myths of Eden and Isis, through the operating adept bearing the name Lilith and working the mysteries of the Black Isis. As we explore the story, we will see how both mysteries come to completion in the final working of Lilith and Rupert in the upper room. In the mysteries of both traditions the issues of fragmentation and loss of perfection are addressed, and in both mysteries the dark divine feminine is the salvic force. There are resonances of the Song of Songs[45] in this book, as well as the unfolding of the temple forms and practices of the Black Isis.

Rupert Malcolm and his invalid wife are in effect a modern Adam and Eve living in the world of separation and fragmentation, unable to make a true marriage with each other: enter Lilith, Adam's first wife and servant of Isis.

At the beginning, however, both Rupert Malcolm and Lilith are struggling with the difficulties of Malkuth. In Rupert's case, added to an unhappy marriage and sexual frustration is having gone as far in his profession as he can and not knowing the way forward—a classic mid-life crisis, in effect. In Lilith's case, she is trying to find a place and partner to work the greater mysteries so that she can bring back the energy of the Black Isis into the world.

There are three major sections to this book:

- **A Study in Telepathy:** told from Rupert's perspective and within which we learn the ways of dreaming in inner and outer life. Here the journey from the outer world through the underworld path to Yesod and onwards through the alchemical path to the temple in Tiphareth is described.
- **The Moon Mistress:** told from the point of view of Lilith, and here we are trained in the mysteries. The process Rupert has been going through is described here from the other perspective. We

45. Also called the *Song of Solomon* from the Old Testament; at one level, a dialogue between lovers.

witness the stages of the incarnation of the priestess: finding and creating the temple, entering the dreams of the priest, and drawing him to her.

- **The Door Without a Key:** told from both points of view, through which we enter into the mysteries of Isis and return with Lilith to the primordial garden.

These phrases can be used for contemplation to help remind us of the deep structure of the book.

A Study in Telepathy

We are encouraged to feel with Rupert his profound sense of frustration and being blocked. We find him at a graduation ceremony with his peers, stripping off his robes, leaving students and faculty, and walking across London to his rooms in Pimlico beside the Embankment. If we are not careful we can miss the threshold that is crossed here, as he abandons his academic gown and breaks his normal routine. For the first time he sets off for the Embankment and begins to engage in "a study in telepathy."

When Rupert removes his robes and walks out, heading towards the river, he is walking away from his everyday life into the depths. He starts to make the underworld journey and moves from the exterior world of Malkuth to the fluid and reflective depths of Yesod via the Thames Embankment and the cloaked woman who walks ahead of him in the mists. By shedding his robes and with no wallet, he is going naked into this place: he is thrown on the resources of his body and must walk home.

We learn that his only solace in his duty-driven life is a recurring dream that comes upon him in sleeping and waking life, of misty landscapes and seascapes and the figure of a cloaked woman with a wide-brimmed hat. Dion Fortune reprises here some of the early parts of *The Sea Priestess* as Rupert communes with the river and lets it carry his consciousness out to sea. The experience of walking at dusk and actually finding the cloaked dream woman walking in front of him catalyses him outwardly and inwardly; she becomes his spirit guide at the very moment that his wife, through her doctor, asks him to stop visiting her.

Rupert is thrown on his inner resources and spends his time revisiting the dreams and waking experience so that the dark woman of the mists becomes more and more real to him. He learns that he cannot command her appearance but must prepare the place by vividly visualising the Embankment and its plane trees, the mist, and the river. Each night before sleep he sets off in imagination walking along the Thames Embankment—a resonance of Lilith taking her nightly path to the temple before sleep. After some time, there is a key moment when he leaves the hospital to see Venus, the evening star, rising. He follows it out, hoping to see the cloaked woman, and although he does not, he notices the church across the river. After this, he follows the woman in the dusk, losing her on two more occasions, until the third time when he follows her back into the darkness of the church, is challenged by her, and leaves.

This is a moment when inner and outer realities come together. Rupert returns to his room and contemplates the church: in an instant he finds himself within and looking into the room of the mysterious moon mistress. This is followed by a direct vision of her face to face, when she tells him all is well, opening a new stage in which he starts to commune directly with her, culminating in her appearing physically in his office.

This first part of the book shows us a powerful inner process of communion between the outer part of ourselves and the deeper aspects. Here in concentrated form are all the processes of the previous books; we address the sense of fragmentation and loss that is both the death and scattering of the union of Isis and Osiris and the loss of the Garden of Eden.

To begin the process of repair, the pain and frustration of the situation must be felt and allowed to impact; then the part of us that is Adam unhappily fused must put off his clothes and connect with the deep river that runs through the centre of the eternal city: it unites the east bank of the living with the west bank of the dead. The stretch of the River Thames that they walk curves to separate east and west, with Rupert's lodging on the west side and Lilith's temple on the east. The process of connection involves going within and, in dream and vision, reaching out for the dark feminine; holding oneself in readiness and persisting, so that eventually we find the way to bridge from the land of the dead to the land of the living, and discover our way to the temple of the dark woman who beckons us onwards. This is the same process that Jung advocates when he uses active imagination to guide him to the lived experience of his soul.

Rupert is living in the temple of Yesod when he is exploring the night side of the mind; the moment of noticing Venus is when he begins the journey along the path from Yesod to Tiphareth. He is eventually led across the bridge by the dark woman to the threshold of the temple, but is turned back. In a sense he waits on the threshold deepening his sense of the dark woman, becoming more and more surrendered to her until she comes to him and brings him across the threshold.

In Rupert's removal of academic robes and letting go, Dion Fortune is describing symbolically a psycho-spiritual process of moving from the world of shells and fragments to a new and living way. This is the process we must follow, moving our attention into the inner, from our side of the river.

The other side of the coin—the side easier to overlook—is the attention coming towards us from the deeper aspect of ourselves in Tiphareth. This is the presence of the moon mistress, first manifesting through the underworld path between Malkuth and Yesod and then more dynamically in the alchemical path between Yesod and Tiphareth. The images here are interesting Qabalistically: we have the fiery red man sitting in the west in the House of the Moon, while the moon mistress sits in Tiphareth, the House of the Sun, making alchemy together.

The study in telepathy the book describes is the communion between the conscious, unconscious, and superconscious parts of ourselves. The meeting of fire and water, moon and sun, man and woman, in Rupert's office creates the catharsis of transition. We can understand what is being described here as a death and resurrection, which also resonates with the Song of Songs—the marriage of the man and the woman—the uniting of the subconscious moon with the super-conscious sun.

At this point we step into the temple, into the presence of the moon mistress; and as readers we sit in the place of Rupert as she draws back the veil of Isis.

The Moon Mistress

Now the figure of Lilith Le Fay is revealed to us, making the same journey as Rupert but from another direction. We begin in the place of mystery where the form of the inner priestess is revealed to us—an interesting parallel with *The Winged Bull* that concludes with the re-vealing of Ursula Brangwyn as the priestess and teacher of the rite. *Moon Magic* continues that story, showing us the figure of Lilith as the ageless priestess. We are told that she is about 120 years old and was once regarded as the priestess of all evil: in the future she expects to be identified with and worshipped as the Goddess. She tells us that she is of Breton and Atlantean blood, a minor adept in the story of Wilfred Maxwell, but now a full adept and priestess of the Black Isis. The Black Isis is Binah on the Tree of Life. What we are seeing is the appear-ance of that priestess through the gate of Daath, and as we follow her she becomes increasingly vivid to us. This is the descent through the desert path from Daath to Tiphareth where we find the temple. In the story this is the unpromising, sinister church guarded by Mr. Meat-yard, the temple and the guardian manifest. Just as she is about to find the church, her path literally crosses that of Rupert.

We are shown the art of building the temple, first on outer levels as the grim and apocalyptic church is transformed under the direction of the priestess. There is a vivid description of her bathroom, place of cleansing and purification, and of the great hall with its hearth. The priestess takes possession of the temple, and as she begins living there she becomes aware of Rupert across the river, and the path from Ti-phareth to Yesod begins to form. There is a very significant moment after a walk in which she considers Rupert and the sense of the frustrated life she senses, and is taken into a deeper contemplation about this blocking of the deep roots of life. When she returns to her hall she finds this:

> Through the high, uncurtained eastern window the full moon was shining. ... A pale Persian rug lay on the dark polished floor and in its centre stood a Moorish inlaid table on which was a broad and shallow glass bowl wherein water lilies were floating. The moonlight shone full on this and a spot of bright light focused on the curve of the glass. The lilies lay colourless on the silver surface of the water but underneath were strange gleams of golden fire. I stood watching this softly glimmering bowl across the wide hall and being raised by the altar steps it was on a level with my eyes. And as I watched it seemed to me that mist was rising from the surface of the water and floating upwards like smoke in still air, and that within the mist there was a Light. Then I knew that all was well, for the power had come down; Isis was indwelling the temple I had prepared for Her and in the language of the initiates, I was on my contacts. [46]

The moment of connection to Rupert and Yesod is paralleled by the opening up of the deeper aspects of the temple. On the outer levels this is the finding of the hidden room within which deep magic can be performed, and on the inner levels, the building of the inner temple. Both these activities are the embodiment of Daath within Yesod; for it is now that the work becomes centred, as Lilith discovers the presence of Rupert within the temple and puts in motion the energies that draw them into communion. In that process, the deeper aspect of Rupert as the sacrificial priest starts to be seen.

This phase of the work comes together in the physical meeting of Rupert and Lilith. They begin working together with three rituals through which Rupert becomes initiated and ascends the Tree. At the

---

46. Fortune, *Moon Magic*, 64.

same time the inner energies, seeking to express themselves through Lilith, descend into expression into the collective soul.

In the first ritual, Rupert enters the outer aspect of the inner temple—the Hall of the Sphinxes—and prays to the Goddess in the form of her priestess, recapitulating the path of the underworld to the temple of Yesod. In response, the Goddess, through her servant, receives him and, through him, all lost and lonely men.

In the second ritual, Rupert goes beyond this to the secret temple and surrenders himself to the Dark Isis, who in return blesses him and all men with new life—the journey of the alchemical path to Tiphareth.

In the third ritual, Rupert offers himself to Isis as her priest and servant, bringing too all the frustrations and struggles of his life and the lives of all men. Lilith, for her part, receives him and takes him and all his struggles into a death-like sleep, watching over him all through the night and bringing him into a new life. This is the entrance into Daath through the desert way.

The Door Without a Key

This, the culmination of the book and the story, is essentially the Ritual of Daath. It begins just after the death of Rupert's wife and is, in a way, his marriage to Lilith. In this book his earthly marriage represents our fusion with things of the surface that do not satisfy us, and the connection with Lilith is the soul connection that aligns us to the source of life. The death of Rupert's wife follows his offering of himself to Isis and represents that freedom that is found as we commit ourselves to deeper life. The style of the book changes at this point, as we now experience it from both characters' points of view and there are parts of the ritual where their names are lost and they are simply called the Man and the Woman in evocation of the Song of Songs.

This ritual is different from the previous three, as here Rupert comes into his own as co-equal with Lilith; he becomes the sacrificial priest in function as well as aspiration. In this process all of his personal issues are included—nothing is left out. There is a key moment in which all the levels of his being coalesce—the outcast sacrificial priest of the past and the great adept he will be; and Dion Fortune tells us that the adept is built upon the outcast.

Another key moment is one in which the ritual becomes reality, as personal and archetypal themes come together and elemental power and personal rage are laid on the altar. The man and the woman find themselves in a cave temple and an alchemical act of death and resurrection is performed in which the rage and power of the man is offered to the goddess through the woman and they become one.

This is followed by a complementary ritual in which she becomes passive and he aligns his nature with Great Nature. He sees her fully as Isis and himself as the longing and fire of the deep earth—as in *The Goat-Foot God*, but on a more cosmic level.

This is the culmination not just of this book but of the whole four-book series: for in Rupert's frustration are Hugh Paston's lostness and feelings of betrayal, Wilfred Maxwell's suffocation, and Ted Murchison's rage; and within Lilith are Mona, Morgan, and Ursula.

The final scenes of the book are worth much contemplation. We find Rupert aware that the power has cleared the obstructions of his nature; he finds himself looking on the face of Lilith and, seeing her as a new Eve in a new creation, he is ready to sing with the morning stars. He sees Lilith unveiled and feels their souls as two centres of radiation interpenetrating each other.

The book ends with a scene indicating the hidden depths yet to be found as Lilith and Rupert stand hand in hand looking into the mirror: "There was nothing to be seen now in the crystalline darkness of its depths, stretching away into a far space in another dimension; nevertheless it seemed to the man that they opened on another world, and that again and again, by the same magic, they could be opened and re-opened. The world of dreams and the wake-world met on that threshold, and he knew now the secret of passing over."[47]

This is a particularly concentrated book, and we are best equipped to use it profitably if we have worked through the previous books.

---

47. Fortune, *Moon Magic*, 235.

From *The Goat-Foot God* we can connect to the living earth and living flesh; from *The Sea Priestess* we have a facility to work with the deep imagination and create and live within the living image; from *The Winged Bull* we can work with opposites and follow the teachings of the hidden priestess into the new world.

In this book, then, everything comes together as we work with the masculine and feminine in our nature, addressing the imbalance in ourselves and the wider world and bringing all into the presence of the Black Isis.

SECTION 2
FOLLOWING

Like the heroes of the four books, we have left home, and all that is habitual to us, to explore the ancient connections of the Tree of Life and bring an understanding of the wider harmony of the cosmos to our lives. We will now follow the stories thematically, through the building structures of our lives, and along the way we will apply the principles we're learning to occult work. Like Rupert, we will follow our anima along the way towards the bridge that leads to life in abundance.

9
The Work of Change

And with the change came a sudden feeling of something dynamic;
of a self-confidence and self-will he had never known before. [48]

The work of change applies both to the fictional characters and to the reader. Reading the stories to find connection, we realise that our circumstances may mirror theirs. Holding the possibility of an initiatory experience, we can expand into magical thinking through studying the texts.

We pick up each of the characters at a point in their lives when they must change. Up until this point they have kept a hold on their lives in a way that society tolerates, but it has been to the detriment of their psychological and spiritual health. Now, their situations have altered in a way that makes their present way of life unbearable to them.

We all have a longing within, coming from our need for congruence between our inner and outer worlds: we feel that they should be harmonious and mutually supportive. This need is uppermost in Dion Fortune's characters, and reading her fiction seems to promise that those yearnings can find resolution in the outer world. Her two aims are to investigate her characters' psychological processes and to prompt psychological responses from her readers *in a particularly magical way*. So every reading gives us the opportunity to start an initiatory journey.

---

48. Fortune, *The Goat-Foot God*, 288.

Dion Fortune warns the student that the occult life requires strength and health. She recommends having the stamina of the blacksmith, so we might feel intimidated and never attempt esoteric study, yet some of the stories have physically weak characters taking important magical roles.

There is a good reason for this seeming discrepancy, concerning the ethics of the occult teacher. Any who disseminate ideas, theories, and practice in nonfiction have a responsibility to the potential student, and so Dion Fortune favoured a cautious approach. Writing fiction allowed her a freedom of expression and explanation without the need for caveats, and the stories seem much truer to Dion Fortune's actual stance. Throughout her life, she made the mysteries as accessible as possible, dependent upon the limitations and talents of the individual.

We meet the main protagonists of *The Winged Bull*, *The Goat-Foot God*, *The Sea Priestess*, and *Moon Magic* at their personal tipping points when a series of small incidents have contributed to an internal revolt against their lives. We learn that the ranks of those who serve the higher powers can—and sometimes must—be drawn from the weak, the profoundly ill, the damaged, the disenfranchised, and those seemingly powerless to cope with the demands of the modern world.

It is reassuring reading to the aspiring student, and a cursory look at the heroes of the four "Qabalah" books shows how very different their psychologies, limitations, and talents are.

Hugh Paston * Wilfred Maxwell * Ted Murchison * Rupert Malcolm

The Goat-Foot God introduces Hugh Paston. Born into wealth, he was married and seemingly successful yet has given up on a life that is unsatisfactory. His mother and sisters and their families batten upon him for money: his marriage financed his wife's affair with his best friend. After a futile attempt to connect to his senses via a Parisian call girl, he has drifted along the path of least resistance. A fish out of water, he feels a faint disgust for the sophisticated manners of London's Mayfair and needs extreme situations, such as big game hunting and driving fast cars, to feel alive. He has no need to earn a living and has been going steadily downhill, until the crisis after the funeral of his wife and her lover, when we meet him.

It is hard to find a less "manly" man than Wilfred Maxwell, hero of *The Sea Priestess*: he is slight in build, henpecked, and has chronic asthma. He is set firmly in middle-class society in a small town, in the bland role of estate agent. Like Murchison, he has been robbed of his youth and freedom by the death of his father—he has had to rescue the family firm. Living in his imagination, he allows his mother and sister to dominate him, like Hugh in *The Goat-Foot God*. Keeping up appearances is their major concern, and, largely through emotional blackmail, they retain control.

Through Wilfred's diary we learn he is a true egalitarian in a small, class-ridden society. Being by natural instinct out of place in his own echelon, he makes friends with waiters in small pubs, the local doctor, and Scottie, the socially inferior partner in the firm. He is pragmatic, quietly subversive, and mischievous. Surrounded by snobbishness, he slyly pokes fun at the pompous and small-minded.

The hero of *The Winged Bull*, Ted Murchison, is a man's man, a warrior who was in his element in the trenches of the First World War. His straitened circumstances preclude marriage, and enforced celibacy does not suit his constitution. Profoundly class-conscious and uncomfortable around women, he's unsettled by the sophisticated heroine, Ursula. He dislikes the idea of both Christianity and marriage, having lived with a cleric brother and his harpy wife. He was cheated of training after he came out of the army and consequently has suffered through a series of dead-end jobs. He is frustrated and dour and possesses huge resources of strength, resilience, and an animal obstinacy.

Rupert Malcolm of *Moon Magic* is a success: an eminent man, a trusted neurologist whose word is law. Yet he is unsatisfied and undeveloped in every other area. He resembles a butcher, grizzled with an impassive, granite-like countenance. He has great physical strength and fitness and an excess of vital energy.

Rupert behaves eccentrically, with no awareness of or consideration for others or the conventions. Yet his persona conceals a child-like simplicity and integrity. He cannot connect emotionally and does not understand his students' worship or his humiliating reprimands by the hospital authorities. His semi-invalid wife and strict moral code force him into celibacy. He has coped by developing a hard shell and a formidable manner, a persona that no one can crack, and his nerves suffer to the point of breakdown.

To sum up, Hugh is a man of independent means, Wilfred has a mid-position in a bourgeois setting, Ted is solidly of the unskilled working class, and Rupert is a respected professional at the top of his tree. This teaches us immediately that magic has no artificial social constraints; it is available no matter where we are in life.

We also note that there are two single men (Ted and Wilfred), one widower (Hugh), and one man with a non-marriage (Rupert): all are celibate, frustrated to the point where they are withdrawing mentally and emotionally from social interaction and life itself. They are lost and isolated, fish out of water, square pegs that society has tried unsuccessfully to cram into round holes.

But despite this similarity, they are very different characters. In magical terms, this means that they have different energetic qualities, which explain how they have lived up until now. Rupert and Ted, who are positive, vital, and energetic, have suppressed their instincts and libido, drawing on their reserves. The receptive, sensitive men, Wilfred and Hugh, who seem powerless in the face of an unsympathetic society, retreat from the world, Wilfred into illness and Hugh into a state that he later self-diagnoses as the gradual disintegration of the personality.

The Need for Magic

So why couldn't these characters sort themselves out by more conventional means? Why the recourse to magic? To answer this, it is worth looking briefly at Dion Fortune's early experience of psychology and psychotherapy.

In her early twenties, Dion Fortune was in the forefront of psycho-
therapeutic practice: she was a lay analyst at a medico-psychological
establishment known as the Brunswick Square Clinic. The clinic developed the first psychoanalytic training programme in Britain, and
was founded by two women, Jessie Murray and Julia Turner. It was
open from 1913 to 1922, meaning that many of its patients were soldiers suffering the ghastly aftermath of the First World War.

Some of the leading lights of the early British Psychoanalytical Society had their first training there, and Dion Fortune was not the only
woman analyst to write fiction with significant psychological content.
The "talking cure" was then being piloted, and was practiced in the
clinic in a variety of ways. In the days of early experimentation, the individual analyst determined the type of treatment. This free approach
was later narrowed down to conform to a narrow definition of the
Freudian approach, and Dion Fortune makes her opinion clear when
Hugh Paston comments in *The Goat-Foot God* that Freud's system
would be better if he had remembered the stature of the priapic gods,
instead of treating them like mucky boys playing with dirt. We can
learn more of contemporary views of psychology from reading the
discussions of Mona and Jelkes in *The Goat-Foot God*.

Dion Fortune's own occult studies, pursued almost concurrently
with her psychological work, opened up possibilities wider than those
then offered by psychoanalysis. Underlying influences on mental and
spiritual health such as reincarnation, non-human entities, mixed-
parentage with non-human races, and the importance of elemental
contacts are all explored in her earliest short stories, *The Secrets of
Doctor Taverner*,[49] which she famously dedicated to her teacher, Dr.
Theodore Moriarty.

She came to significant conclusions when contrasting psychological and magical approaches in prompting change. Fortune was a forward thinker and the first to acknowledge that ideas and theories could
develop for the better. Her stories seem almost to anticipate the direction psychology would travel, into areas that might now be described

49. A collection of psychic physician short stories published 1926. See bibliography.

as spiritual psychotherapy. In light of these developments, it is probable that if she were alive today she would change the opinions she formed then of psychology and psychotherapy:

- That analysis alone does not effect cures
- That there are more things in heaven and earth than are dreamt of in the psychologist's philosophy

The stories show clearly her belief that it is through dealing with underlying occult causes that people can be healed.

Psychology in her time was in its infancy and was intent on gaining its credentials through strict adherence to the scientific method: it is within that model that Fortune made her pronouncements. As she heralds the possible harmonizing of the magical and psychological methods, we can assume that she would have welcomed psychology's progression in favour of fluid and intuitive approaches in tune with magical precept, and its increasing effectiveness in treating the mind, psyche, and soul as a result.

So although each character is going through a dramatic psychological awakening, Fortune's message is that the magical component is also necessary to effect a transformation. The magical aspect of their cures, including glamour in no small measure, is what halts them as they teeter on the brink of catastrophe, and then redirects their journey to wholeness.

In the liminal spaces of the mind, it is the opening up to uncertainty that allows magic to enter, that activates a response from the universe and increases synchronicity in their, and our, lives. In the mundane world, each hero's journey is expedited by the following:

- The total removal from normality and everyday concerns
- The glamour of the unfamiliar
- Being introduced to a deeper way of thinking about life
- A burgeoning awareness of life's interconnections and unfolding possibilities
- Becoming fixated on new projects

All these aspects speed each hero to the conclusion of this part of his life story.

Essential Character and Our Place in Magic

Dion Fortune's writing promotes a subtle difference in the way we think of the characters: Wilfred and Hugh, weak and ineffectual in the apparent world, are referred to by their first names, whilst the manly heroes have their surnames, Murchison and Malcolm, reinforced by the text. But from both the psychological and the occult viewpoint, their importance is not how they appear in the everyday world. The essential ingredient is quality of each of their natures: positive, outgoing, and energetic or negative and receptive.

These are their links to the universe, the qualities that place them in their own sphere on the Tree of Life. These dictate how their understanding develops through magical work. They are qualities, unrelated to gender, with which we can all identify and that link us to the greater society of life.

By placing ourselves in the place of each character, Dion Fortune intended that we should undertake the magical journey with them. Through working with their unique gifts they will become "joined up"—within themselves, to society, and to the greater cosmic life of the universe. From a starting point of no connection, pushing themselves until they "run on empty," we see them developing relationships in both the inner and the outer world. And they gain an understanding of the interactive, energetic nature of the universe, the "reality behind the reality."

Working with the Qabalah can bring the balancing and integration of the personality, which goes hand in hand with an understanding of the harmonious interaction of microcosm and macrocosm. As we reread the books, we respond instinctively to the underlying message driving the story, which is that our spiritual task is to work towards a state of congruence, within and without. Our job is to remain aware of the magical possibilities of life in abundance. Dion Fortune plotted meticulously and deliberately for psychological effect—both on the characters and the reader—and this is the reason that the books have captivated generations of readers over seven decades.

Although the contrast between the inner and the outer self is most marked in Rupert Malcolm, all of the men possess a childlike simplicity. Each has a nature that cannot attune to the dictates of a society that Fortune makes plain has an unnatural and superficial morality. So they are constantly at odds and are baited by uncongenial companions—frustrations that we all know only too well. The vital connection to life that will complete them, and the psychological and magical journey to this sense of completion, is an aspiration that we share, making us deeply involved in the journey.

Microcosm to Macrocosm— The Ills of Society and the "Sex Question"

Fortune introduces the idea of finding a way of living life in abundance in an artificial world through romantic fiction. She uses the examples of working magically with a member of the opposite sex, or "polarity magic," to illustrate how we can all make connections with our inner and outer selves and our relationship with the world.

Through the romantic story, she can clearly allow her individual characters to embody and express the dissatisfactions of society as a whole. For the time in which she was writing, it is an impressively forward-thinking approach, and her main commentator, Gareth Knight, has postulated that the magical work of Dion Fortune and her Society in the 1920s and '30s was responsible for the sexual revolution of the 1960s.

Reading the books encourages us to examine the mores of our own society, and to be reminded that their rules should not run counter to our own instinctual, naturally moral stance.

But it is important not to interpret the books' messages too literally. The emphasis on male/female magical working, necessary for a good story, is not the only way to work magic nor the only valid expression of intimate relationship. The novels should not encourage us to be "on hold" until our occult soul mates magically appear in the world: that is to misunderstand their message.

For through the various devices of each plot, the psychological changes throughout the stories are *within the person*; and so it can be with us. Regardless of gender or orientation, the changes to our view of the world and our relationship to it must happen internally. We will lose the opportunity for magical change if we simply wait for a literal reenactment of the novels to act as a catalyst. That's not to say that such a thing is impossible; who knows what might happen in an instant in our extraordinary world? But if we do wait, we are using the books as an aid to daydreams—tools to distance ourselves from reality.

Instead, we will read in a way that will set the process in motion regardless of physical circumstances; we will stop procrastinating and start to help ourselves. And in the magical way that the world has, synchronous events do seem to indicate when we have made an internal connection and are on the right lines. A tiny example: in *The Goat-Foot God*, Mona finds the statuette of Pan when she starts to decorate Monks Farm as a place for his worship.

Remembering Dion Fortune's strictures on the hard work involved in magic, we need not only to read and dream but to make a commitment to disciplined work. Our engagement with the novels must progress to active and inner work for our own journey to a magical life. The gods love the smell of human perspiration, and we don't work up a sweat by sitting waiting for our magical mate to materialize.

The stories explore polarity from a traditional stance, but even the most superficial readings show us that there can be equal and complementary connections between people of varying degrees of "masculine" and "feminine" qualities. The strong female characters alone make these designations seem old-fashioned and redundant. Thoughtful reading shows us that the qualities of activity and receptivity within us all are not necessarily gender-based—a point illustrated conclusively by the designations of the Tree of Life.

Our personal connection to the stories focuses on our yearning for fulfilment. But, as part of that spiritual development, Dion Fortune has a greater message, implied through all her fiction and a major theme in *The Sea Priestess* and *Moon Magic*: that the personally satisfying effect of magic is a byproduct of the greater work, performed for the benefit of all society.

If we choose to be co-creators of our own world, we have to have thought out what we are trying to achieve. And the main reason for magical work is take a share in the ongoing journey of humanity. The chief tenet of Dion Fortune's vision was *I desire to know in order to serve.* In claiming her fiction as a valid teaching material, even though we are learning from her at one remove, it behooves us, her present students, to tread the path in the same spirit.

Our first stage is accompanying the characters through each story, along the middle pillar of the Tree of Life. This diagram is drawn as a fixed template, but we do not work with it as a static tool: we will find that the Tree is infinitely fluid and relational, as we compare the four stories. Revisiting the stories with this understanding will help us to integrate the theory and practice, just as Dion Fortune promised.

— 10 —
First Steps on the Path

There is to every man's mind a part like the dark side of the moon that he never sees but I was being privileged to see it. It was like interstellar space in the Night of the Gods, and in it were the roots of my being. [50]

The heroes of the four books, in a deeply introspective mood, weigh up what has brought them to this place in their lives. In so doing, they open up the deeper aspects of their natures to us. This review process reveals their underlying emotional states and is essential for the clarity they need to move forward, and we learn a lot about their characters in a very short time. We will examine these briefly now, and place them in the context of their present lives. For after skating on the surface of life, the characters will begin to feel connected with a deeper purpose, and we can join them on their journey.

In Qabalistic terms, this is our entry into the bottom sephirah of the Tree: Malkuth, also called the "kingdom." This happens through paying attention to our bodies and the messages of our senses, an apparently simple process that is our first vital magical tool.

Dion Fortune divides her heroes by energetic qualities—two positive and two negative—but all are in hostile circumstances. The positive characters—Ted Murchison and Rupert Malcolm—resent and stolidly endure. Rupert overworks to suppress his demons, and Ted

---

50. Fortune, *The Sea Priestess*, 4.

deliberately turns from his known world when he reaches the end of the line. The negative men—Wilfred Maxwell and Hugh Paston—have their sense of themselves gradually eroded. Wilfred gives up life in favour of dope-induced dreams, and Hugh withdraws before collapsing in a crisis. They are at the point of having given up life as a bad job; each has done all that is expected by society, yet had no recompense from life.

The plots quickly move them: the positive Ted and Rupert of *The Winged Bull* and *Moon Magic* stay in the city, whilst Wilfred and Hugh of *The Sea Priestess* and *The Goat-Foot God* are quickly removed to the country.

Here are more useful messages. First, we do not need to wait for ideal circumstances to start our inner work. The work will create the circumstances. Second, whilst an isolated place may be the ideal for occult work, the demonstrations of magic in action show how diverse those places might be in practice. They invite us to be creative, to search out and develop our own magical working spaces. The importance of the space, wherever it is, is in the dedication.

Feeling at home and being embodied are primary requirements to coming to a deep connection with the world. We must experience the sense of space and place fully in the stories for the subtle interplay to work as Dion Fortune layers sensual impressions to seduce all our senses, to build magical dwellings that live deep within our imaginations.

The Hero at Home

By contrast with the ideal of the magical dwelling, our heroes feel that there is nowhere to call home. They are emotionally and spiritually adrift, and go through a series of significant physical moves that mirror their psychological journey. All are in painfully restrictive circumstances, and they are searching for "the hint of escape—a glimpse of fire from the heart of the stone—the gates of life ajar,"[51] which hints of a world of greater, and magical, possibilities. It is not accessible

---

51. Fortune, *The Goat-Foot God*, 10.

through the normal channels of society, but is what our heroes crave. It is a craving many of us share with them.

All four men live, and all four books start, in urban environments, which are worth comparing.

Acton and Dickford:
The Winged Bull and *The Sea Priestess*

Ted Murchison lodges in Acton, where the petty rules reflect a narrow thought and meanness of spirit that mirrors Dickford, the small town where Wilfred Maxwell (*The Sea Priestess*) markets his properties. The vicar (Ted Murchison's brother) and Wilfred the estate agent inhabit a grey area above working class but very definitely not of the top drawer: a division of the class structure would have been instantly understood by Fortune's original readers. Acton and Dickford are restrictive societies encouraging the aspirational snob, an accurate description of both men's relatives.

London: Mayfair and Gloucester Road:
The Goat-Foot God and *Moon Magic*

Hugh Paston, the man of means, is a drifter around Mayfair, of the privileged, bored, and disengaged class. Their manners and morals are despised by the educated and artistic Jelkes and Mona, and friendship blossoms when it is clear that Hugh agrees with their judgment. Hugh's salvation is escaping the artificiality of Mayfair to the homely, organic nature of Jelkes's shop.

Rupert Maxwell, the successful professional, has two dwellings, in London and by the sea, but feels at home nowhere. His digs by the River Thames are devoid of comfort or companionship: his house by the sea is home to his invalid wife and her companion, to which he is a barely tolerated visitor. His harsh manner alienates him from friendships, even among the professional class.

To sum up, both Ted and Wilfred have their powerlessness and disconnection pointed up by malicious servants in league with their womenfolk: Hugh is unaware of his wife's infidelity, though his housekeeper knew of it; Rupert has no dealings with those who serve him and resists any effort to change or improve his cheerless conditions. The lack of the sympathetic influence of women in their lives is a grave imbalance.

Their Response to the World

Ted Murchison is the bull of the title, but tethered and baited, stolid and powerless. Unable to earn enough to make a life worth living, he exists in his brother's overcrowded house with a ghastly family and a sister-in-law who believes in kicking a man when he is down as the best way of helping him to rise.

Hugh Paston is valued only for his money and initially feels that is appropriate; he suffers with a mother and grasping sisters who exert a kind of moral blackmail. He has faded out of his own society, just going through the motions. He wants nothing, and his housekeeper sees him going downhill, heading towards mental trouble.

Wilfred Maxwell's position in the household is undermined by the servants' allegiance to his sister's petty morality. Highly imaginative, he becomes quietly subversive. He pricks the pomposities of society, subverts his sister's charitable schemes and daydreams.

Rupert Malcolm exists in a bubble of overwork, unaware of his effect on the rigid medical establishment: he offends against the rules and barges his way through life. He follows the dictates of society to the letter, doing his duty by his wife and career, and becomes a workaholic to escape the need to engage with any form of empathic human interaction.

They have all been in these situations for a long time, so that stasis is now causing sepsis. In each case, a life poisoned by circumstance has reached a crisis point, and something must happen.

The Hero's First Journey

In both the outer and the inner world, all the heroes travel to meet their fates—even the chronically ill Wilfred, whose physical journey is a walk of a very few steps.

Crossing a large courtyard in the fog, tramping the city streets, discovering your own back yard, or walking by the river might seem insignificant actions, but each is cathartic. The inner journey of discovery is reflected in the real world, and each walk has a profound effect. And Dion Fortune tells us these walks are significant because each hero acts *out of character*, prompted by a deep instinct that cannot be explained rationally. It is that instinct to enter the dimly sensed larger reality behind the real world.

Walking is a valuable psychological tool, its repetitive nature inducing reflection. During their walks, the heroes examine their past lives.

Ted's musings tell us that he has been brave, charismatic, and a leader of men, and is still an upright, soldierly man with his integrity intact; he has refused criminal work, although his jobs have been a series of seedy dead ends. Absorbed, he is in a highly sensitive state when he reaches the British Museum.

Wilfred's journey is into the imaginal realms, when he is bedridden by severe asthma after a family argument. He is exposed to the moon, and his weakness and heavily drugged state lead to a deep connection to a cosmic reality behind the everyday. To escape his relocation into "a dungeon" of a room in the main house, his physical journey is to the bottom of the garden, to find the old stables where he will live.

Hugh Paston has the clearest boundary between his present and his future life: the funeral of his wife. Highly sensitised, conflicted by bereavement and his sense of betrayal, he has a revulsion against staying in a house that seems dead and empty.

Rupert Malcolm, like Hugh, leaves precipitately—in his case, from an awards ceremony—without a hat or money, in his hurry to meet an appointment with fate. His inflexibility makes him irritable and a restless sleeper, and his reserves are running low.

For the first time, Rupert walks along the deserted Embankment to get to his lodgings: the glamour of the water reminds him of his earliest ambition to work with ships. It is as he explores this inner dream-world of seascapes by the side of the River Thames that he remembers the mysterious woman's figure in his dream, and is thrilled to spot her actually walking along the Embankment, far ahead of him.

And Then We Have the Mist...

Like a thread running through all the books is the use of time and weather—both frequently liminal—which have a profound effect on both characters and reader. Place is most definitely a character in the books, and each can be a boundary space to aid the process of initiation. Through reading we are encouraged to open to the universe and recognise the influential forces of our surroundings, thus fulfilling in part Fortune's hope that the novels will initiate an inner change.

The weather is often referred to as "the elements," which are the building blocks of the natural world and magical practice. And of all the natural states, mist indicates liminality, the in-between state that allows possibilities that the known world can change and transmute, from whence one could emerge transformed into a new world.

Mist is endemic in the British Isles, and the Romans recorded the weather wisdom of the ancient Druids and their ability to conjure magical mists. Despite the stories' emphasis on named gods from Egypt and Greece, they contain a remarkable amount of arcane lore of the British Isles. One feels that the "sea of wonder"—the low-lying sea of mist covering the land described in Fortune's *Avalon of the Heart*[52]—and the other atmospheric conditions Dion Fortune experienced around Glastonbury Tor in the 1920s made a profound impression. It is worth remembering that, at the end of her life, her focus—including that of the magnificent meditations of the war years—was upon the Matter of Britain.

Today, thanks to private transport, sophisticated buildings, and a largely interior lifestyle, we are inured to the effects of weather. It is hard to imagine the "peasouper": the London smog (fog mixed with coal smoke) during which people could literally not see their hands in front of their faces. Deaths directly from smog led to the Clean Air

---

52. A book about Glastonbury, first published as articles in the Society of the Inner Light's magazine. See bibliography.

Act in the 1950s, and Dion Fortune, having lived in London since 1906, would have known it well. But we have only to drive, alone, at night, with ghostly tendrils of mist curling through the beam of our headlights, to become conscious that our world is not as secure as we had formerly thought; a new element of uncertainty has intruded. We have entered liminal space: the place of both danger and new possibilities. It is a place that the author exploits most effectively.

In each book, the overwhelming need for change is aided by the weather conditions: the liminal times and states of dusk, dark, rain, fog, and mist. Most magical workers today will recognise this seeming reflecting of the inner and outer states at times of magical change: it is the beginning of the harmonising of the self with the larger workings of the universe. Once experienced, it changes our view forever: the world is seen from a larger perspective and becomes a backdrop that impacts every area of life. This understanding and feeling of connection is what will make life worthwhile, moving both the characters and the reader from spiritual impoverishment to abundance.

Natural Talent, Unnatural Circumstance, Dangerous Consequence

The characters are all new to occult studies, but all seem to have a natural talent for contacting the unseen. Yet we would be wrong in envying the characters their ability to access extraordinary gifts, which comes from their extreme emotional circumstances. The gradual disintegration of their hold on life allows their subconscious processes to rise and become active, but this—loosening the hold on mundane life—is a very dangerous state.

The fact that they are such a disparate bunch, all very much "in the world" but in differing ways, shows us that Dion Fortune saw these capacities in all people, waiting to be developed. But the extreme way that happens in the books is something she expressly cautioned against in her nonfiction.

It is easy to overlook, on a cursory reading, the dangerous fragility of the main characters. But their worlds have turned upside down, and the descriptions, although brief, do not pull any punches. We must not underestimate the heroes' damaged state—a state that Dion Fortune regarded as most dangerous for occult work in the real world, but one that allows her to accelerate each hero's development under guidance.

Ted steps away from the path to the centre of the museum courtyard into the "primordial soup" in such a reckless spirit that Brangwyn later checks with him, "Had you said to evil, Be thou my good?"[53] The result of Brangwyn's sudden appearance in response to his invocation of Pan was that "his wits were astray in the fourth dimension.... His mind had turned bottom-side up with the shock and reaction...and for the moment subconsciousness had superseded reason."[54]

Wilfred, deeply drugged, comments upon the "curious inverted sense of reality. Normal things were far away and remote and didn't matter: but in the inner kingdom...my wishes were law."[55] Hovering between life and death, he feels no attachment to living, and experiences "a profound sense of release; for I knew that the bars of my soul would never wholly close again."[56]

Hugh is fading away, withdrawn from the decadent lifestyle of the bright young things: he notices his own state of capriciousness, instability, and feverishness and recognises the signs of an impending breakdown. Having followed the vogue in reading psycho-analytical literature, "It amused him to realise that he...was now getting a close-up of the disintegration of a personality."[57] But disinterest changes to concern at the end of his walk; facing the bookseller, "For a moment Hugh Paston did not know what he had come for. His mind was slipping its cogs and it scared him."[58] He realises how tenuous his hold on life has become, and that he can see no roads to travel to the future.

---

53. Fortune, *The Winged Bull*, 46.
54. Ibid., 14.
55. Fortune, *The Sea Priestess*, 13.
56. Ibid., 4.
57. Fortune, *The Goat-Foot God*, 13.
58. Ibid., 14.

Rupert deliberately courts his obsessional vision until he frightens himself with semi-manifestations. Because of his medical training, he, unlike the other heroes, knows very well what he is doing. But he still continues deliberately to court Lilith, who, evoked from the depths of his soul-longing, has become indispensable to him. Like Wilfred, Rupert feels no attachment to life; gazing into the river, he confesses to Lilith that it is only because he is a strong swimmer that he hasn't tried to plunge to his death in the Thames.

This is why Dion Fortune recommends attempting mind-expansion methods only with a trusted teacher. As examples of the inherent dangers, she instances gaining control over the autonomic nervous system—obviously essential if we are to keep breathing *without* our conscious control. And the danger of allowing the subconscious free rein in the everyday world, without the controlling influence of the conscious mind, goes without saying.

The tide in exploring the mysteries has turned since her day, and the fashion for being completely passive—as were the trance mediums of the day—has passed. As students we will find a balance between the inner and outer worlds in our studies, a sustainable place, as at the conclusion of each of the novels.

Awareness and application can be safe ways of inducting us into life in abundance. This becomes a dynamic dance, where we find that living with an enlarged perspective actually *increases* our ability to live fully and effectively in the world. The trauma and bereavement we can all expect from life will challenge and develop us for good or ill, and these are not times for occult experimentation: but the path of awareness and persistence is a gentle, enriching, and sustainable way, and is open to all.

Reaching a breaking point within the safe confines of fiction allows the portals between these places in the mind to open, and each character's positive reaction aids the acceleration of what would otherwise be a slow process of psychic development. Dion Fortune advises us in her nonfiction: when faced with these experiences, either embrace them and make a contact or bolt from them like a rabbit down a hole, but do not linger in a state of uncertainty in that strange territory. All of our heroes embrace the challenge, and all subsequently meet their mentor, in the inner and outer worlds.

Ted Murchison calls on Pan, via the winged bull, the doorkeeper of the gods, conjuring up Brangwyn to transform his life; Hugo's striving for depth of experience to give his life significance is taken under Pan's protection and leads to Jelkes. By his intimate communing with the processes of the universe, Wilfred has been taken under the auspices of the moon; he meets Vivien and, later, the Priest of the Moon. And Rupert Malcolm, through synergizing his dream lady with the Goddess, is rescued by Lilith and is accepted into the service of Isis. All thus escape the fetters of society.

The heartening message is that a combination of time, place, and circumstance will manifest to further our true work, if we take the time away from the everyday to dedicate ourselves to the path and open ourselves to connection. Brodie-Innes, one of Dion Fortune's early spiritual elders, was of the opinion that whether the unseen realms, gods, and discarnate entities exist doesn't matter. The only thing we need to notice is that when we act as if the unseen greater reality is real, the universe seems to respond as if that is correct.

Our heroes have taken their first journey into the magical unknown. They have reviewed the past and acknowledged the reality of their inner connection and so have set out on adventures to transform their lives on the physical plane.

─────11─────
The Emotional Connection

The lives of a man are strung like pearls on the thread of his spirit; and never in all his journey goes he alone, for that which is solitary is barren. [59]

Dion Fortune has told us that she viewed her fiction as if on a screen. The images arose and she transcribed what she saw—as the psychology of the characters gradually opened to her, dictating the action of the plot. And each of the characters was simultaneously Everyman—the typical human on their journey—and also of heroic stature: a representation of the possibilities within us all.

Archetypal Resonance

It is easy to categorize three of her characters: Ted is the Warrior, Wilfred the Artist, and Rupert the Priest. Hugh is more difficult, having made no independent mark in the world. Absorbed by his journey of integration, he is initially led by Mona and Jelkes. But as his alter ego, Ambrosius, becomes integrated into his psyche in a healthy way, he soon starts to make things happen: he becomes the archetypal Active Man of Earth who crafts the work of change.

The archetypal resonance of each character is mediated by their upbringing and experience, and, in stories where even the domestics

---

59. Fortune, *The Sea Priestess*, 163.

are well sketched, these main characters have an authentic presence that provokes our empathy.

Ted

Ted needs to strive for goals, to dare and achieve—all of which has been denied him in peacetime. Altruism is an essential part of his psyche: he needs to be loyal to a cause, to be of service, and to protect. We feel the frustrations of a strong, dependable person tethered by circumstance. His transformative power is anger—at injustice and at abuse of the weak—and whilst this warrior energy can be utilized productively in peacetime as in war, it requires the right opportunities.

Ted has experienced the energy of the warrior in the inebriation of battle, in protecting Ursula: then, he loses his self-doubts and inhibitions and is completely effective. The only time he makes this transition without the catalyst of anger or emergency is in the early rituals, where his emotional connection to a primal level of consciousness makes him a worthy Priest. For the first time with awareness, he courts, submits to, and experiences divine inebriation, and becomes one with the greater life. He becomes the vehicle for Horus, and everything that is Ted Murchison is swept away. He feels himself reborn in the knowledge of ritual from the oldest times.

Wilfred

It is the artist Wilfred's "dynamism" that makes him so useful for magic. His priestess Vivien notices that despite his illness, he has an amazing store of it. His magnetic vitality increases in relation to the depletion of his body. Through the freeing nature of his illness for his psyche and his imagination he can regain past-life memories: but as artist, he needs to work under the direction of a muse, and his emotional connection to her underpins his development. Surrendering to her influence opens a creative path: his achievements are recognised by the artistic world as well as by the priestess in the sea fort. His other latent qualities slowly begin to emerge, along with his artistic and ritual development, so that by the end of the book he is transformed into a councilor and city father. More importantly, he develops the capacity and depth to adopt magical principles in his marriage, making it the highest and most complete union.

Wilfred's passive nature is important to the relationship of muse/ artist, which is essentially magical and a reversal of traditional gender roles. In the relationship of Wilfred and Vivien, she inspires him, and he gestates and gives birth to artistic expression. His negative temperament is perfectly suited to this role, in spite of his anger at Vivien's insistence on his many feminine qualities. Having lost his attachment to life, he, like Ted and Rupert, becomes aware of his sacrificial role, and is the one whose temperament allows him to submit most gladly to it.

Hugh

Hugh is the most profoundly negative of the characters, both temperamentally and through circumstances, relying on external stimuli such as big game hunting and car racing to start to feel at all. He cannot access his deeper levels; the personality generally on show, nervous and inhibited, is the result of the inquisition he suffered before his last death. He is tall and stooped, with jerky, awkward movements. Everything is uncoordinated and he has no stamina, subsisting on nervous energy that burns out quickly. His mastery of fast cars is a result of his past-life persona, Ambrosius, coming to the fore in the heat of excitement. Later he will find a connection to those deeps through internal processes. Hugh's past-life recall develops throughout the book, and his personality changes as he absorbs Ambrosius into his psyche. As with the other male characters, it is through his priestess that he can harness the depth of emotion he needs, through anger at his frustrated life—in both incarnations—and at the thought of her being taken from him. To access that subconscious part of his personality, he realises, requires danger or the threatening of his relationship with Mona.

Rupert

The outwardly dominant Rupert has a taste for martyrdom: he no longer wants to fight to protect the weak, but to put himself in the hands of a woman who will make demands on him. After a wasted emotional life, he has had his fill of giving where his gifts are not appreciated. He wants to know what is required, but he is the most generous in his giving: Lilith's strength provokes a willingness in him to "pour out his life like wine"[60]—like Wilfred, to surrender completely. Lilith delights him because he can never conquer her.

Influenced by a strict upbringing, Rupert would never countenance an affair, and that, combined with a huge reserve of life force that must have an outlet, makes him ideal for magical work. He is Lilith's equal intellectually, and his medical training mirrors the dedication of her occult path: he soaks up her teaching. It is when he submits completely to her in a perfect sacrifice, even at the risk of his death, that he achieves greatness, and becomes the powerful priest that Lilith needs.

So far we've seen that a spontaneous shift of perspective, time, and space combine to allow the characters to progress. One very natural reaction to these unsettling experiences might be to switch on lights and radio and return to normal as quickly as possible: for they are all aware of the potential danger of their fragile states. Rupert particularly strains to return to his usual habit through focusing on his work. But, with nowhere worth returning to, all are impelled by extreme need. The next stage will be making time and space for a more considered exploration of what they have experienced. And, if the voice of our inner need is not to be swamped by everyday concerns, we need to find hints in the texts to maintaining our own practice.

The main component in their, and our, development is accessing the imagination, and wedding it to the emotions. A strong emotional attachment is essential if magic is to work. The fiction tells us that the pump must be primed; the characters must be in the right state if they are to have the right responses, and so must we, the readers.

---

60. Fortune, *Moon Magic*, 28.

Emotional Responses

In all the books, there is a rhythm to the prose and a mantra-like repetition of words to build atmosphere. Words such as *tranquil, lull, drowsed, aromatic, sweet, shadowy,* and *gleaming* form a ribbon of rich vowel sounds, which we could repeat to form an effective relaxation exercise.

Reading key paragraphs aloud from any of the books can have a profound effect on listeners, and extracts from Dion Fortune's stories have often been used for this purpose. We are drawn into the characters' emotional responses, and how we react depends on what the author makes overt through the text.

As Wilfred's prose style echoes the rhythms of the sea, so Rupert's journey between his inner and outer worlds is rhythmic, ebbing, and flowing, but all the time gaining in strength. We remember the liminal state and how we can progress whilst in it, and what is possible for us, as we read these texts. We also realise, by contrast, the strong drag and pull of our habitual, rigid thinking. Liminal space is fluid—an organic process of flux and reflux, not a forward-only linear progress. Considering this through reading helps us in developing an understanding of the relationship between our inner and outer states, and the appropriate parameters for each.

This fluid water/moon effect is reinforced in *Moon Magic*, when we regularly return to revisit scenes from the perspective of the priestess, and past lineage connection is so very important.

In the first of these books that Dion Fortune wrote, *The Winged Bull*, the magical component, after the first profound ritual, is not stated until much later in the text. Ted's journey is literal, and the recurring imagery is vehicular. Ursula's state is described as a car smash; Ted's conversational powers are like a car that is a poor starter and so on. There are long car journeys across the country from east to west and back again, and Dion Fortune makes it clear that Ted's response to the land affects his behavior.

This is valuable food for thought for all of us in the modern world, where so many of us feel uprooted and constant travelling is seen as necessary. For Ted to be secure in the liminal state he needs to feel at home physically, a space that he finds only at the very end of the book. Through him, we are invited to consider these questions: What are the optimum conditions, the right places, for our own practice? Where are we truly at home and empowered?

With Hugh, we have a satisfying example of a dormant priest and the relationship necessary to realise his potential. *The Goat-Foot God* explains the feminine fecundating principle that will transform him, and we are pulled into the mystery of his inner work of incorporating Ambrosius, whose nature is left open. Is he a dissociated personality, spirit control, or previous incarnation? *What is Ambrosius?* is the question that exercises Mona and Jelkes: they decide, with the voice of the pragmatic lay-analyst Dion Fortune—or Miss Firth, as she was known at that earlier stage of her career—that whatever theory they choose, for all practical purposes the result will be the same. We embark on our own personal quest to find our inner priest and priestess. We are *not* trying to find answers, for we are not dealing with the world of absolutes, and literalism will stop the magic dead. Our job is simply to work, to embrace the mystery and find our right place within it.

The First Deep Connection

With reference to the Qabalah, the first connection that each of the characters makes is along the path that brings them to the sphere called Yesod. This is also often called the underworld journey, reminding us that the journey along the paths of the Tree of Life can be considered not only *up* the Tree but also at the same time deep *into* the more profound parts of ourselves. They are two ways of relating to the Tree that the student holds simultaneously.

However we look at it, the heroes come to a special place, to the experience of Yesod, meaning "foundation." For Ted Murchison, it is the British Museum; for Hugh, Jelkes's bookshop; for Wilfred, it is his bachelor flat; and for Rupert, the Thames Embankment.

Here, as we journey with the characters, we directly encounter our unconscious selves, our images of ourselves and of the world. Yesod has the title "the treasure house of images," as it is the repository of our life experience. It is also the place where we start learning about, and working with, the deep imagination and the archetypal world. As we become established in Yesod we develop a depth of connection to our inner life, so that thoughts, feelings, and the intuitive ground of our being become more tangible and vivid.

Hugh

Hugh begins to emerge from his emotional anesthesia with raw emotions. He looks for diversion beyond his experience of everyday life and finds it in Jelkes's lamp-lit bookshop, in the shape of books that were commonly available at that time: *The Prisoner in the Opal*, describing the feeling of being imprisoned and the need to break out into a larger unseen reality; *The Corn King and the Spring Queen*, about the magic of ancient Sparta; *The Devil's Mistress*, about Scottish witchcraft, and the black magic of Huysmans's *Là-Bas*. These flood his imagination with occult images and rhythmic prose. Their influences, in a place so different from his normal surroundings, are powerful calls to revision his world that he responds to wholeheartedly. Reading that scene is a powerful call also to the reader.

The profusion of stimuli acts like a psychically resonating mirror. The shop is mysterious and redolent with the smell of old books and incense; Hugh feels that the "shell of the world might crack and some streak of light come through."[61] This corresponds exactly to his moving to the Qabalistic place of the imagination: Yesod. His soul is stirring after a lifelong dormancy, and the books literally surround Hugh with new avenues for exploration. The shabby inner room represents the acme of comfort and warmth, and its apparent disorganisation is gradually revealed as a simple system for living. Hugh judges the hollowness of Mayfair by comparison with Jelkes's arranging his life to his priorities, reading and thinking. The shop is the polar opposite of Hugh's fashionable home, whose brightness, sharp lines, and ugly furniture and textiles are so upsetting to his senses. In the shop, plain

---

61. Fortune, *The Winged Bull*, 6.

food and simple comradeship minister to his soul; he rediscovers his appetite.

Fired up, Hugh's starved senses want sensationalism: the Black Mass. Like a pendulum, he needs to find his level between apathy and recklessness. He is taken in hand by the bookseller out of sheer humanity, and led gently to a connection with life—the deep connection that has been hitherto denied him.

In the seedy nobility of a four-poster bed, he visualises, a contact is made, and his real inner work begins.

Wilfred

Wilfred constructs a place of privacy and nurture in which he can learn and investigate properly after his spontaneous connection to the moon. How he goes about it, exploring without any help or advice, provides practical hints as to how we can proceed.

His "journeys" have been inner dialogues with the moon: because of his illness and the effect of his medication, he is the only character to make a connection with the deep imagination before finding his own sanctum.

Wilfred feels that he has gained a relationship with the moon, learning about the secret laws of her strange kingdom and influence of the cosmic tides. Alone of all the heroes, Wilfred is also an author, and he tells us that his writing echoes the deep, rhythmic pull of the tides. We accompany him on his visions, sharing his fascination and his experiences. And the lesson we learn is that by simply allowing space and time, we can access a deep emotional response. This can give us a genuine experience of connectedness and start to erode our habitual sense of separateness from the world.

Through Wilfred's development, we learn what to expect when we study: not a smooth progression, but a pattern of advancing followed by a period of consolidation until the next impetus to growth. Wilfred's solitary training is eclectic and reminds us of Dion Fortune's dictum that there must be an intellectual component to the path of the adept. Wilfred responds to the magnificent literature of the Old Testament and flirts with Theosophy, which he finds disillusioning. To this material he adds moon communications; he daydreams and devises reincarnation stories when halfway between sleeping and waking. He notices especially vivid dreams when he slides from there into actual sleep, as does Hugh Paston.

Wilfred especially develops "my power of 'feeling-with' nature-things."[62] His body has attuned to the tides through the tidal nature of the stream running under his window. He is pulled in imagination to the drowned-land mythos of his region, in his bachelor flat, his own place of Yesod.

Through his imagination and connecting to a place in himself that is not bounded by space and time, Wilfred visions the practices of the earliest peoples on the drowned land. It is after a vision of a flaming pyre on the sea edge that he takes his most significant journey, a fully realised reincarnation dream, just before he meets Vivien, his mentor and priestess.

Ted

We might tour a museum many times with only the mind engaged, but Ted Murchison in the British Museum is primed for a profound emotional experience. The warmth and dim light encourage his senses to reach out. The wreathing fog along the corridors fuels his, and our, imagination. In an unfamiliar and exotic Otherworld, the logical side of his brain is in abeyance, allowing an instantaneous communication with the huge carved winged bull guarding the doorway—a good-humoured and probing personality, which has vital life lessons for him. Ted feels he has more in common with this ancient carved figure than with the humans in his life. In his heightened state, the museum exhibits begin to come to life: the huge red granite "hand of power" exudes benign divinity, the Egyptian gods brood quietly, and the aboriginal "godlets" reek of blood.

Retreating, Ted longs for a life worth living, as he remembers the glory days of his army life. A long-suppressed part of his psyche is

---

62. Fortune, *The Sea Priestess*, 14.

awakening and he takes charge: he senses a portal of opportunity and deliberately plunges into the pathless way.

Like Wilfred, Ted gains an awareness of the dawn of creation. But unlike Wilfred's moon-influenced vision of the mechanics of the starry heavens, the thick fog fires Ted's imagination to the void before creation, and the glory of great winged bull-beings as they manifest. Ted is disorientated, and, not knowing which spirit might appear, he takes the initiative, choosing that it will be a mighty arm cleaving the darkness. Freed from his inhibitions, rapt in the emotion of the moment, he calls out for the fullness of life he craves, in an invocation of Pan. And the call, of course, is answered instantaneously.

Rupert

With Rupert Malcolm, Dion Fortune intensifies the experiences of her earlier heroes, so it is worth using his experience to put them all in context, cranking up the emotional pressure almost unbearably. Rupert is the culmination, the evolved priest, existing not for personal happiness but to fulfil the esoteric work of the aeon. His story is given further emphasis by our reading it twice; first from his point of view and then from the viewpoint of Lilith Le Fay. And, although an adept, Lilith is not infallible. Her worry about her personal fondness for Rupert is misplaced: by the end of the book she realises that for the magic to work, her emotions must be engaged.

Rupert has a strong visual sense and the habit of intense concentration, and his ruthless control of his mind to subdue the "beasts of Ephesus"—his libido—has developed it further. Combined with an intense emotional need, his is potentially a very dangerous mental situation. Thus, "A Study in Telepathy" begins. In it, the natural boundaries between the worlds will be eroded, as Rupert's stabilizing beliefs in the twin responsibilities of job and marriage begin to crumble.

Rupert suffers a depth of agony to reach the state that will make magical work with a priestess of Lilith's stature possible. Like Hugh, Rupert is feverish and vacillating, but to a greater extreme; his first glimpse of her thrills and intrigues him, banishing his boredom.

Straight after this, his wife's doctor discharges him of any emotional responsibility to her. He is free, yet anchorless, and at the mercy of every wind that blows. Pursuing his dream woman provokes obsession, agitation, ecstasy, and nightmares. Deciding to sacrifice his fantasy, he realises that she "had wrapped herself round the very roots of his being."[63] The depth of his emotional range is insisted upon, for great capacity is needed for great magical working.

Dion Fortune's tenet is that sacrifice is necessary to magical work, and nowhere in her fiction is this more starkly depicted. Fuelled by Rupert's extraordinary strength of will and capacity to endure, his deep well of suffering is an integral part of the process of bringing forth the power needed by Lilith, and an indicator of how powerful that is.

Rupert Malcolm strives for vision and the recurring dream that comes in that mysterious place between waking and sleeping, until eventually he oversteps the bounds of reality and gets manifested sensations. These lead to the second stage of his understanding, the most valuable for the work to come, and for us too. He learns that he can experience the presence of his priestess but never possess her. This is partly a reflection of the precept that the adept can have the use of everything yet own nothing. It says clearly that although the work is fuelled by intense emotion, we must transmute that into a dedicatory experience of service if we are to achieve anything of worth.

After Rupert's profound experience of "blessing and peace"—the sensation of sleeping on a woman's breast—his conscience tries to force him to relinquish his inner life. This leads to an upheaval of the soul, a compulsive call for help to his mentor to rescue him. After months of visiting the half-world where they can meet, she determines to grasp the nettle and introduce herself in the real world.

The Four Characters

Rupert shares many resonances with the characters of the earlier books. Like Hugh, he is not valued for himself by the professional

---

63. Fortune, *Moon Magic*, 24.

world or respected by his wife. Like Ted, the lost dreams of youth activate his imagination, and watching the ebb tide of the Thames brings back his fantasy of life as a ship's officer. In a reflection of *The Sea Priestess*, the sea motif coalesces around Rupert as it has with Wilfred, before either of them meets their priestess in the flesh. Rupert shares Ted's frustrations, but as he is successful in the world, they focus on his private life. And his mentor, like Ted's, is working magic that is an energetic catalyst. Ted's invocation is simultaneous with, and a response to, Brangwyn's magic to find him, which is the reason Brangwyn was in the British Museum. In the same way, whilst Rupert is transported by his imaginings, he is being summoned by Lilith's work on the inner planes. Rupert shares with Wilfred a reincarnation memory of torture, but it is only in *Moon Magic* that this physical suffering is emphasized. The other characters have a straightforward response to suffering. Ted's is the egotistical reaction of a man disadvantaged by birth, breeding, and money in the presence of a cultured woman. His wish is to respond tit for tat, to denigrate Ursula in a chauvinistic way, proving his mastery, just as Wilfred belittles Vivien by fantasising about having an adventure with her. Rupert, immune to such pettiness, views the possible loss of his dream with desperation and the urge to murder.

Hugh's escape has been from the deeper emotions. He has been branded a cuckold in the national press, yet it is Rupert, because of his struggles with his restrictive Presbyterian upbringing, who undergoes a purgatory of humiliation and self-reproach.

Lilith remarks that both Rupert and Wilfred suffer the restrictions placed upon a man's soul by early influence—in Rupert's case, his father's rigid morality—as a tree grows bent according to the prevailing wind during its growth. We need to become aware of the restrictions caused by our own upbringing, and this is the reason for the dictum "Know thyself" as a requirement for occult training.

The Imaginative State Needed for Magical Work

To reiterate some very important points of the previous chapter, these examples are not suggesting that we need to experience a psychic upheaval in the way that the characters do; far from it. Dion Fortune has written elsewhere on the dangers of breakdown through Rupert's type of experimenting. Both Ted and Hugh are desperate and reach out blindly for whatever occult help is at hand; but, in life, our integrity does not mean that the right influences will respond, and there is no guarantee that we, if we attempt magical work whilst in such a state, will be as fortunate. Dion Fortune's strictures on drugs in occult working were also strict, and we see how even medicinal drugs have Wilfred hovering on the cusp of life and death.

We may approach aspects of the sphere of Yesod, the imagination, through story, myth, and archetype. Coming to it through the senses and the inner world, we need then to ground it in concrete experience. Yesod carries with it the danger that we can become lost in fantasy, causing a split between inner and outer experience, and all the characters run this risk. It is important that all of the exercises suggested in the third section of the book should end with the experience of grounding and the integration of the inner and outer.

Magic needs a head of emotional steam to function, and with the safeguards of ritual we can deliberately construct the right mindset using various techniques. We are at first fired by a longing we share with the characters for fullness of life. Our best course, after setting our intent, is then to engage all of the senses. This has happened most sensationally to Rupert Malcolm, with his visual and tactile sensations of a woman's touch. Even the down-to-earth Ted responds to the sensual experience of colour and texture, and wakes to a vision of Ursula's face, whilst Wilfred and Hugh's inner work is "real" enough to manifest the smell of burning wood, from a sea-dowsed pyre and from smouldering cedarwood, respectively. These experiences are based on the actual experience of Dion Fortune and her colleagues, and are documented elsewhere.

As the four men enter a phase of more guided development, their senses will become ever more engaged. We have to work hard these days to do the same thing, as our senses are jaded and overstimulated by colour, spectacle, sound, and the widespread exoticism in the present world.

It is worth trying to look back into the mind of the reader of the 1930s when we read the stories. Imagine for a moment, in those conventional times, how strange and exotic the books' locations and clothing are, and what a revelatory effect they would have on men from mainstream society. The characters experience saturation of the senses, underpinned by scents, for the sense of smell is closely connected to the emotional centre of the brain. Brangwyn's and especially Lilith's use of perfumes and incenses is a useful hint, and as we read all these evocative passages we can mentally plan how sensory stimuli might support our exercises.

The habit of connecting through our senses to feel in an authentic way comes as we learn to relax and notice our responses to the real world. And regularly accessing an emotional rapport with our inner state will not take us away from real life. Rather, it will help us to relate to the world *as it actually is*, not as we usually see it, through the spinning wheel of melodrama, judgment, and past assumptions that is assumed by the outer world to be the only way to respond. We return from each experience of our inner state ready and able to progress, like Dion Fortune's characters, with clearer sight and a more grounded, prepared attitude.

12

Thresholds, Guardians, and Obstacles

The thing in which he was really interested, the thing for which he had bought the book—was its title, 'The Prisoner in the Opal'; the hint of escape—a glimpse of fire from the heart of the stone— the gates of life ajar—. [64]

A good place to work is tremendously important, for it should allow our minds to expand into a wider consciousness of the reality behind the reality. When it comes to choosing the physical space, we find that the characters' needs mirror ours. One thing that makes the books so satisfying is the time spent setting the scene, with every detail chosen for its resonance. Characters and readers respond on a deep level to the concept of "home." But for each of our characters, there are initial obstacles to be overcome if they will cross the threshold into magic.

Guardians and Obstacles

In occult books, as in magical reality, there are thresholds to be crossed, and wishing to pass does not guarantee admittance: we must prove our worth to the guardians of any path. There is a tradition of guardians who hold the portals of the inner planes, but it is sensible first to consider that what stands in our way are demons from our

---

64. Fortune, *The Goat-Foot God*, 10.

own subconscious, in spite of a sincere wish to advance. Projections of our personalities, desperately trying to keep the status quo, are adept at preventing our progress.

Dion Fortune, far from mythologizing her characters' psychological states—with dragons at portals, for example, as in popular fantasy fiction—writes clearly about them. We need clarity of mind for magical work and must be able to identify our own weaknesses; reading about the characters' shortcomings invites us to examine our own.

We notice in the stories how often, after a breakthrough, the characters revert to their former blinkered thinking. This is part of the gradual nature of magical change that reminds us of our own psychological patterns. We cannot eject our rigid ways of thinking once and for all; it takes sustained effort and awareness to progress, for they constantly try to reassert themselves.

Hugh's deep instinct takes him to Jelkes's shop, but he is turned back from the portal after entering. When Hugh inquires about the Black Mass, Jelkes becomes the obstructing guardian of the mysteries: his face closes like a shutter and he repeats that there is nothing written on the subject. Hugh finds himself out of the shop, making his way through the darkness and rain to the hotel. As he skims the book he bought earlier, we see his facile approach; he is intrigued by the Black Mass but regards it simply as "music hall." He has no understanding of the psychology behind it—and, by implication, the magical connections forged, whether ritual is considered black or white.

Hugh has been ejected from the shop because of his lack of understanding and his search for sensationalism. But his deeper instinct prompts him to go back, in a more appropriate state of mind and on foot, a traditional and humble way to approach something sacred.

The return walk plunges him into examining his neglected inner self, and the moment he realises that his real problem is not his marriage, but his life, he finds himself back at the shop. Both his leaving and returning seem a destined path—he returned without knowing how he got there. In his altered state, he felt his mind slipping its cogs when challenged, but stumbled through an answer. He found the door unlocked, Jelkes welcoming. He is literally allowed through to the inner sanctum at the back of the shop: he has arrived.

Hugh recognises the relationship they fall into as intimate, something on a deep level that his been denied him in adult life. He begins the experience of treating his inner life seriously and seeing what is authentic, of dreaming and allowing his intuition to lead him forward. He begins to listen to his dreams and unprompted thoughts. The process of treating his inner life seriously creates a basis of integrity that is the foundation for Hugh, as it will be for us. The setting of the shop is profoundly therapeutic and sets him on a path that has hitherto eluded him. It has carried Hugh through his crisis, removing him from a sterile environment to one that is rich and organic. His new possibilities are symbolised by the books, which are repositories of ancient knowledge and wisdom. Jelkes stands for the grounded, sane, and puritanical mentor: his relationship with Hugh is that of a father. He guides Hugh's reading and experience; he sets his feet firmly on his new path and introduces him to Mona, who will be his magical partner.

Hugh will leave Jelkes and Mona only to put in train the packing up and selling of his Mayfair house. He is free to pursue his new life.

From now on, Hugh's main limitation or obstacle will be his lack of self-worth. He cannot imagine anyone having any use for him, except for his money. His is a journey to his deep self—of power and potential. And we find, as in *The Winged Bull* with Ted, Ursula, and Brangwyn, that once a magical connection has been made with the magical partner, the mentor will increasingly take a back seat, leaving the student to the full flowering of his abilities. And so Jelkes quietly disappears back to his bookshop to leave the way clear for the conclusion of the story.

Wilfred seems set fair for his story when, from the deep promptings of his subconscious, he sets up the practical steps that give him independence. His hidden refuge at the bottom of the garden comes complete with the guardian his sensitive nature needs—the ancient Sally, who guards the door from his family. On her death, the support he needs changes from the purely physical to the empathic and emotional barrier that the love of his secretary, and later wife, Molly, supplies. Like all of Dion Fortune's main characters, Wilfred attracts the help that he needs.

Wilfred's main obstacle to a relationship with Miss Morgan, who will become his priestess, Vivien, is his estate agent's small-town mentality. Before meeting her, his fantasy life was focused on an escape to London and the literary scene—artistic fulfilment, adventures, and fascinating women. Vivien is just such a one, and he is unprepared for the collision of his daydreams and everyday reality.

Time and again in their early meetings, his pragmatic side is uppermost, mixed with his limited knowledge of "women of the world." Wilfred suspects Vivien of trying to "vamp" him, and of a lightning change of tactics when she sees this is not working. He retreats into estate-agent mode frequently, ignoring her friendly approach. He realises, "Theoretically I am entirely unconventional, but never having had anything to do with unconventional women, I was thoroughly off my stroke with her, and as prim as a curate. ... This was the very thing that I had wanted to go to London for, and yet I couldn't break out of my shell and meet it half-way."[65] The word "shell" reminds us again of the world of illusion and scattering before we start our exploration of the Tree. Shortly afterwards, the drugs in Wilfred's system override his caution, and he shares his vision of the sea cave with Vivien: it is the first evidence of their telepathy, a theme thoroughly explored later in *Moon Magic*.

Yet his habitual small-town stance returns with his health. The chauvinistic attitude to women that Wilfred, and Ted in *The Winged Bull*, sometimes assume is unattractive. They are still paying homage to the status quo in a society that says that the man must be the top dog; they vacillate between this state and a more enlightened relationship as they get to know their priestesses. In Wilfred's case, he decides to "bet" on Miss Morgan, for either a genuine fourth dimension experience or a bit of vamping; pragmatically, he is prepared to pay for his fun, but not to overpay. This distasteful attitude comes from his fantasies, not his present reality, and he feels shamed by Vivien's sincerity.

---

65. Fortune, *The Sea Priestess*, 32.

Through an act of petty subversion typical of the small-town mentality, the deus ex machina who ensures Wilfred's first more intimate meeting with Miss Morgan is the office boy, who shows her to Wilfred's flat. Wilfred is weakened, his guard drops, and he shares past-life memories, reverting again to his habitual state as he recovers. His earlier solitary training helps him to overcome this finally: because he has already been getting in touch with the nature side of things, his perceptions alter completely as they cross the bridge into the marshes. Entering the liminal land of his earlier vision, away from the poisonous atmosphere of the town, his mood is liberated and he discusses, with absolute naturalness, their meeting in his vision. Exploring the site that will be the magical temple, the scene of the next stage of his spiritual growth, they get into rapport.

Ted's advancement could not appear smoother: he is welcomed into Brangwyn's flat and is quickly accepted as a student and potential magical worker. Having been down on his luck, suddenly his fortunes have changed in every respect; the work should be plain sailing. Yet his relationship with Ursula suffers fits and starts that keep halting its natural progression. The guardians are not those protecting any inner magical plane, for he takes naturally both to mythological study and to the imaginative work of ritual.

Ted's need and Brangwyn's work in the British Library have together ensured his contact with the inner worlds. Even before they meet in the courtyard, the sincerity and focus of them both—Brangwyn's search for a student, Murchison's for entrance into an enlarged life—have synchronised to ensure the magical meeting.

Both Ted and Ursula suffer from the guardians of proper behaviour—the ogres of conditioned responses to class and appearance in their own psyches. Coming together and the accommodation of opposites is the novel's theme, and Ted and Ursula are evenly matched in the entrenched societal attitudes that prevent the work from flowing. Their magical mentor might have smoothed their way, but Brangwyn, the adept, is "in the world but not of it." He has higher priorities and an income that bolsters him against the diktats of society, so that he can't relate to or understand the pressures and motivations of the two. He doesn't understand Ted's resentments, nor his invidious and inhibiting position as employee, but Dion Fortune's original readers certainly would: and they would probably be far more in sympathy with the snobbish Ursula, repelled by Ted's shabbiness, than we might be. It is impossible for us today to understand the importance placed on appearance in that society, but being correctly clothed so as to identify oneself to one's peers was so fundamental that it was often a main theme in light romantic fiction in the inter-war period. As a social indicator, it was vital; witness Hugh Paston's instant assessment of Jelkes's "honest" tweed jacket.

The inexperienced Ursula fails, through a lack of discrimination. She judges Ted solely by his outward appearance. Her more authentic, deeper response to him is revealed later: when the cause of the grime on his trench coat sparks childhood recollections of exhausted soldiers, she remembers how highly she valued them for shielding her from an unknown terror. She is aware of her own shortcomings yet is powerless to overcome them, despite such moments of awareness.

Ted's resentment of Ursula makes every talk fraught with awkwardness, and he recognises early on that their easiest communication is through physical contact. In comparing himself to a gigolo, Ted is putting the world's worst construction on Brangwyn's plan for him, but it shows that we, like Ted, can advance in our magical work only as far as our understanding will allow. It is Ursula, not her brother, who gently helps his worldview to shift. Ironically for an inhibited man, the leveling effect of discussing sex and the breeding question puts him more at ease; for the first time the two relax and talk as equals. When Ted forgets that she is an attractive woman and talks "man-to-man" to her, they break through the barrier into authentic communication—foreshadowing Ursula's magical teaching on the subject of sex that eventually causes Ted's final transformation.

Ted's task is to embrace his role as the man of action and recognise that this is the way forward for their relationship, not by intellectual rationalizations. By saving himself, he will save Ursula. Action on the outer plane must come from Ted, and on the inner from Ursula. The book emphasizes Ursula's need for the protection of the soldier, but his hostility delays the sacrificing love-element of their magical working. The ogre of class consciousness prevents his going through the portal to the next stage. Yet every time he is activated by compassion, his instinctual and higher self together ensure that he acts impeccably.

Finding a way past society's differences to the nature of true connection will be the culmination of the book. And it is in the sanctum of Brangwyn's flat that Murchison learns the techniques that will aid him in the journey.

The Relationship in Qabalistic Terms

Ted and Ursula are the clearest example of what happens to us all when we begin to develop a connection to our inner life. We become aware of the experience of opposites within us, and in particular the interrelationship of thought, emotion, and image.

In Qabalistic terms, we touch on the sephiroth Hod (related to thought) and Netzach (related to feeling). Their relationship is one of a spinning wheel of tangled associations in which image (Yesod) stimulates thought and feeling, which in turn stimulate the other two spheres ad infinitum. This tangle of inner material relates back to past experience rather than treating each new experience on its own merits: it holds the momentum of our lives. It is the source of our habitual thinking and explains the resistance Ted and Ursula constantly encounter when they sincerely seek to penetrate more deeply into their inner lives. Understanding this will help us look more deeply into the journeys of all the other characters.

All these sanctuaries are stopping points along the way. The flat of *The Winged Bull* is Brangwyn's home, not Ted's. For Wilfred, the age of Sally—the servant/guardian who ensures privacy from Wilfred's family—will always mean that his tenure of the flat must soon end. The bookshop of *The Goat-Foot God,* so primitive and basic by Hugh's usual standards, can only be a temporary measure, as Jelkes realises immediately. And the surroundings are too limiting: the characters need a broader stage in which to fulfil their potential.

Rupert Malcolm's threshold moment is clear: he literally forces his way across the threshold to Lilith's private home, is turned back by her, and flees, ashamed—yet that act advances his clairvoyance. His other psychological thresholds occur as he rationalises the "daydreams" that he is pursuing.

Rupert's puritanical upbringing and high moral sense mean he suffers even more than Wilfred in synthesising the real woman with the fantasy of his dreams. And the problem is exacerbated by their erotic quality; he has never fantasised even about his wife in a way that might offend the bounds of propriety. The shock of meeting his dream woman provokes an instant connection with his past life: thinking that her reality will destroy his dreams, he looks with the eyes of the butchering priest—a reflection of his actual role in the distant incarnation when he first knew Lilith.

Fear of the strength and violence of his own reactions holds him back. Humiliation and his rending emotions resonate deeply with the torture that put him to death in that past life. Eventually that process and the blessing of Lilith starts his reintegration. She is ruthless in pursuit of the higher aim, and needs to unlock his strength, generosity, and talent for the "great work" of helping to birth the new aeon.

Rupert is Lilith's equal from the start, through his strength, discipline, and intelligence. He is also a catalyst, for it is only after nearly knocking him down that she recognises the building that she has previously rejected. Rupert's perception of Lilith as a priestess is necessary for her to access the magical personality: it is the fuel for her part of the work.

Significantly, Rupert's next advance is when he is criticized at work —the one constant marker of service in an unbalanced life. When that criticism shakes his self-confidence "to its foundations," his mystery woman at last appears much closer on the Embankment walk. His pursuit of her along the River Thames—from Blackfriars to Lambeth Bridge —has the recklessness of desperation. Through memories of his reincarnation as the butchering priest, we know that Rupert has lived this pursuit of a priestess before and committed desecration.

Rupert is constantly at odds with his own nature. He is both affronted and relieved by Lilith's disinterested kindness, a response to his emotional upheavals that removes any moral pressure. He dislikes Lilith's distance, her cold surgeon's instinct, and distrusts her past worldly experience. But speaking man-to-man on all topics, especially about sexual and emotional needs, is the portal to their intimate relationship, for authenticity of communication is a constant theme in all the books. He struggles throughout with Lilith's essential adept's nature, which makes romantic attachment impossible. He will not come to terms with this or the conflict of being a puritanical man in love until he experiences the profound peace their magical work brings. Ultimately Rupert capitulates completely to the work, as he has already done in vision. He may not possess Lilith, yet he is completely satisfied by becoming subsumed in the work.

When they finally meet in his consulting room, she leads the way to her car and takes him to his spiritual home. Thereafter, their rapport is limited only by his conscience. She explains the finer points of magical working as she allays his fears, and we can all benefit from her exposition. Rupert's gradual understanding of Lilith's cosmic responsibilities and the part he can play brings a conclusive final ritual. The implications are more far-reaching than in the other books, for the story doesn't end by earthing the magical current in physical marriage but promises ongoing magical activity.

The process for the hero as student, or for the reader, is to begin to move fluidly, gradually overcoming obstacles and opening the pathways between the planes. We can become aware of our own inner dialogue, that habitual "spinning wheel" of reactions based on memory of past experience and programmed responses. We can learn to look gently at our defects of personality and ingrained attitudes.

Simply becoming aware of our limitations and examining them kindly, coupled with the wider perspective gained from inner work, helps to disperse the rigidity that may have hindered our progress in the past. And our first task will be to designate a nurturing space in which we can relax into allowing...

We need to allow the space and time for the development of imagination, to make a pathway of emotional connection with our inner life, to unravel ourselves gently from our habitual responses and habits. Finding the time need not make unrealistic demands on us, although the effect, as with learning any new skill, will be in direct relationship to the effort we put in.

As within, so without; as our attitudes change, so our lives will become more magical.

And, emulating the characters, once we start to free ourselves of our psychological constraints, we can begin to engage with the sacrifice necessary for all true magic: in our case, the making time and space and the willing surrender to the mystery of deep connection, which is the precursor to a joined-up and magical life.

—13—
Magical Space

There were only half a dozen candles in high ecclesiastic candle-sticks ranged in a circle round the room, but walls, ceiling, floor and every article of furniture was painted in a shining golden hue, and the light of the candles reflected back again and again till the very air of the room seemed to glow with golden light. [66]

Dion Fortune says of occult work, "We mean much more than a course of study. The Path is a way of life and on it the whole being must co-operate if the heights are to be won." [67] And she demonstrates this in the books, as the work completely takes over the lives of the characters. Swiftly, they find permanent temple spaces suitable for deep magical transformation.

We will probably not be fortunate enough to have a place solely for magical work, but whatever space we use and whatever its mundane function, it must represent for us a place of rapport. As in the stories, it must be harmonious and expansive. And we can interpret that as simply being a clean and tidy area for meditation, in temporarily dedicated time and space.

---

66. Fortune, *The Winged Bull*, 113.
67. Dion Fortune, *Esoteric Orders and Their Work & The Training and Work of an Initiate* (London: Thorsons, 1987), 120.

In terms of the Qabalah, this withdrawn working space represents Tiphareth, the central sephirah of the Tree of Life; its planetary correspondence is the Sun. It is a place of balance, resting at the centre of the Tree and between the two side pillars; the midpoint between the deeper and outer parts of the Tree of Life.

Here, we can work with differing elements, placing them in appropriate relationship: it is a place that allows disparate parts to begin to interact harmoniously.

It would be wrong to assume, though, that a temple space will be a shield from all friction and discomfort. No change comes without reaction, and the vibrant action of psychological process and of magic makes it inevitable. It is only in this way that elements can be resolved within our psyches. Rupert's losing control in ceremony and chasing Lilith round the altar, and Ted's wishing to humiliate Ursula during their first ritual, show just how powerful our warring emotions can be.

A feeling of support and engagement is fundamental to our relationship with our space. It is the seat of a healing and teaching presence sometimes called the Holy Guardian Angel. This is not an objective being but represents our deep, more aware nature; it functions as a centre of stillness and secret life. It is not designed ready-made for us or bought from shops: its rituals are not templates found in books—not even those of Dion Fortune. For each of the heroes, as for Fortune's latter-day students, the meeting, melding, and progressing place is handcrafted.

Ted's entrance into another world is Brangwyn's flat: it is the security of a sanctuary, on every level. The house is the manifested dream of Brangwyn, who has elevated the mechanics of life to an art form. We might feel the superlative decor and the golden silken curtains permanently closed against the outside world somewhat overwhelming: the down-to-earth Murchison certainly does. The rarefied atmosphere, whilst enviably luxurious, is symptomatic of the main problem that is Brangwyn's idiosyncratic relationship with the real world. It is both his strength and weakness.

Murchison finds that the flat's ambience expands his spirit, but the atmosphere is stuffy. Away from the hustle of everyday life, time hangs heavy and he retreats outside frequently for his constitutionals. Fortunately his self-contained apartment has access to the roof garden, allowing him elemental connection and a wider viewpoint. It is in these more homely surroundings—small rooms, a gas fire framed with childhood books—rather than the grandeur of the downstairs apartment, that he pursues most of his studies.

It is worth considering Brangwyn's approach to life to see just how far we think it reasonable. We also need to rate all the everyday requirements of our lives. We need to set up simple systems for sustaining us in the world, to free up the time we need to work unhindered. We are more aware of life choices and their global and ecological implications than Dion Fortune's original students would have been. We make choices as far as we can to set up our everyday lives as we wish. That is relatively simple; but having made our lives simpler, we still need discipline to maintain our focus for magical work. For when we've made our altar/meditation space, we will still probably find it difficult to sustain a daily practice.

Dion Fortune tells us to dedicate a place, even if only a shelf or cupboard, and to pay attention to it, to nurture and clean it every day. This advice is so simple, yet many of us will be glancing at dusty candlesticks as we read. We need cleanliness and clarity to assist our tuning in, and our failures show the weaknesses that we need to address. Brangwyn's example as an adept is before us here. Even in the demoralizing atmosphere of the trenches, he maintained his standards, and we are never in any doubt that, although the staff keep his domestic machinery running, he keeps punctiliously to his own rigorous regime.

From here, Murchison travels to Wales, to the withdrawn sanctuary that has been created for Ursula; and we are invited to contrast its clear simplicity with the slovenly, seedy grandeur of the house of Astley, the black magician. The message is clear: choose less, but of better quality, if you are in the service of the gods. And as domestic help is very much a thing of the past, it is sensible to heed that advice.

Naturally active, Ted needs the contemplation of books and pictures and the practice of inner visualising to balance the warrior energy he is constantly expending. His creative instinct only finds expression at last in his homemaking on the East Coast. He has never had a proper home as an adult, and it is when he selflessly concentrates on fitting out a house for the Brangwyns that he constructs the perfect space for the magically fulfilled life he will share with Ursula after their marriage.

Compare his temperament and needs to Wilfred's, discussed next, and remember the adept's dictum, "Know thyself." We must find our own balance of inner and outer work, of practical and imaginative exercises, if we are to progress in the mysteries.

Wilfred's "bachelor flat" at the end of the garden seems to have been waiting especially for him. The bolts and locks are no barrier, light floods into the building, and its position by the tidal river supplies the vital elemental contact. This basic building fulfils all his simple needs: a magical apartment habitually overlooked, hidden in full view, where he can give his daydreams the attention they deserve. Even before he meets Vivien, he is temperamentally suited to start his studies direct with the powers of the cosmos. The flat becomes a haven where he can do just that: collect books, think, and be assured of privacy away from his family. Only two men, the doctor and his business partner Scottie, are allowed access, and both are as happy to sit in silence as to talk. The writing acts upon us psychologically. It awakens in our imagination just what it means to feel truly at home, what our deep nature needs to blossom. It is from here that Wilfred will advance to his temple.

The discovery and re-equipment of the old fortress as a sea temple for magical work is a major investment of time and energy. It is no wonder that Wilfred undergoes profound changes masterminding this huge project. Like Hugh and Mona in *The Goat-Foot God*, Wilfred and Vivien together transform an everyday space into the temple they need for spiritual work, devoted to the moon and to Isis. We note how they do it, and the story shows just how powerfully the method works.

Wilfred's absorption in supervising the building and his flowering as a mystical artist reflect his strengthening connection to the Otherworld. He needs practical work to ground his contemplation of the cosmos and earths his inner experience in creative expression—another message to us. Creativity is essential for magical work, so we must find our own creative outlet. Wilfred expresses himself in producing architectural plans, later reproduced in an art magazine—in designs for balustrades, carvings, arts and crafts hinges, and the frescoes that act as a magical portal. And Vivien's wholehearted admiration is an important component to his development in all areas.

Unlike Wilfred, whose priestess already owns the sea fort that will become the temple, Hugo must hunt for his place of deep work. Through Mona's instruction and their discussions, Dion Fortune teaches us much about the sacred geology and its effects on magical practice. *The Old Straight Track*[68] was published around eleven years earlier, but Fortune's cogent exposition of prehistoric tracks as lines of earth energy takes the premise of the earlier book far further. Her instructions for choosing a place on the landscape suitable for esoteric work are simple, logical, and masterly. They also give us a rare instance of the author speaking directly, from her experience of working with Bligh Bond, whose excavation of Glastonbury Abbey was aided by a band of discarnate monks: "You will find that people living at these power-centres simply hate any mention of the Unseen. It rubs their fur the wrong way.... Ask Glastonbury what it thinks of Bligh Bond if you want to see people really savage."[69]

The land beneath our feet is at the start of *The Goat-Foot God*, and it should be the starting point of our magical work. Like Wilfred at the sea fort, Hugh's work on the house reflects the inner work that will transform him. The building he and Mona find is a complex of

---

68. Alfred Watkins, *The Old Straight Track* (London: Methuen & Co., Ltd., 1925). This book was the first to explore and map "ley lines"—prehistoric straight trackways marked by ancient mark stones, mounds, and moats in Britain.

69. Fortune, *The Goat-Foot God*, 86.

monks' and abbot's lodgings and church. Its layout is deliberately vague, focusing on key aspects for their psychological effect.

As with Wilfred's flat and the sea fortress, the temporary shoring that bars access to Monks Farm is easily dismantled; in an orgy of tearing down and clearing away, the sound structure of the original dwellings is revealed. These buildings mirror our internal worlds, sound and whole but shored up with the unstable fixings of the assumptions of modern life.

All these locations have the potential to be transformed into spaces fit to interface with the more-than-human energies of the cosmos. Our personal imaginal realms, activated in the service of magic, share that same potential. All the practical work of making the temple can be read simultaneously as a satisfying story and as an allegory for the magical path.

Making the temple harmonizes humanmade and natural elements, as a sculpture is worked to reveal the inner essence of the material, just as Brangwyn, ripping out and adapting his slum property, has revealed its possibilities before the start of *The Winged Bull*. Each building reflects the character of the owner: Brangwyn's select flat and Ted's deeply rooted farmhouse; Wilfred's flat and Vivien's sea temple with visionary carvings and otherworldly frescoes; the gothic complex anchoring Hugh to his medieval incarnation and the timeless temple/church that Rupert finds, ready for occupation by a goddess.

Each act of discipline in preparing our temple space is getting back to the clean, stable bedrock of our beliefs. Each magical lesson we internalize is building the temple within, and every temple is completely individual.

Rupert Malcolm has no hand in the practical construction of magical space; he is incapable of attending even to his basic comfort. Yet, through Lilith, *Moon Magic* becomes a magical handbook on constructing magical space. Without disguise or ambiguity, Dion Fortune tells the student all they have to do to make and inhabit a temple. Rupert's first sanctuary, after his blustery walks by the river, is Lilith's spacious, timeless main room, and he feels immediately at home there. Here is no stuffiness, no gadgets, fussing servants, or extraneous detail. Lilith has described the making of her house and temple with the skill of a master magician: it is impossible to read the description without actually longing to see it.

Through Lilith Le Fay we learn how to make suitable magical surroundings and the effects we may hope to achieve. This is psychology and magic in perfect synthesis; she is as frank with Rupert as with the reader, making no excuse for psychologically manipulating effects that help achieve her results.

The writing is like watching a stage magic show and simultaneously going behind the scenes to examine the apparatus. But Lilith uses psychological tools to the opposite effect to the stage show: she is not creating illusion, but revealing truth. Through making an interface to contact the higher realms under conscious control, we strip away the artifice of the real world and contact the reality behind the reality. It is the real thing.

Rupert is the soul yearning for such contact and only needs to be introduced to it. By a combination of past and present circumstances, his spirit ranging free in search of it is the entire subject of "A Study in Telepathy." Lilith describes first of all her "manufacturing" of an appearance fitting for the work. As without, so within; and as she transforms, so she is honing her magical personality, whilst waiting for the arrival of a suitable dwelling to house the work. Its fitments and development are an extension of the manufacturing of the self, and the indwelling of the goddess—described in a brief paragraph of the most evocative magical writing—rewards the labour.

Having our senses and emotions stirred so deeply inspires us to change. It is a process within that can be activated by Rupert's story.

Vivien Becomes Lilith: The Development of the Priestess

We can contrast Lilith's openness in *Moon Magic* with her more reserved attitude to the world in *The Sea Priestess*: there, as Vivien, the adept in the final stages of constructing her magical personality, her life is more withdrawn. The difference is clear in her secondary relationships: *Moon Magic* places her firmly in the world through her relationship with the local police officers, visits from her magical colleague, and visits to the dentist—all homely touches missing in *The Sea Priestess*. And her relationships with the domestic staff, the Trethowens, with the inestimable Mr. Meatyard of *Moon Magic*, are very different. The first are sketched in to take care of the practical aspects of life at the sea fort, but Meatyard is very much a co-worker in Lilith's enterprises, albeit of the practical variety, and to an extent he is a confidante.

It is refreshing to read about the intimate social relationship of a priestess about cosmic business and her favoured factotum, with his winks and innuendo and tarred bowler hat. Meatyard has depth and, like Lizzie and Bill, the domestic help of *The Goat-Foot God*, he has character. The relationship tells us much of Lilith's humanity; it gives a modern feel to the book and injects a vernacular style contrasting to the high prose of the magical passages. Down-to-earth, intimate, and picaresque interaction in the everyday world is important to the magical student. One world is not favoured over the other: a balance is maintained between the two.

Having enjoyed *Moon Magic* for the sake of the story, we then reread the text as a magical workbook. Every hint and suggestion can be acted upon as we construct our own places, within and without. Our inner selves know what we need to grow, what circumstances will allow our spiritual development.

Transformation

It is worth noting now how the heroes of each book are transforming.

The inner connection Ted makes with Ursula through ritual tells him that he must take charge and brook no interference. His changing self-image is reflected in his outward appearance and affects Ursula. He buys clothes of a decent quality—a superficial but vital change that shows Ursula the error of her initial assessment. His self-assurance grows when he plans to double-cross Astley, and his selflessness finally brings Ursula to her senses, so that she can rescue him during the ritual of the bull.

Wilfred's confidence is fed by critical acclaim, and as an artist, he assumes an equal position with Vivien. This stands him in good stead for the ritual work, where his intuitive faculties make him a worthy partner in the invocation of Isis through the sea and moon connection.

Hugo, whilst learning from Mona, intuitively follows a route of solo meditative work. Through it he integrates his past and present incarnations, gaining the confidence of Ambrosius at the height of his power. With Mona's support on the inner and outer planes, he is able to grow and take his proper place in relationships and in the world.

When Rupert realises that he is free from emotional responsibility and meets his priestess, he then has to release himself from the shackles of his Presbyterian upbringing. Lilith unlocks the set muscles of his psyche—an excruciating process that leads to freedom. Lilith redecorates his rooms in a pleasing domestic passage, but apart from that, Rupert's inner changes are reflected in his relationships to the world. He has little in common with his peers, but learns the joy of creating a rapport with his students. The man self-confessedly "sick of the nervous system" gains a new source of stimulation in imparting his knowledge to others. This is the immediate result of the soul finding its yearnings assuaged, and the man coming into his correct place in the world. It is the result of Lilith guiding his spirit to a safe haven, where he can learn to submit, to release, and to allow, in order to be of service.

All of the characters develop methods of touching the strata that makes life worthwhile to them, that allows them to express creatively what is in their innermost nature. And all of this work happens in temple space.

It starts with a sanctuary, a place of spiritual space and peace, and progresses to a place of deep rapport in which to develop the connections of the inner self. This is the nature of the ongoing work until it ends, unfinished, at our death. From developing a kind and impersonal understanding of our personality-selves, we then go on to find the inner temple and to craft it to our requirements.

Moon and Sea, Sun and Earth

Our characters have an incredibly fertile creative relationship with their temple spaces, which constantly develop and change.

Lilith's is the most stable temple, but the emphasis on moving the temple fittings—the mirror, altar, couch, and so on—demonstrates the flexibility of the type of magical space within which the author herself worked. Withdrawn from the world, it will continue well into the future, to adapt to any ritual demands.

At the other extreme is the partial destruction of the especially adapted sea temple—a temple of Yesod, of the imagination, the moon and the sea, brought into being on the earth place, which disappears back into the imaginal realm after its purpose is served by the great ritual of the book.

The sun and earth temples in *The Winged Bull* and *The Goat-Foot God* endure, being rooted in earth; both the house by the sea of Ted's childhood and Hugh's farm are ancestral dwellings that have grown from their surroundings and the work of their forebears; and enduring also is the final temple space of the farm that Wilfred crafts with Molly, the Priestess of the Earth. Rupert we leave to the sanctuary of his lodgings, redesigned by Lilith, with his open invitation to visit the withdrawn temple to join Lilith in the ongoing higher work of the aeon.

All magical spaces come into being to fulfil the higher purpose, and ours will develop as we progress. A temple may not be permanent, or we may construct a space so accommodating to change that we will inhabit it for the rest of our magical lives. Our only concern is to craft it for the immediate task, for the continuance of our interpretation of the greater work.

—14—

The Mentor and
the Threefold Way

He felt that in the shadowy cloaked figure he had found a kind of
spirit-guide through the bewilderments of life. [70]

"When the pupil is ready, the teacher will appear" is a Theosophical
adage that first appeared in the 1880s, and literal belief in it has been
the excuse for procrastination for thousands of occult students.

Our characters show that the one valid connection to be made to
the mysteries is a direct one. They strike out prompted only by inner
guidance, for occultism is an active path, not relying on another to
mediate.

The wish for spiritual companionship is strong within us all, but
the stories challenge us, showing that even this relationship, which we
might tend to idealise, can be problematic. Ultimately, any mentors we
find will be flawed, by virtue of their being human; and our prime connection will always be through the bridge of the body and the senses
into the internal realms.

We might also find helpers throughout our lives, and there are many
real-life stories of such synchronicities, but rarely will these be lifelong
mentors. A part of us will always long for this external ratification of
the inward process: how satisfying it would be. But putting our energies

70. Fortune, *Moon Magic,* 15.

into looking for such meetings is putting the cart before the horse, and waiting passively until they appear is abnegating our responsibility to our spiritual development.

At the start of our personal adventures we must follow any hints with conviction, remembering that we have the knowledge that we need and a perfect teacher within us. We must slow down, wait with an open attitude, and give our studies our time and attention. As Wilfred explores every avenue, so must we. Develop that inner relationship, through commitment, and the rest will unfold. We become reconciled to the fact that our guides and helpers along the way may always be internal, and this will stand us in good stead if a teacher does come along. With confidence in our own abilities, we can look with Dion Fortune's well-loved clear common sense and not be glamoured by false gurus. She saw clearly that her own early teacher—whom she admired greatly—was not perfect, and stresses that mentors and even adepts are also flawed human beings and capable of mistakes, limitations, and doubts.

Having said that, each of the main characters does meet his mentor. Dion Fortune's stories chart the progression of the spirit; we are re-reading with the understanding of a deeper process at work, to learn lessons for our own lives.

The mentor figures of Jelkes, Vivien, Brangwyn, and Lilith illustrate the teaching aspect of Tiphareth, but that relationship is fluid and can be shared. There are crossovers in the mentor role, so that it is initially Brangwyn who teaches but then is superseded by Ursula; Jelkes who leads but relinquishes the role to Mona; Vivien who initiates but Molly who takes over to complete the cycle for Wilfred.

Unlike the characters, we should not be in desperate circumstances when we start the work: we will foster gently our instinct for the fullness of life. Like Wilfred, Hugh, and Rupert, there might be aspects of reincarnation to our lives, which will influence relationships in our present life, but this is not something to focus on. The stories tell us that when the tide of life is right, memories might emerge gradually and naturally. Perhaps the most difficult part of the training is learning not to interfere but to stand back and allow things to flow. This is a spiritual Catch-22 situation; without that trust, we might never make the space for allowing Otherness to be active in our lives, and we must have the experiences to gain the trust.

There is a warning in *Moon Magic* about allowing the logical mind to interfere. Rupert drives himself into a dead end trying to explain away his experiences: he tries to force his life back to reality with sessions with a "New Thought" therapist, even whilst he knows that he should trust his deeper instinct. When he allows events to take place, all is well: the process, available to us all, is not of controlling circumstances by our outer actions. It is human impatience and lack of trust that sets us striving after what might be false paths. Our daily challenge is to accept the way of the mysteries as just that, and not try to define it by logic or pursue it in the way that causes Rupert Malcolm's succubus to withdraw. Like Ted, we take our development into the mysteries one stage at a time, and ground each stage in the everyday world, trusting that the inner forces will take care of the journey.

Relationship with the External Mentor

To create the story, the inner processes are externalized, and so we meet the glamorous, intriguing, ancient-in-wisdom mentors who take the protagonists away into a world of magic. A close reading shows just what a complex relationship each hero has with his esoteric tutor, involving the same ups and downs as any other. Most interesting is the occasional revulsion of feeling for the mentor that the pupil has, and the ways—sometimes manipulative—by which the teacher prevails.

Dion Fortune writes of symbiotic relationships. In occult fiction contemporary with her novels, the guru-pupil relationship often puts one on a pedestal and infantilises the other. Dion Fortune's teachers' needs are as great as their pupils'. Each teacher is aware of the weight of responsibility on their shoulders, and each needs the pupil's particular qualities if the magic is to be done. Although one person is further along the occult road and guides the other, there is equality between them; it is in their service to magic, whose axiom is to fulfil the needs of the cosmos, to play an active part in the development of the race. *I desire to know, in order to serve.*

The Character and Needs of the Mentor

As we look now at the adepts' particular qualities, we remember that we have all of them within ourselves. Looking at their range of very special talents, we also listen for the voice of our intuition. In this way we assess our strengths by seeing which resonate most strongly within us.

T. Jelkes, Bookseller

Jelkes is the focused mystic, philosopher, and clear thinker. He is educated and a gentleman, a specialist and a scholar. Beneath the slovenly dressing gown, he is wearing the clothes of an educated man. Quality shines through. He is a theorist on magical matters, a collector of philosophical and spiritual material on life, and, like Brangwyn, has elevated the mechanics of life to an art form, although his takes a more homely expression. He has enough for his simple needs, allowing maximum time for his intellectual studies; he is a priest in his heart, and temperamentally is a mystic, not a magician. In *The Goat-Foot God*, Jelkes seems at first self-sufficient, motivated just by human compassion towards a fellow creature in trouble.

Yet, like Brangwyn, he already has a pupil who is suffering, and one whom Hugh will save. It is not for himself, but for his "niece" Mona, the impoverished artist whom he is powerless to help, that he needs a man of action.

In an echo of Brangwyn's schooling of Ursula, Jelkes has guided Mona in the studies that have cured her crippling headaches and developed her artistically. As her mentor, his is the responsibility of opening up the spiritual reality behind life, and setting her on a path that can only be concluded by the arrival of a priest. Both Ursula and Mona suffer for want of a magical marriage: the one half-alive and a cipher, the other starving in a garret. Both are completely emotionally isolated.

Although Jelkes is compassionately resolved to see Hugh through his crisis, he views him with suspicion, and Hugh's interest in sensationalist books doesn't inspire confidence. He despises the manners and morals of the Mayfair set and assumes that Hugh will be an example of them. And Jelkes distrusts Mona's honest, raffish morality, which is the opposite of society morals. He is of a different class, tradition, generation, and temperament to Hugh, but they settle quickly into a relationship on a deep level that has been denied Hugh in adult life: Jelkes seems to see into Hugh's soul. The old man and his surroundings are immediately therapeutic, the first steps on a path of life that has hitherto been missing.

Jelkes is the guide who turns Hugh in a different direction, clearing the fog of his habitual ennui and wiping his obsessions away instantly. Through Jelkes, Hugh arrives at a state of quivering anticipation, through the accumulated knowledge stored in his shop. Jelkes is a compelling figure who allows access to a strata of life that had previously been unsuspected by Hugh, and sets the appropriate parameters for him.

The tussles between Jelkes and Hugh result from the intellectual theorist being dragged into the actuality of practical magical working, an area where Hugh and Mona's combined gifts make them the leaders. Eventually they reach the position where Jelkes must retire in order not to inhibit the free flowing of the magic. He calls himself an unregenerate old pagan, yet is unable to pass beyond his earlier Jesuit training. As Hugh journeys to his deep self of power and potential, Jelkes quietly disappears back to his bookshop to leave the way clear for the conclusion of the story.

Jelkes represents the activity of Tiphareth operating through the sphere of the mind in the arena of Yesod, the place of imagination and images. He is scholarly and focused but also compassionate, and we see him in the novel helping Hugh to heal and teaching him through the medium of story. We might all be able to recognise that activity in our life when we think of stories that have awakened us or helped us to heal.

Vivien Le Fay Morgan

Vivien emerges as a contacted priestess in *The Sea Priestess*. Wilfred's business partner Scottie sees her as an aged adventuress, but in the course of the story she is transformed into a priestess beyond time, of magical stature. Vivien Le Fay Morgan is exotic, veiled, and exciting: we can trust Wilfred's intuition about their rapport and his judgment that there is "something fine" in her. Like H. Rider Haggard's *She*,[71] Vivien can open a curtain to reveal a very strange reality; and like that eponymous heroine, she has a ruthless streak, which will be made even more apparent when we meet her in *Moon Magic*. She glamours and overwhelms with her will, yet beneath the glamour she is trustworthy and has knowledge to share that cannot be understood by the uninitiated.

Her chanting conjures a magical world, evoking an instinctual response in Wilfred that insists she is truthful, although there would be no way of proving what she says.

Vivien needs someone intuitive, artistic, and possessed of a magnetic quality to come fully into her magical personality. Overtly, the story is Wilfred's, but Vivien's early biographical account is also an example of magical development; and Dion Fortune continues this teaching in *Moon Magic*. Yet despite their early bond, Vivien's attitude affronts Wilfred's masculinity, and periodically he revolts at her cold-blooded nature. To her credit, Vivien shows distress at the drowning of the craftsman's son, for, with her Atlantean legacy of ancient sacrifice, the book touches on ethical ground that is shaky, to say the least. It is not until *Moon Magic* that Dion Fortune makes crystal clear that the initiating priest/ess must always take the responsibility for the work, and put themselves forward in the place of sacrifice. Vivien's human side shows in her genuine affection for Wilfred and her ongoing concern for his welfare after her disappearance. It is because of her belief in the reciprocity of magical work that Molly learns to come into her

---

71. In H. Rider Haggard's novel *She: A History of Adventure* (which was first serialised in *The Graphic* magazine from October 1886 to January 1887), an explorer finds a primitive tribe ruled by an imperious, magically eternal woman.

power from Vivien's letters, and Wilfred is repaid in full for his willingness to sacrifice himself to her.

In contrast to *The Goat-Foot God,* here Vivien represents the activity of Tiphareth mediated through Netzach, the sphere of feeling, once again into Yesod, the place of deep imagination. The deeper mentor figure who shows the mediating aspect of Tiphareth is the Priest of the Moon, the inner teacher who shows the movement from Tiphareth to Daath and engages Wilfred with the cosmic background of the work.

Alick Brangwyn

Brangwyn has stature. He is mysterious, solitary, and a marvellous handler of men. In the trenches of the First World War, he adhered to a standard of behaviour, integrity, and care for others that the younger soldiers responded to with hero worship. He controls the first part of *The Winged Bull* and he needs help badly.

In her instructional books, Dion Fortune talks of the wise adept surrounding himself/herself with helpers, to act as a buffer with the outer world, and Brangwyn certainly needs one. Fortune is referring to the adept's sensitivity and possible lack of understanding of human nature, and on the inner planes, Brangwyn has provoked a situation that he cannot rectify. He has trained up his sister and a former pupil, Fouldes, for the Winged Bull ritual, a rite originally planned for Brangwyn himself and his fiancée who died. Through Fouldes's defection, a black magician now has access to Ursula, and the fault is laid firmly at Brangwyn's door—"The Adept who accepts an unsuitable pupil is guilty of cruelty just as much as the rider who sends a horse at a fence it cannot take,"[72] says Dion Fortune. Yet Brangwyn was motivated by both duty and compassion towards Ursula, who was about to enter a convent before she had known any life—a reminder of the youthful Ambrosius, who took the same route in medieval times in *The Goat-Foot God.*

---

72. Fortune, *Esoteric Orders,* 67.

There are two casualties of Brangwyn's experimentation: Frank Fouldes, artificially empowered by drugs and magic, and Ursula, the result of a psychic car crash.

Brangwyn and Ted will never have an ongoing magical relationship, for the direct Ted distrusts the magical experiments that have left Ursula a wreck. They work to achieve Ursula's salvation, and there is a mutual respect and trust between them. Brangwyn trains Ted ethically, with the warning image of the black magician Astley's methods, where one partner is sucked dry and the other swelled up with poison, before him. Brangwyn is masterly at conjuring the ambience for magical workings, but willingly hands over responsibility on the outer plane to his more practical pupil. It is with relief that he cedes the initiative, gently steering the action to allow time for Ted to work out his fate.

Ted's final abnegation of self in service to the beloved is the preparation of the home that he does not think he will share. Seeing it, Ursula takes up the reins to advance their mutual magical development and they enact the ritual privately: they have now gone beyond the mentorship of Brangwyn, who we assume will resume his studies in London.

The relationship between Brangwyn and Ursula as mentors shows us two different approaches to mentoring. Brangwyn shows us the activity of Tiphareth acting through the sephirah Hod, the sphere of the mind, while Ursula shows us the activity of Tiphareth reaching through the sephirah Netzach, the sphere of feeling. At a key point of development, Brangwyn is left behind and the deeper aspect of Tiphareth leading to Daath is mediated through Ursula.

Lilith Le Fay Morgan

Lilith's every aspect is devoted to the work of the greater humanity. She has dedicated herself to cosmic evolution, and any human concerns are totally subservient to it. She is Dion Fortune's vision of the fully fledged adept of the aeon. She is virgin in the ancient spiritual sense of the word: autonomous, answering not to any other human, but with a responsibility only to the relationship to the Divine. Through her, we learn some of the daily routine of the ancient priestesses in the house of the Virgins, and of the concealed mysteries of the Veiled Isis, who stands behind the Isis of Nature.

She has built her magical personality and developed her practice as Vivien in *The Sea Priestess*, so that she can communicate with those on the higher planes and become the avatar of the goddess Isis. But she now needs a priest for two reasons: first to fuel the work of the race, and second to be her foil for the particular polarity magic in which she is engaged. Her remit is to introduce a fresh impulse for sane and free relationship between men and women into the folk soul, where it will work like yeast.

The ongoing relationship between Lilith and Rupert is of utter willing capitulation, one to the wishes of the other. In Rupert she is well matched and constantly surprised by his intuitions, drawn from deep memory, and her respect for his many qualities and his potential is apparent in her writing.

Yet even such a rarified being is not exempt from anxiety and insecurity. She doubts her abilities in the long wait for her priest, and misses the opportunity to meet him by deliberately avoiding contact on the Embankment: she suffers from nerves before each major ritual. She is as capable of mistakes as any student.

Lilith shows brilliantly that being a high-grade adept does not exempt anyone from human weakness. No matter how high the calling, we will all always share blindness in the human aspect of relationships. Lilith is frequently drawn, against her sense of caution, to respond empathically to Rupert, in surges of tenderness she finds worrying, although she handles his emotional upheavals with a disinterested kindliness. It is worth reiterating that we readers must understand that these instincts are actually her saving grace. Feeling and expressing loving compassion is an essential component for magic to be effective.

The magical work brings relief and profound peace to Rupert's frustrated longings, and she appears to him as the Goddess in ritual; they both receive the blessing of Isis on their work, and together they expand to the furthest realms of the cosmos in a magical mating.

Rupert taking his full part as an equal in Lilith's cosmic work brings it to a conclusion—with implications more far-reaching than in the other books. It is the only story that doesn't end by earthing the magical current in physical marriage.

There is a way here in which Lilith embodies the activity of the other mentors, representing Tiphareth in its fullest working with mind, emotion, image, and even body. In the background is the deeper teaching figure of the Black Isis, who arises out of the depths of Daath.

Moving Beyond...

And then, at the end of each book the characters move beyond the place of Tiphareth—to the place of deep mystery. Tiphareth brings us into a deeper alignment of opposites. It prepares us for the desert path leading to the encounter with mystery at the sephirah Daath.

At Daath we work with the still small voice of inner-tuition: we are led away from dependence on outer things and towards the resources of our inner spirit. Finally we can sit in the cloud of unknowing, in service to the divine mystery concealed within it. This seems far removed from life and the practice of magic, but is at the heart of both. Paradoxically, it is a process that will ultimately bring us back to being more at home in the world.

Resting in the Place of Daath

Ted finally finds his own territory on the east coast of Yorkshire, where his familial and cultural history is held, where he is remembered. Despairing, he looks up to see the sun lighting the windows and knows that this will be the property for Brangwyn and Ursula. Here he soars beyond his earlier thinking and fully understands what Ursula is telling him. In a space that becomes a timeless connection to the greater life, the magical marriage, the Rite of the Winged Bull, is finally performed.

Hugh finally breaks through his medieval incarnation. He emerges into the bright sunlight of the spiritual heritage of Pan and conducts his own marriage rite, not in Greece but in the sacred yew grove planted many of hundreds of years earlier by Ambrosius for just this occasion.

Wilfred finds acceptance in the outer world in Dickmouth, and in the farm in the marshes, on the land-end of the escarpment that has seen so much magical activity. There, with Molly, he consolidates his magical lessons, and she is taught by the Priest of the Moon to sound the call on the inner planes that transforms them both.

All inherit "ancestral" territory, through past-life or heritage connections. Rupert continues in his refurbished rooms, visiting the hidden temple in an ongoing relationship that will be based purely on magical working.

All become "in the world but not of it," a basic requirement for the life of the initiate. Their final dwellings reflect this, being in liminal space: Ted's and Wilfred's farms are between the elemental contacts of earth and the sea, Hugh's abbey and grove are centred between the artistic life of London and the wildness of nature, whilst Rupert, living in the heart of London, has lodgings and temple that both overlook the elemental contacts of the tidal Thames. These places allow them a continuing, fulfilled "life in abundance," which is both the culmination of their work and the ongoing challenge of the rest of their lives.

It is the process of internalising guidance and finding home ground from which to work that concerns us in the third section of this book, as we learn to apply these methods in our own lives.

SECTION 3
CROSSING THE BRIDGE

——15——
Magical Work:
Guidelines and Boundaries

Our early forays into magical work come from a very personality-based place. Often, the experiences we have can be likened to looking through a kaleidoscope of exciting internal effects to provide new experiences—and like Wilfred at the beginning of his studies, we wonder how authentic these are. Cut off from our proper relationship to feeling, we, like Hugh Paston, need sensation to prime the pump: like Wilfred we may crave excitement, to try to redress the sense of imbalance we have about our position in the world. None of this is of concern if we trust that these surface reactions mask a profound and holy intent: to come into a harmonious working relationship with the evolutionary current. We can call this nature, or divinity, or leave it unnamed, and can picture it in whatever way helps us explore that process.

Now the way to learn to make bread is not to read a hundred recipes, but to try making bread—and to keep on trying. Similarly, it is through practice and experimentation that our underlying vision gradually comes into focus. That vision has been concealed because its scope is so awesome as to make us shy or embarrassed about acknowledging it, for we arrive at the idea of the connection to divinity, which has been so misused and subverted through the ages.

Dion Fortune is waiting to fine-tune our intent when we come to that place:

We take spiritual initiation when we become conscious of the Divine within us, and thereby contact the Divine without us.[73]

Then we are about the true business of the soul, and, instead of an internal kaleidoscope, we discover a telescope to the relational nature of the worlds, which will faithfully report on the cosmos, bringing distant vistas into sharp focus. It will allow us to connect our lives to the wider whole and the spirit that is the inspirer.

Hopefully this workbook will aid in the process of initiation that started—maybe many years ago—with being moved by the stories, just as Dion Fortune intended. Consciously now, we will work, through our engagement with the structure and pattern of each story, to interpret those themes through the fluid connections of the Tree and reach a place of deep and authentic internalisation.

Before starting, we need to remember the basic guidelines of magical work by asking simple questions about the stories as we read them:

1. How Often Are the Characters Interrupted in Their Magical Work?

The only example of interruption or disruption is in the black magic ceremony in the Winged Bull, when Ted infiltrates the ritual. It is a sloppy, showy performance, to pander to a dissolute audience. It comes from the wish to impress, with the eye very much on the main chance—a cheap aim that dishonours the sacred nature of ceremony.

So, by default, we learn that the ethos supporting true magical work is discipline and integrity, not personal advantage. We set up our space to be private, as the work deserves. Our motivation is to align with the progressing current of the cosmos, and our evolution as a species, and we set our intent before every ritual.

---

73. Fortune, *Esoteric Orders*, chap. 2.

2. What Emphasis Is Placed on the Magical Temple?

The making of the temple is a core element in each book; it is both actual and externalises an inner process: making the temple changes the characters into the priests and priestesses fit to inhabit it.

We also will make or adapt real space, and construct one on the inner planes.

The making of the inner temple rewards the student in direct relation to commitment and energy expended: these things build up gradually. And what should it look like? There is no right answer. The "temple" is crafted by *you* to be an intimate and safe space: it does not conform to any stereotype. Allow it to unfold in the inner realms, and allow it to be whatever it is—a pavilion in the forest, a cave with natural pillars ... even an Egyptian temple, as in *Moon Magic*! You will construct it as a unique expression of your dedication. And here is how Lilith tells us to do it:

> So I ... let him get used to things, and waited. We described our visions to each other—the visions I built and the visions he saw, going over the same ground again and again till they were utterly familiar to us both. This is the mise-en-scene of magical working that creates the astral temple. Our temple was now built, though Malcolm thought it was all imagination, and the next stage was ready to begin—the stage of making a priest of him. People try and make priests of themselves in order to be fit for the temple, but it should be the other way about—make the temple first, and then make the priest. There are good reasons for this.[74]

---

74. Fortune, *Moon Magic*, 187.

3. How Do the Characters Make Time for Magical Work?

Swathes of time are made available to them, whilst we have the problems of many legitimate calls on our time from family and friends, which must be honoured. So we must put thought into this: what, from the areas of our lives that we can legitimately simplify, are we willing to sacrifice, to free time up?

Read the previous passage again, noticing the slow, repetitive nature of the building of images. If we read between the lines of the passages dealing with the training of the characters, we find that a few paragraphs actually indicate weeks and months of dedicated work. In *The Winged Bull*, for example, Ted studies until the images become a background to his waking life. He is not confusing the worlds by this extra awareness; rather, through internalising the images, he has successfully awoken the capacity for another way of understanding that in most people is permanently dormant. It is a slow, organic process.

We need to address our time-poverty attitude, determine to make space, and decide how to structure our lives to make time: regular time, no matter how short each day. The reward is that with dedication come the synchronicities that smooth the way for us—not as drastically as in the books, perhaps, but significantly.

Maintaining a regular practice is the most difficult aspect of esoteric training, so two considerations might help.

First, be aware that it is more difficult to do now than in Dion Fortune's day. We have a million more possible distractions—our mobility giving more opportunities, more disposable income and time for leisure pursuits, iPads and their like, home entertainment systems, and a more stressful work environment and increased communication making us available 24/7.

Second, remember that *slowing down is a subversive act*. By going contra to the treadmill of mundane life and asserting our right to claim time free from pressure, what we are doing will benefit society, our families, and us. We must keep looking to the wider, deeper, more nuanced and mysterious world and the other planes to remind ourselves why.

From our reading we get our first guidelines:

- We must be committed to our practice.
- We must be ethical.
- We must make an internal/external space fitting to the work.
- We must be free from interruption.
- We must make time.

The next question then is ...

4. What about Doing Mundane Business Whilst on the Magical Trail?

The answer is that the characters never mix the two—although the magic they set in train will be working in their lives all the time. They interact with the everyday world but are secluded for their magical work, not only physically but also mentally and emotionally.

It is a matter of spiritual hygiene to be clearly in or out of the appropriate space for the differing aspects of our lives, and opening and closing procedures that take us from, and bring us firmly back to, our mundane selves are essential. You will find reminders to this effect repeated throughout the chapters that follow. The state of "in-betweenness" can be very alluring, but is at best self-indulgent and unhelpful to the serious student, who concentrates on clarity and intent in every area of life.

We must keep our differing states of consciousness separate, and develop the habit of clarity about what we're doing and why at all times.

5. How Do the Characters Begin and End Each Ritual?

The wonderful descriptions in the books clothe the essential guidelines of magical work. The preparation to the rituals need not be taken literally; rather, it is indicative of basic guidelines. Nothing mundane, says Dion Fortune, should be taken into the temple, which we can interpret as our inner state rather than as a strict clothing guideline. We need not have dedicated robes, though they are helpful in making the psychological and magical shift. But we should have a way of symbolically divesting ourselves mentally of our mundane encumbrances. Washing hands, cleaning teeth, taking off shoes, or donning a special scarf or garment are all physical acts that can help to move us into the right mental space. They are the first stage in allowing the temporary quieting of the mundane personality, so the magical personality can blossom.

Then each time we go through the same mental and emotional process to open to the inner working temple. The pathways and structures hold us securely and bring us back safely each time. Like Wilfred in his back garden, we "break trail" through the undergrowth to make a track that, with use, becomes an easy path for us. In our expanded state, we recognise Dion Fortune's evocative descriptions of travelling, of ascending to upper rooms, reaching out to liminal space, and descending to the deep inner temple as representations of our inner experiences in picture form.

> **Our ritual acts of preparation, opening, and closing make the chalice that holds our work. They are essential to supporting us and enabling us to shift through the planes easily and effectively.**

6. With Whom Do the Characters Discuss Their Magical Work?

This inner world is withdrawn from, and never discussed with, the servants, the shopkeepers, and the everyday characters who people Fortune's fiction.

Our culture has trampled boundaries so we live in the context of sharing every aspect of life as the norm, with celebrities as role models, selling their most intimate secrets. But magical work, like any personal undertaking, deserves and needs respect and discretion and privacy. There is nothing "secret"—in the way that implies "shameful" or "wrong" about it—but magical students do not apologise for respecting their own sense of privacy, and will only discuss work with colleagues of like mind. Anyone can read this book, but only those who *do* the work will gain anything from it. The secret of magic is that it is experiential. As Hugh says, objective evidence may be lacking, but no one can doubt the profound changes this work effects when they have committed themselves to it.

This comes with a proviso, of course: it is wrong to wilfully withhold information from our loved ones, who are entitled to be interested in what we do. Magic is not about power plays or indulging a self-conscious mysteriousness for effect, but there is no need to discuss the minutiae of your work with people of a different persuasion. Just explain that it is *the experience* of meditative techniques that is important, and that they can try them for themselves if they wish. Usually they just want reassurance, a broad outline, to know that you are safe and that they're not excluded. Be kind, be fair, be sensible.

Discretion is the watchword.

7. What Guidelines Do the Characters Have?

They work from their own deep inner instincts, and the more they trust them, the more these become a vibrant conduit for messages from the wider world, indicating the path ahead. If it is legal, sensible, safe, and fair, we owe it to ourselves and the greater work always to follow our instincts.

We will always be guided by our intuition and common sense.

Preparing to Use the Workbook

With these guidelines in mind, here is the workbook for your use.

The ideas are not to be copied slavishly, but held lightly, handled and examined, experimented with, explored, and made your own, so you will develop other guidelines or instinctively find your own way of doing things. And you will adjust the suggested timescales—you will know when a section of work is complete and when more is needed.

Unlike most magical workbooks, this one invites you to sit quietly and regularly with uncomfortable, challenging aspects that find their reflection in the stories, so the preparation exercises and the Body of Light exercise are vital to the process.

In our everyday state, we frequently rehearse/reprise arguments, supposed slights, and frustrations in our minds—a process that feeds these feelings, leaving us churned up and with no resolution. This is part of the internal "spinning wheel" dialogue (described in section one) that blocks our progress.

By engaging with difficult emotions through the body of light, we can calmly observe the underlying feelings that prompt our reactions. Really working at simply holding and observing them in the crucible of our awareness then becomes an alchemical process. We allow space, and find that, gradually but magically, they begin to change. It is a sure incremental process, and the time it takes is the reason that so many fall by the wayside in magical studies.

Going back to the "common sense" clause just discussed: the challenging nature of the work means that current stress and trauma are a *clear signal not to engage with inner work,* but to deal with your current situation and resume only when your emotions and your life are back on an even keel. First and foremost, magicians take responsibility for their own wellbeing.

Being in the right state for the work, with the template of the Tree and its paths to our deeper understanding before us, we can allow time to explore, and to return again and again. By so doing, we are parting the veil and allowing the influence of a deeper, more connected and more profound energy to permeate and inform our relationship with the everyday world.

In conjunction with what is given in this section, we can use a number of techniques to encourage the emotional response that magic demands. Some might be ...

- Reading selected passages out loud
- Cultivating creativity—draw, sing, dance, make music
- Using the mysterious place between waking and sleeping
- Following Dion Fortune's lead—exploring the mysteries of our own lands, wherever we may live
- Allowing and expecting the process to be organic, not mechanistic

"The gods ... are lenses that wise men have made through which to focus the great natural forces," which are made of "thought-stuff,"[75] we're told in *The Winged Bull*. But our connection to them is activated by "feeling stuff." By head and heart, by logic and emotion, combined with a deep embodiment and firmly held by the real and more-than-real world, the elemental makeup of our land, sea, and sky, we join ourselves up with the quivering web of the cosmos, to fulfil our potential.

75. Fortune, *The Winged Bull*, 126.

—16—
The Qabalah Applied

The work of polishing the rough block of temperament into the finished Ashlar of character is achieved by dwelling in meditation on the ideal you have set for yourself, and by thought control. Control the imagination and you control the emotions. Build daily; build steadily; build systematically. Do not accept your feelings as your masters: learn that feelings can be mastered by the higher mind, and bring them into subjection to your directing judgment. This is the work of the Exempt Adept.[76]

Setting the Scene

When Dion Fortunes quotes Jesus, "Know ye not that your body is the temple of the Holy Ghost,"[77] she gives us the clear message that the involvement and consideration of the body is essential to the training of the esoteric senses. The invitation is not to separate ourselves from the world, to transcend the physical or favour the spiritual above it, but to engage with every aspect of our being, so the physical and spiritual are integrated as we use them in balance. This is our starting place.

We are about to work with her formula in a practical way, taking the themes and journeys of the novels and combining them with the earlier Qabalistic analysis. Thus we will create an ongoing practice that

---

76. Dion Fortune, *The Magical Battle of Britain* (Bradford on Avon, UK: Golden Gates Press, 1993), 93.

77. Fortune, *The Sea Priestess*, foreword.

engages our senses and body and inner vehicles in such a way that we become the living temple through which the wild freedom of the spirit can manifest.

The four books describe the establishment of the middle pillar within us. They each take us through a journey, which begins in places of fragmentation and confusion and the separation of the masculine and feminine principles.

Regardless of our gender or orientation, each journey begins with the wounded masculine and involves the emergence of the empowered feminine as teacher and guide and concludes with a marriage or union that resolves the dilemmas presented in the beginning and opens up a new life or way.

Reinstating Lilith Le Fay

The presiding genius of this whole work is none other than Lilith Le Fay. She has been a controversial figure in esoteric circles, having been ritually banished initially from the Society of the Inner Light and later by another prominent occult group. There are many stories of her malign influence and suggestions that we should be very wary of her. There is no denying that Lilith Le Fay, as the dedicated priestess of the Dark Isis, is a powerful archetypal presence and, like any other essence or being from the archetypal realm, should be worked with respectfully and with an understanding of the clarity, discipline, and parameters that are the safeguards of this type of work. Dion Fortune showed clearly in *Moon Magic* the techniques used by Lilith to create mood and a suitable response, and use of these is part of a magician's repertoire. We, who through doing the work are privileged to see behind— or rather, beyond—the scenes do not need to fear the effect upon us of the "'special effects." Rather, we can accept them at face value, and with common sense, love, and trust use the imagery of the books to take us to a place of deep connection.

We remember always that our concern is not with the imaginal form of the priestess but with the current of revitalising spiritual energy—the reinstatement of the ancient Goddess of Life—of which the figure we know as Lilith Le Fay is an archetypal aspect.

This book was inspired by a group meditation on the Dion Fortune material, which led to a spontaneous experience of Lilith Le Fay emerging from the inner planes to guide the direction of the meditation. It was a powerful and utterly benign experience for all concerned. Since then she has remained as muse and guide of the work, and, when approached with genuine inquiry and respect, has always responded in a similar way, with no remit to control or overshadow. As in the books, it is the work that is of importance, not the personality or ego of any student or discarnate entity. She holds the deep intention of the work laid out by Dion Fortune of uniting the masculine and feminine in a sacred marriage that will regenerate the world and make concrete and visible seeming abstractions.

Rules of Engagement: More on Spiritual Hygiene, Potential Pitfalls, and Basics

Intention is fundamental to the practice of magic, so we begin there.

In any magical order, one of the first questions a prospective initiate should be asked is "Why do you want to do this?" And before beginning this work, we have to ask ourselves the same question and be honest about the answer.

In ritual lodges the usual answer is a variant on "to serve the light," but that same issue is addressed by Dion Fortune in the novels in a much more concrete way. The men pursue their quest because they are blocked or frustrated in their lives in some way and are looking for resolution or deeper meaning. As within, so without: by healing themselves, they are addressing the healing of society; their personal work has a wider remit. Similarly we must find our motive—our dissatisfaction and our need. By letting it guide us into the way, within the context of the wider spiritual remit of service, we trust that our actions may also influence the evolutionary current and work like leaven in the cosmic mix as they are benefitting ourselves.

Having established a clear intention, we must then create a structure of engagement: regular times to practice the exercises, contemplations, and rituals suggested.

The rule is regularity. Better to meditate for ten minutes each day than for long but irregular sessions. It is common to begin with enthusiasm under the novelty of the material and then lose impetus, so we should begin slowly and build up momentum and a regular practice we can sustain in some form, through the times when even a small effort can seem too great.

With an archetypal figure—Lilith—as psychopomp, we must be aware of the dangers of literalism and glamour. The great occultists were firmly wedded to the real world and its responsibilities. Magic is no escape route from these; rather, inner contact renews and refreshes us for further work on the earth plane. Rupert Malcolm's experience is a good example: through his magical work, his humanity and personality flower, and for the first time he is able to empathise with patients and to form relationships with his students.

By being well-rounded people who take responsibility for active lives with families and the usual commitments in the world, we keep the boundaries between the realities clear. To each world its own rules: it is simply hygienic to open any interaction with other planes of reality with awareness and commonsense, and to be sure to close down in the same way.

Preparatory Exercises

1. Sensing the Body

Inner work starts and ends with the body, and becoming present to our bodies is the fundamental beginning exercise. One recognised way to calm the body is by consciously tensing and relaxing each muscle of the body, beginning with our toes and working up the body to the scalp.

Then spend some time breathing slowly and rhythmically: breathing in to a count of four, pausing for a count of two, and breathing out to a count of four, at a speed that is comfortable for you. This has the effect of deepening the sense of contact with the body and opening us to the inner worlds.

2. The Interwoven Light

Having come into relationship with your body, the next step is to energise your inner vehicle: an important discipline called the practice
of the interwoven light.

Here the middle pillar of the Tree of Life is built within the inner
structure of your body.

Either sitting or standing, we begin by sensing the central axis of
the body from the crown of the head to the feet and let our body align
to it, letting the structure of the spine hold the weight of the body. If
sitting, it is important that you are not leaning back and that your
spine is as upright as possible.

Visualise or sense just above the crown of your head a sphere of
brilliant, whirling white light. This is your connection to the sephirah
Kether, the crown of being.

Vibrate the vowel sound **U (oooo as in "you")—sing it gently but
powerfully, with a relaxed throat, to the length of your breath, and
repeat if you need to, up to five or six times, to build your sense of
resonance** with the sphere. Then sense a pillar of incandescence moving down through the central axis, forming a sphere of grey/violet lumi-
nescence at the level of the throat. Here vibrate **E (eeee)** in the same way,
then follow the pillar to the level of the heart, where it becomes a miniature sun, and chant **I (eye)**. Follow the pillar down to the level of the
genitals and see a sphere like the moon emerge and chant **A (ah)**, and finally follow the pillar to just below the feet, to a sphere of autumn earth
colours—citrine, russet, olive, and black forms: here chant **O (oh)**.

Sit quietly after this exercise and gradually let your sense of your
everyday awareness reestablish itself.

For the first week of the practice, do no more than the preparatory
work and establish the pillar.

Then, to add to those exercises, proceed to the Fountain exercise:
Begin by centering in Kether, and on an in breath let your awareness
sink down to Malkuth, just below your body, resting there for an in
breath and an out breath to activate the sphere.

Then, on an in breath feel the energy rising up the middle pillar, piercing each of the spheres and ending in Kether. On an out breath visualise a fountain of crystal light cascading down through the aura and collecting in Malkuth. Breath in and feel the power rise again to Kether, and as before establish the circulatory current. Do this no more than six times.

Take time to establish this discipline. It will deepen as you progress in the work, giving you an increasing capacity to connect the inner and outer planes. With this you will start to internalize your understanding of the Tree not as a static model but as a living glyph of fluid, interactive, and interrelational energies.

3. The Body of Light

Visualise or sense yourself putting on an indigo hooded robe and placing around your neck a pendant in the shape of a circled equal-armed cross. Feel the encompassing quality of the robe; feel the weight of the pendant and the intention it holds of participating in the cosmic life.

Let the power generated by the interwoven light energise and bring into being the magical identity represented by this form. It is as if we step into it and it enfolds us. It becomes the locus of our consciousness and we sense with its senses.

Take a little time to experiment with being in this body. You may want to walk around your room or you may find that it gives you a different relationship to time and space and its senses operate differently from your physical senses.

As you deepen into awareness of the body of light, your sense of the physical body will lessen, being more in the background. Contrary to glamorous accounts of astral projection, you do not lose awareness of the physical body, but your major focus is on the body of light and the inner planes. On completing your work, feel the body of light sinking deep into the structure of your body.

These exercises will precede all others specific to the books, throughout the course.

Preparation for the Lilith Meditation

Now that the preparatory work has been established, the first meditation involves linking with Lilith as guide and initiator.

This meditation is written simply, to allow your own imagination to fill in the scenes; in this way, they will become alive to you. Engaging with all the senses will help to evoke a strong sense of the essence of the spiritual current that Lilith represents. Remember, time is the gift that occult students give themselves. Read through the meditation (in the next section) a couple of times, so it becomes familiar, and then trust yourself to direct your own journey—although you can tape it for yourself if you prefer. *Do it far more slowly than seems usual or even reasonable at first.* Most of us race through all our activities too quickly to get the full benefit from them, and it is a challenge to break this habit.

Beforehand, decide how long you will allow for the meditation—twenty minutes is plenty after your initial preparation—and then stick to it, allowing space for each image to rise and gain strength before proceeding. Remember, it can help with initial impatience to regard slowing down as a subversive act, a reclaiming of our own internal space from the everyday world. Allow time to completely relax into the experience and to gently return and journal afterwards, and ring-fence it. Conversely, it is unsustainable and probably unfair to your other life commitments to allow too much time for the process, so be realistic, decide on your time, and stick to it.

If you know the books well, then it is likely that the images of *Moon Magic* have already become internalised, and even the first reading will begin to wake them to life within you.

After completing the preceding preparatory exercises, perform the Lilith Meditation.

The Lilith Meditation

You form and step into the body of light and connect to the ancient city of London, walking along the banks of the Thames on a misty evening.

Feel the rhythm of walking into the mist, into mystery and silence … A little way ahead of you, become aware of the figure of a woman with a broad-brimmed hat and a black cloak.

Let yourself follow her—your rhythm matching hers as she leads you onwards, across a bridge to the other side of the river.

She leads you to an old gothic-looking church dimly seen through the mist … and you pause at the entrance as she turns to face you, shining a crystal-clear light into your face, asking, "Why have you come? Why do you seek entrance here?" Answer spontaneously, and if she is satisfied she will invite you in.

You find yourself in a large room with high windows, lit by moonlight slanting across the dark polished floor. There is a great hearth and a fire in which aromatic woods are burning.

In the centre of this otherwise bare room are two chairs: one simpler, in which you sit, and the other like a throne, with many images carved on it. On this sits Lilith Le Fay, a priestly, still, and potent presence. Between the chairs is an octagonal Moorish table with a great blue bowl filled with water and having a lotus flower floating in it.

A strange smoke or mist hovers over the bowl, and as you sit opposite Lilith she invites you to look deeply into it.

As you look into the waters, you see sparks of golden light within the water and the silvery mist that is rising. You feel as if you are sinking into the deep sea of the beginning, touching the source of all life, feeling the sea, the moon, the deep flowing tides of the universe in which we live and move and have our being.

Behind Lilith you sense a vast veiled shape: the Deep Mother, the Dark Isis, and through her priestess, Lilith Le Fay, you connect to the continuing spiritual current of the work of Dion Fortune and commit yourself to the work.

As you do so, in your own way, you may be shown scenes or images relevant to the work and to aspects of your life, or you may just sink into the relaxation of acceptance into service.

At a certain point you will feel a change, the pull of the outside world and the impulse to leave. So, saluting the priestess and the

Goddess she serves, you find yourself outside the church door and thoughtfully retrace your steps, crossing the bridge and walking along the Thames, allowing the scene behind you to fade back into its own realm and your awareness of the everyday world to come to the fore, until you find yourself back in the room you started in.

Take time to return, grounding and orientating yourself to the outer world.

You will use the early part of this meditation each time you connect to the current of the books in the inner realms.

The work that follows allows two to three months for each of the novels. Take your time, explore the journey, and enjoy!

──────17──────
Working with Malkuth and *The Goat-Foot God*

Number of meditations: 8 + Ritual
Possible time frame: 2–3 months

Having established the basic preparatory exercises and made contact with Lilith, we are now ready to start working with the novels and the Tree of Life as per Dion Fortune's formula. We begin at the bottom, or outermost part, of the Tree, with Malkuth and *The Goat-Foot God*.

Before Every Meditation

Work with the preliminary exercises and the interwoven light, sensing the body, the interwoven light, and then stepping into the body of light.

Then, after you settle in for the meditation, you will start by repeating the first part of the Lilith meditation:

You form and step into the body of light and connect to the ancient city of London, walking along the banks of the Thames on a misty evening.

Feel the rhythm of walking into the mist, into mystery and silence … A little way ahead of you, become aware of the figure of a woman with a broad-brimmed hat and a black cloak.

Let yourself follow her—your rhythm matching hers as she leads you onwards, across a bridge to the other side of the river...

Meditation 1: Entering Malkuth

As you cross the bridge, that scene fades, and you allow feelings or pictures to arise on the screen of your mind—a strong sense of place and person as you contemplate the scene at the beginning of the book: Hugh Paston sitting in a house and life that is empty to him, feeling betrayed and purposeless.

Colour the scene with the description in the book: harsh light; a small, comfortless electric fire; and jagged and discordant furnishings and furniture. As you empathise with Hugh's discomfort, you let his situation meet the similar places in your life and experience. Feel safely held, and gently and dispassionately open to the ways in which your life has given you similar wounds or beliefs.

Like Hugh, feel the restlessness, the need for *more*, and let that need take you deep into the body, showing you the trapped and blocked life force. Take time to establish this feeling. We are using Hugh Paston and his world as a magical image that can help us see that outer things in themselves cannot help us.

Let the image of Hugh fade, and as you turn and walk back across the bridge, find yourself sitting robed and hooded in the body of light and contemplate the resonances in your body and your life. Let the body of light and its experience sink deep into the structure of your body. Open your eyes and be aware of the outer world.

This meditation should be pursued for about a week, and it is good practice to write notes afterwards. It can also be helpful to explore the experience non-rationally afterwards, through drawing, colouring, movement, or music.

Meditation 2: The Path to Jelkes's Bookshop— Malkuth to Yesod

After the preliminary exercises and after following Lilith along the Embankment, the next step into the meditation is to imagine yourself as Hugh leaving your house and walking, following the restless trapped energy as you relax into the body.

Feel yourself walking the rich streets of Chelsea and Kensington, walking out of the known places into the mean streets, the places on the edge, in effect entering the underworld. Let yourself wander the night side of London, like Hugh, finding it intriguing and fascinating. Coming unexpectedly upon Jelkes's bookshop, see the worn sign "T. Jelkes Antiquarian Bookseller" above the door and the secondhand book bin lit by a street lamp. Get interested in the scraps of paper and worn, old books that emerge as you rummage, then find a book with the title *The Prisoner in the Opal*. Looking into the book you find these lines: "The affair gave me quite a new vision of the world. I saw it as a vast opal inside which I stood. An opal luminously opaque so that I was dimly aware of another world outside mine."[78] Become aware of that feeling within—the sense of being the prisoner in the opal: sense the greater, richer world outside you but touching you with luminosity. Feel the threshold of the door but do not cross it. Let the images fade, and sit in the body of light, feeling the weight of the pendant over your heart. Contemplate the journey and the new, expanded vision of the world. As before, let the body of light and its experience sink into the physical body and open your senses to the outer world.

Do this for about a week before taking the next step.

Meditation 3: Jelkes's Bookshop— The Temple of Yesod

After the usual preliminary exercises and following Lilith over the bridge, you find yourself standing on the threshold of the bookshop door. As you open it, you set off the warning bell, and you pause on the threshold. The shop is in darkness; you feel the piles of books all around you, and as you step forward you sense rather than see an inner room beyond a curtained doorway. You hear a match striking, and

---

78. Fortune, *The Goat-Foot God*, 5.

through the curtain an old man in a voluminous dressing gown appears, holding a lamp.

Feel yourself in the place of story, standing in front of the collector of stories who can show you the story that will lead you on. In kaleidoscope images flitting across the hanging curtain, the Black Mass, the spoiled priest, the Virgin and Satan, the Corn King and the Spring Queen, and the goat-foot god Pan in a sylvan setting all form in your mind, shifting and changing in turn. Sense these seed images in the story of Hugh Paston and feel their resonance in your own story; allow yourself to consider each one in turn, and when you are ready ask the teacher and guardian of this temple for help to pass beyond the curtain.

Pause and notice his response and then let the images fade and sit in the body of light again, feeling the weight of the pendant, and contemplate crossing the threshold and the nighttime temple—the stories that free and the stories that bind and the encounter with the inner teacher. When you are ready, absorb the body of light and allow the outside world to reestablish itself.

This meditation also should be pursued for about a week.

Meditation 4: The Inner Room

After the usual preliminary exercises and the walk across the bridge, you enter the shop to find that the curtain is open and there is light streaming through it. You step through it and find yourself in a small room lit by golden-green light, with two people standing at the far end on either side of French windows of stained glass.

On the left is the familiar figure of Jelkes, a large, craggy, and unkempt figure in an Inverness cape like a robe. On the right is Mona, small and with shining dark hair, in a long, emerald-green leather coat. Between them in the greens and blues of the stained-glass window you see a road leading to an old monastery and a wood. Stand between them and feel their energies, thoughts, and suggestions; this is your opportunity to dialogue with them. Jelkes is the teacher of symbol and story, the structures of inherited wisdom deep within, and Mona is the green muse, connecting you to the fluidity and energy of the green life. As you listen, you feel those two strains of energy gently mixing within you and finding their own balance. Spend this time getting to know the teachers and making yourself known to them.

Explore this for about a week.

Meditation 5: The Alchemical Path— Yesod to Tiphareth

After the usual preliminary exercises and crossing the bridge, you stand in the inner room, between Jelkes and Mona, in front of the stained-glass window. You link hands with Jelkes and Mona, aware of their supportive energies, and focus momentarily on your earlier sensations of the energies mingling within your being. At a motion from the two, you step together into the scene in the glass.

Feel your need to move more deeply into the inner world in search of the mystery of the goat-foot god. You sense the focused mind of Jelkes and the green fountain of Mona, letting them intertwine within you, supporting your intent and will. As you walk together, your will builds and sharpens; there is a feeling of passing through a barrier or obstruction. The world shimmers and you find yourself at the entrance to a medieval monastery of grey stone, in the shadow of an old wood.

Notice the carvings upon the door and the entranceway. These will be personal to you, although you may not immediately recognise their shapes or understand their meaning; simply notice them. Like the dynamic of the journey itself, they may fluctuate and change each time you revisit this place.

Let the images fade, and as usual sit in the body of light and contemplate your experience before returning to the outer world.

Meditation 6a: Monks Farm— The Temple of Tiphareth

Before this meditation, reading chapter 10 of *The Goat-Foot God* will prime your imagination, though it's not essential.

After all the usual preliminary exercises, the scene on the bridge fades and you find that you have passed into the courtyard of the ruined monastery. The delicate pillars of the cloisters surround you on four sides, with gaps for access.

Explore the ruins at your own speed. Attached to one side of the cloisters is a long range of low stone buildings. Through a gap on another side, you reach a handsome, two storeyed house. Turn the corner to find a huge barn that has been a chapel.

With Jelkes and Mona, take a circular tour of the outbuildings and the chapel. Let Mona and Jelkes lead you through the chapel, with its painted eastern wall and zodiacal paving. There, in the centre of the symbols of the harmonious universe, contemplate the figure of Ambrosius, the imprisoned abbot, and his monks, letting his story touch yours. Move on to spend time exploring the monastery, the clean, bare living quarters and the great winding staircase that leads to the abbot's room and the monks' cells. Contemplate the peace of Ambrosius's sanctuary room, and walk down the corridor, feeling the resonant memory of the monks, confined in their cells.

Complete this stage by spending a week renewing the chapel. You might spend time repainting the faded colours of the Tree of Life as a meditative exercise, feeling as if you are making a bridge to Arcady, the inner Greek landscape.

You remember Hugh's first visualisation: the firs and their resinous smell, the sunlight and heat, the wine-dark sea, the flocks of goats, and the buzzing of the insects. The sense of freedom washes through you as you work, making the bridge between the inner and outer worlds. Then stand in the circle of the zodiac before the altar with the statue of Pan upon it, arranged so that the sphere of Malkuth is behind the statue of Pan on the eastern wall, and settle into that experience, allowing it to sink deep within your body.

As always, let the images fade and sit in the body of light and settle your experience before returning to the outer world.

Meditation 6b: Descending into the Cellar

After the usual preliminary exercises, you cross the bridge to find yourself sitting in meditation in the cellar in a small, dark, bare cell. Contemplating Arcady and the medieval church's wounds, we may consider the loss of the older world in whatever way that has affected our life—consider guilt and shame we have inherited or have learned from others' worldviews, and look dispassionately and with a wider understanding at any that we have caused ourselves.

These are all aspects of our own life force that live in prison.

As we sit in the midst of these meditations, notice that simply observing the past is causing a mysterious shift, as if a regenerating spring breeze of change is blowing. The door opens and Mona enters as the green priestess; this is the beginning of the polarity working that we will consider from both parties' points of view.

Sit quietly and allow your attention to fluctuate and shift, one moment being Hugh, the next Mona, bringing the masculine and feminine archetypes, the feeling of the structure of your life, and the essential fluidity that drives things forward into balance within you.

Contemplate the monk and the succubus, the priest and the priestess. When we have reached a state of equilibrium for this session, we follow Mona up the stairs to the ground floor.

Meditation 6c: Ascending the Stairs

In the next stage we go from the ground floor up the great winding staircase, feeling the power of the priest and priestess of Pan within us, building and energising us as we climb.

We go up into the abbot's room. It is a small, bare room with a great chair in the centre. Take your seat and contemplate the imprisoned monks in their cells. Feel the prisoners within you and, like Hugh, think backwards; follow the river of your life back to its source. Explore the events of your life in reverse order and uncover the foundations of your house of life. Begin by contemplating the events of the day in reverse, and with each meditation let your awareness go back further in time.

As you do this, engage with the deep river of your life force, noting how it has been split and dammed through your reaction to events. Bring a compassionate intention into the work and free the prisoners of the past.

Let the images fade, and as usual sit in the body of light and contemplate your experience before returning to the outer world, to journal before returning to everyday life.

Meditation 7: The Desert Way— Tiphareth to Daath

After the usual preliminary exercises, the river scene fades and you find yourself sitting in the dim chapel with Mona and Jelkes contemplating Pan and the Tree of Life. Feel the freedom of the life force within and the deep will freed by the meditation in the abbot's chamber.

As you do so, it is as if the walls of the chapel dissolve and you find yourself walking into the pine-scented forest in the soft evening light, letting go of the forms and structures and stories that have restricted you and being totally open to the experience of the moment. A little ahead of you is Mona, leading you onwards; feel the presence of the wild, of the deep green life, and follow her.

Feel the longing for more life as you move ever deeper into the forest, coming at length to an ancient grove of yews sealed with an old oak door. Stand with Mona before the door, taking your time to feel the presence of the forest and your proximity to sacred space. You are on the edge of mystery: pause to absorb your relationship to this timelessness.

Then gradually let the images fade and sit in the body of light and contemplate your experience before returning to the outer world.

Meditation 8: The Mystery of the Grove— Daath

After the usual preliminary exercises, the bridge leads you back again to the oak door that seals the ancient grove. As you renew your commitment to explore the current of Malkuth, the ancient studded door opens easily.

You enter the grove formed of ancient yews, their red-brown trunks and boughs delineating the shape of a lozenge, or the centre of a vesica piscis, in the heart of the forest. It is protected and set apart, with a waist-high stone pillar at its centre. Enter as both Hugh and Mona, masculine and feminine, priest and priestess. Contemplate the grove, the priest and priestess, and await the coming of the God. A breath of cold air stirs, as if feeling you, bringing fear and exhilaration as you realise that you are presenting yourself for the blessing of Pan.

Feel both the longing and the freed life within you; let the priest and priestess be one within you; feel the rising of the inner sun.

Between the completion of this main practice and the next, final ritual, you will find many side issues, ideas, and byways that the story has planted in you. Hold them lightly but with focus. Pursue them in meditation, visualisation, and contemplation until you feel complete enough in this phase of the work. There is no rush.

To compete the work with Malkuth, perform this last ritual.

The Ritual of Malkuth

This deceptively simple ceremony completes the work of this sephirah. Through the magical relationship of story and the imaginal sense, you may sink into an appreciation of the sacred marriage within yourself. As always, ensure that you will be free of interruptions, and allow time to prepare and wind down afterwards, to make notes and gently return to the everyday world.

You Will Need:

- Space that you have cleared in preparation and with awareness
- Comfortable seating
- A green candle
- Low light in the room—sufficient to read easily
- A copy of *The Goat-Foot God*
- Optional: pine oil in a burner/pine cones/a branch of fir

Make yourself comfortable in a clear, clean space in front of the candle and with a token of the breath of Arcady present—pine oil scenting the room, with a fir branch, twigs, or scented cones, or whatever seems right to you. Light the candle and sit with your spine straight, thinking of the lowest sphere on the Tree of Life, as you repainted it in the chapel.

Perform the relaxation exercises and the interwoven light, and call into being the body of light. Let it settle around your physical body and feel the energy of the wild. This manifests in a green glow that spreads until it surrounds you with the light, sun-fused atmosphere of Arcady.

Remain aware of this imaginal space as you pick up *The Goat-Foot God* and riffle through the pages. Take time to read odd paragraphs as they catch your eye, retracing Hugh and Mona's journey. Allow the images and scenes to resonate with your own experiences stored deep in the body—there is no need to remember them with the rational mind—and feel them resettle in a harmonious shape...

Relax completely into the experience of magical reading, and as the scenes become more vivid, turn to the last chapter and quietly read it aloud to yourself, in that place of inside and outside discernment—a mirror of the way that the books were written by the author.

As you finish reading, allow the ancient cry "Hekas, hekas, este bebeloi! Be ye far from us, oh ye profane!" to fade into the silence, and sink into a rich, profound stillness. Within this, feel the masculine and feminine energies within you, the satyr and the maiden, the sword and the chalice, the active and the passive principle of pursuing and yielding, dance and align themselves. The green-gold threads of nature permeate you, unifying the whole glorious complexity of your psyche in a constantly fluid, shifting pattern around a central core of spiritual life; the living caduceus of the sacred marriage.

Sit with the energies, becoming aware also of natural forces pouring into you, supporting and energising the process, and feel, almost simultaneously, the need to give them back to nature, so that they flow in and out in a never-ending stream, for the benefit of all and the evolutionary current.

Slowly this feeling stills, and you respond to the pull to return to the everyday, bringing back your feeling of harmony with the nature of all things.

Respect the end of this section and your own inner process: ground it with journaling and walking in nature. Give yourself time and space to settle within.

When you are ready, you will move on to contemplate the sephirah Yesod and the book *The Sea Priestess.*

18

Working with Yesod and *The Sea Priestess*

Number of meditations: 8 + Ritual
Possible time frame: 2–3 months

Moving from Malkuth to Yesod, we take the work deeper, addressing the foundations of life and magical identity and learning the art of the magical image. The nature of the work encourages fluidity, yet still we keep our barriers clear between our inner and outer states.

As before, use the preparatory exercises, and before beginning this sequence perform again the meditation on Lilith (from chapter 16), for she is the guide and psychopomp in this work. Let her advise you as to how to begin this stage and build on the work of Malkuth. Be prepared to sit with her and do not be concerned with explicit instructions that might or might not come. Instead, trust your feelings, instincts, and intuition.

When you feel ready to embark, you will repeat the first part of the Lilith meditation before every meditation:

You form and step into the body of light and connect to the ancient city of London, walking along the banks of the Thames on a misty evening.

Feel the rhythm of walking into the mist, into mystery and silence...A little way ahead of you, become aware of the figure of a woman with a broad-brimmed hat and a black cloak.

Let yourself follow her—your rhythm matching hers as she leads you onwards, across a bridge to the other side of the river...

Meditation 1: Wilfred Maxwell's House— Malkuth of Yesod

You find yourself stepping into the beginning of *The Sea Priestess*...Sense that you are in a small town, confronting a Georgian house of two storeys, with an open front door that leads into a hall.

On the right is the main door to the offices, and opposite it on the left is the front door of the home Wilfred shares with his mother and sister. Begin by seeing Wilfred Maxwell as he walks from one door to the other, feeling his sense of entrapment due to his father's legacy and his mother and sister's incessant demands. As you did with the figure of Hugh Paston, let Wilfred's life meet yours, feeling the sense of blocked life and frustration as he roams round the anodyne office and prowls round the pretentious, stuffy furnishings of the family home.

Contemplate all in your life and environment that imprisons you.

Contemplate Wilfred's mother and sister and his inheritance from his father. Where are these figures in your life? What is the inheritance that keeps you chained? What roles have you been expected to adopt?

Explore Wilfred's family house and feel into his persona, his vital energy and psychism. Walk up the staircase to his bedroom, the one place where he can have space. Yet even here, feel his sensitivity and the negativity of his personality that makes him unable to activate his will in these surroundings.

Be aware that by simply identifying and noticing, you are starting a process of personal change that will free up your creative connection to your present life.

Let the image of Wilfred fade, and as you turn and walk back across the bridge, find yourself sitting robed and hooded in the body of light and contemplate the resonances in your body and life. When you are ready, consciously let those feelings sink deep within. Allow the presence of your physical self to reestablish its supremacy and rejoin your normal life. Through your awareness, the process of integration has begun.

This meditation should be pursued for about a week, and it is good practice to write notes afterwards.

Meditation 2: The Underworld Way— Malkuth to Yesod

After performing the preliminary exercises, the next step into the meditation, after following Lilith along the Embankment, is to imagine yourself as Wilfred lying on his bed and contemplating the night sky. As you lie there, it is as if you are floating on a deep black sea, and within this womb-like stillness you witness the rising of the moon.

Meditate on the moon, contemplating the bright moon and the dark, the waxing and the waning.

Then contemplate this phrase each time you revisit the meditation:

I let my mind range beyond time to the beginning. I saw the vast sea of infinite space, indigo-dark in the Night of the Gods; and it seemed to me that in that darkness and silence must be the seed of all being. And as in the seed is infolded the future flower with its seed, and again, the flower in the seed, so must all creation be infolded to infinite space, and I along with it. [79]

Centre yourself in the body of light and return over the bridge in the usual way, allowing the body of light to sink deep into the body.

Spend at least a week on this meditation.

Meditation 3: The Sanctuary of Yesod

Follow Lilith across the bridge as usual and allow the scene to change so that you are again lying in bed contemplating the moon. Rise from your

---

79. Fortune, *The Sea Priestess*, 4.

bed, descend the stairs, and go out into the back garden. As you step through the door, you are stepping into the garden, finding a long-lost overgrown path that leads to the bottom of the garden. Push through the overgrown laurels until you come to a brick wall with a small door with a pointed arch, like a church door. Pause on the threshold of Yesod.

As you open the door and step forward, you find yourself in the sanctuary of Yesod. Sitting in the kitchen by the hearth is an old woman with bright button eyes. She keeps the hearth and feeds the fire; she has seen all the cycles of the moon and knows its ways. Commune with her for a moment, and take the stairway up to the first storey.

Here you find a room with a peat fire burning on the hearth and a chair placed in front of a lectern with a great book upon it. Sit in the chair and open the book, seeing in it scenes and images from your past. Look deeper into the book and you may find or sense scenes from your past lives and the life and history of the land. Step into the images of self and world and learn the secret ways of the dark side of the moon; feel your place as an ongoing part of the hidden processes of the universe.

Conclude in the usual way, coming back easily to your everyday state of awareness in a relaxed way that allows you time to record your experience fully.

Meditation 4: The Road to the Sea Fort— Yesod to Tiphareth

After the usual preliminary exercises and crossing the bridge, allow the scene to change and find yourself in Wilfred's garden sanctuary. As you go upstairs, you notice a window formed of a thick blue-green glass, and as you look deeply into it you see beneath the house a ravine with a tidal river flowing in it. Let your attention rest in the ebb and flow of the water connecting the land and the sea: hear the tidal surge, and follow the ebb tide flow out to the Atlantic. The images through the distortions of the glass remind you of the moon tides of the cosmos, and you let your awareness descend into the deep. At the deepest point you perceive the image of a woman—the sea priestess—enthroned in the temple of the sea and stars, Vivien Le Fay Morgan. In that moment, if it feels right, you see and are seen, are chosen and assent.

You rise with her out of the depths and find yourself in the dragon boat coming towards land. You see in front of you the peninsula of Brean Down lying like a lion with its back to you, and you are dimly aware of a car making its way through the salt marshes and along the shore to the Down. As the boat touches the land, there is a sense of transition—a stillness and a movement—and you find yourself in the heart of the ruined sea fort witnessing Wilfred and Vivien coming together in the decision to build the sea temple here.

Meditation 5: Rebuilding the Sea Temple— Tiphareth

This meditation is in two stages. Progress to part 2 after a few days, when you have internalised the feeling of the sea fort as the meeting place of earth, sea, and sky—the creative coming together of form for a higher purpose.

Part 1

Crossing the bridge, you find yourself at the end of the Brean Down peninsula, with gorse, furze, and hawthorn clinging to its sides and rocky cliffs leading down to the swelling sea. You walk with Wilfred and Vivien around the ruined sea fort, feeling the rock beneath you vibrating with the intensity of the waves, feeling the intersection of sea and land.

You witness the fort being repaired and restored; see Wilfred at his work supervising repairs while Vivien looks on. Look through his eyes and Vivien's, feeling the coming together of the sea temple. Contemplate the façade of sea creatures and the death of the craftsman Bindling's son—what is the sacrifice that potentises the temple? By your attention, know that you are also bringing into being your temple within, and that every gain means a sacrifice, a shedding of something. What will you willingly give back to the sea, the primordial mother?

Part 2

Go to the sea temple once more, to be with Wilfred as he paints the walls of the temple. As the paintings come to life under his skilled hand, contemplate the four panels on the seaward side between the windows that depict the following:

- Wave piled upon wave, seeing the life of the sea elementals in froth and ebb and flow—the sea in sun
- The mysterious misty sea with the Flying Dutchman upon it
- The stormy sea with the sea horses and the battle riders
- The still and moonlit sea and the face of Morgan Le Fay

Feel the moods of the sea and find their correlates within you.

Meditation 6: Lighting the Fire of Azrael

Before embarking on this meditation, you might want to reread Wilfred's vision in chapter 16 of *The Sea Priestess*.

After the usual preparations and crossing the bridge, sit with Vivien and Wilfred at the hearth as they light the Fire of Azrael. Bring to mind the juniper of the chalk and the green west, cedar from Lebanon, and sandalwood from the Far East. Let the essences of these trees combine together in fire, the sandal and cedar burning steadily, the juniper catching in showers of sparks until its ashes lie in a fine golden net above the red embers, and let Vivien lead you on a spirit journey that travels backwards in time to ancient Atlantis. Contemplate the rise and fall of civilisations—the use and abuse of knowledge, and the saving and furtherance of all that is noble and good from ancient times, made relevant for our use in the present time, and yourself on the path of service.

Accompany Wilfred as he paints the great sea palace on the landward side of the room: see the throne and the figure of the Moon Priest enthroned on it. Commune with the Priest of the Moon and let him teach you.

Come back gently across the bridge, allowing time for this experience to settle down into your being and journaling quietly to ensure you ground yourself before resuming your everyday life.

Meditation 7: The Road to the Sea— Tiphareth to Daath

This meditation is in two parts.

Part 1

As before, let Lilith lead you across the bridge and find yourself in the sea cave of Bell Head. Sit upon a stone throne, contemplating the table altar and the two braziers at the cave's mouth. The indigo robe of your preparatory work has become a heavy deep-blue velvet cloak around you, held with a massive silver trident brooch.

Look deep into the sea at night and slowly witness and become absorbed in the rising of the moon. Feel the connection between the moon, the sea, and the inner earth. Contemplate the priestly throne and the altar of sacrifice.

Let this meditation build for seven days before moving to part 2.

Part 2

Prepare... and sit in the cave. Feel the full moon flooding the cave with light and see the moon path across the sea to the horizon. Rise from your seat, make your way to the top of the cliff and then along the down, over the springy short grass following the moon path to the sea fort. As you enter the temple, you find Vivien seated on her throne, veiled and crowned with horns and the moon, and you take your seat opposite her, feeling the sea palace around and the Priest of the Moon behind you.

Feel the interplay between you, the sea priest, and the sea priestess.

Within your being you are aware that, as Wilfred, you offer all: as Vivien you receive all, and become more vivid and somehow larger...

Vivien receives the presence of the Goddess into her body, drawing on the life within you to become the Goddess made flesh. As she manifests, the tide turns and the blessing of the Goddess rests on you in a reciprocal flow as you are claimed and live by and through her.

Behind her the window and walls dissolve, and it is as if the sea and the stars flow into the room. You are held in place by the presence of the Priest of the Moon, and you watch as the sea priestess steps into the deep beyond deep, being absorbed into mystery.

Conclude as usual, coming back easily across the bridge to your everyday state of awareness.

Meditation 8: Daath

Follow Lilith across the bridge and find yourself sitting in the sea temple feeling the presence of the Priest of the Moon behind you. As you look the walls of the fort seem to vanish and you find yourself in the midst of the sea. Contemplate the sea beneath you and the sea of stars above you. Feel the absence of the sea priestess and look into your heart. Contemplate the Deep within, feeling the inner tides and the outer—the tides of sea and cosmos. Dedicate yourself to the service of the cosmos.

Meditation 9: The Crowning Experience

As before, cross the bridge, and this time find yourself in the farmhouse at the foot of Bell Head. There is a feeling of settled harmony in the living room, and the Fire of Azrael is laid in the hearth.

Feel the density of the stone walls and the depth of earth beneath you. Light the fire and await the turning of the tide: as the moonlight strikes through the open window, you hear the rustling of the tide on the shingle. Above the fire place is a picture of the enthroned Priest of the Moon sitting between the black and silver pillars, and as the fire burns the smoke rises like incense and the picture becomes a three-dimensional opening out into the seascape, so that the Priest is enthroned on the western horizon and behind him is the vast shape of a woman.

As you sit and witness, the woman comes to shore along the moon path of the water. The tide flows in until it laps into the cottage around the base of the hearth fire, which is not extinguished but burns brighter in the rite of the cosmic earth of the great Goddess who rules both land and sea.

Sit at one with the sea, at one with the fire, at one with the woman.

Feel and see the union of Wilfred and Molly, the union of the deep earth and the sea of stars, and in your witnessing, be the enthroned Priest of the Moon and set a tide of divine creativity free in the world.

To compete the work with Yesod, perform this last ritual.

The Ritual of Yesod— The Culmination

As with the culmination of the work of Malkuth, this simple ceremony completes the work of the sephirah Yesod. Your deepened imaginal sense will combine in magical relationship with the story, in this, the natural home of the imagination.

The ceremony need not take very long, but as always, ensure that you will be free of interruptions and allow time to prepare and to wind down afterwards, to make notes and gently return to the everyday world.

You Will Need:

- Space that you have cleared in preparation and with awareness
- Comfortable seating
- A candle the blue-green of the sea, rising from a bowl of water
- Essential oils of juniper, cedar, and sandalwood, and an oil burner
- Low light in the room—sufficient to read easily
- A copy of *The Sea Priestess*
- Optional: sea salt in a shell

Make yourself comfortable in a clear, clean space in front of the candle: light it with the intent to experience the culmination of the sephirah of Yesod and sit with your spine straight, thinking of the next sphere on the Tree of Life, as represented by the Moon.

Mix together the oils of juniper, cedar, and sandalwood, and light the oil burner.

Perform the preliminary exercises, aligning the body with the central axis and performing the middle pillar exercise. Summon the body of light so that it coincides with the physical body and focus your intent to manifest the energies of Yesod. Around you see a sphere of silver-mauve light spreading until it surrounds the room you sit in, and sense the mysterious ebb and flow of the cosmic tide. Feel safely held, aware of the indigo depths beyond and of the harmony of the universe, and your place in the stars.

Sense the presence of Vivien Le Fay Morgan behind you and, behind her, the Priest of the Moon. Feel the earth and solidity of the room you are sitting in, and invite in the sea and the moon. Let your attention travel to the west, to the great deep where drowned Atlantis waits, and create the connection. Find the plain of basalt beneath you, the circle of black Doric pillars around you and the moon above you.

Slowly, with attention to detail, read the final chapter of the book, with the witnessing part of you aware that you are receiving wisdom from the wellspring of deep connection.

Take your time and hear the final phrase echoing in your ears; feel it sinking into your being as the crucial teaching: "Take up the manhood into Godhood, and bring down the Godhood into manhood and this shall be the day of God with us; for God is made manifest in Nature, and Nature is the self expression of God."[80]

The silver of the moon mingles with the indigo vastness of the universe, permeating your being, and you are simultaneously human and composed of a million stars, with your own unique place in creation and the ongoing unfolding of the universe. The tide of your being ebbs and flows, now physical, now spiritual, constantly in flux and each part feeding the other. You are fluid and take and give for the benefit of yourself and all beings, constantly regenerating as your vital, creative self.

Sit with the energies, for a timeless moment, a still point in the flow: rest in the presence and bless the world.

---

80. Fortune, *The Sea Priestess*, 235.

Slowly this feeling stills, and you absorb the body of light into the depths of the body.

When ready, move on to contemplate the sephirah Tiphareth and the book *The Winged Bull.*

19

Working with Tiphareth and *The Winged Bull*

Number of meditations: 8 + Ritual
Possible time frame: 2–3 months

As before, use the preparatory exercises, and before beginning this sequence perform again the meditation on Lilith, the guide and psychopomp. Let her advise you as to how to begin this stage and build it on the work of Malkuth and Yesod. Be prepared to sit with her and do not be concerned with explicit instructions: connect to a feeling of beauty, harmony, and the wider life, and trust your instincts and intuition.

When you feel ready to embark, you will repeat the first part of the Lilith meditation before every meditation:

You form and step into the body of light and connect to the ancient city of London, walking along the banks of the Thames on a misty evening.

Feel the rhythm of walking into the mist, into mystery and silence …A little way ahead of you, become aware of the figure of a woman with a broad-brimmed hat and a black cloak.

Let yourself follow her—your rhythm matching hers as she leads you onwards, across a bridge to the other side of the river …

Meditation 1: Ted Wandering in London— Malkuth of Tiphareth

Follow Lilith across the bridge and find yourself wandering around London with Ted Murchison, down at heel, hungry and chilly in the dusk. Feel his restlessness and absence of place. Contemplate his brother and sister-in-law, the moralistic vicar, and the censorious vicar's wife. Be aware of the strength and energy of his body and the absence of any direction: feel his rage and resentment.

Let the image and felt experience of Ted in his discomfort of body and mind bring you to the similar places in your own life as you become the wingless, chained bull. Maintain a detached awareness in your body of light as you ask yourself, what frustrates you and makes you feel helpless in the world? From the distance of this safe internal place, allow that image to embody in you and notice the response of your deeper nature. Be aware that, by simply identifying and noticing, you are starting a process of personal change that will free you from the accumulated resentments of your present life.

Let the image of Ted fade, and as you turn and walk back across the bridge, find yourself sitting robed and hooded in the body of light and contemplate the resonances in your body and through your life. When you are ready, consciously let those feelings sink deep within. Allow the presence of your physical self to reestablish its supremacy and rejoin your normal life. Through your awareness, the process of integration has begun.

This meditation need not take long, but it should be pursued for about a week, and with each repetition you will feel a shift that gradually prepares you for the next stage.

Meditation 2: The Underworld Way— Malkuth to Yesod

The Journey to the British Museum

From the bridge, walk in your vision through the misty streets of London, feeling the chained and restless bull within you. Surrender to its energy and let it lead the way past leafy squares and along a row of tall, black railings dripping with fog dew, until you turn into a large gateway.... Find yourself in the huge expanse of the courtyard of the British Museum, seeing its frontage like a Grecian temple with pillars and portico. Let the mist embrace you and watch as it swirls around the pillars. You feel in limbo.

Stepping forward with a sudden resolution, you walk through the pillars. Notice how the mist comes with you into the museum. Feel the dim warmth, and, through the wreathing mist find yourself suddenly encountering the winged bull of Babylon, guardian and gatekeeper of the temple. Feel how the chained bull within you responds as you gaze up at his stern, kind face.

Let the images fade and sit in the body of light, feeling the weight of the pendant over your heart. Contemplate the journey and the challenge, before concluding in the usual way.

Meditation 3: The British Museum— The Temple of Yesod

After the usual preliminary exercises, your accustomed walk over the bridge leads you back into the British Museum, where you have reached an understanding with the gatekeeper, the winged bull. Something in you has answered his challenge, and with a nod of recognition you pass him. You are free to explore, here in the treasure house of images: wander slowly through the galleries, through the pantheons, through Greek and Roman, Celtic, Meso-American, Pacific Islands, Mesopotamian, and Egyptian. You study the gods and as you do so, it is as if they come to life and study you. As they do, you touch the reflection of them within you. You find the quickness of Hermes, the sexuality and beauty of Aphrodite, the potency of Zeus. You come across one section where the gods seem misshapen and unformed, and here too you find reflections of your nature.

You are deeply aware of the chained and wingless bull and the absence of direction. You wander into the Egyptian gallery and your attention is drawn to a fragment. It is a vast, clenched hand of rose-red granite—a hand of power, which you feel emerging out of the mist of the beginning times. In that moment it holds all that you lack, and for a moment the bull within you has wings and feels held in that hand.

Do this for seven days; contemplate the gods and witness them coming to life and contemplating you, and deepen your contact with the hand of power, returning each time in the usual way, back across the bridge, and concluding and grounding.

Meditation 4: The Straight Way to the House of the Sun—Yesod to Tiphareth

After the preliminary exercises and river walk, follow Lilith across the bridge and find yourself again before the hand of power. As you study the huge, ancient red granite, it is as if something ignites within and you hurriedly retrace your steps, through all the corridors, through the great door and down the steps. You step out of the museum straight into a deep and impenetrable fog and stride until you are no longer sure of your bearings. You feel the presence of the winged bull and you spontaneously ask him to open the door to the inner worlds. The darkness ripples, and you feel the winged bull emerging behind you and the presence of the great rose-red arm stretching out and opening the way. You cry, "Rushing with your bull foot come: Evoe, Iacchus! Io Pan, Pan! Io Pan!"

There is a moment of great stillness and then a voice out of the darkness says, "Who is this who calls upon the Great God Pan?"

Respond in whatever way your heart prompts you.

As you do so, the fog thins, and walking towards you is the figure of a man, though for a moment behind him you see the image of a woman wearing a winged-bull pendant. He cannot be seen clearly but comes and offers to guide you through the city to a place where you can rest. Let yourself relax into his guidance, following him from the known places to the unknown, feeling his familiarity and strangeness, for at times he seems to shift into the image of a dark-haired woman. You come at last to a shabby, terraced house with peeling paintwork and dirty windows; above the door is a small niche with a statue of the winged bull. On the threshold your companion turns to you and you see for a moment a man and a woman standing on either side of the door. They invite you to enter.

Pause on the threshold and contemplate the journey before returning to the everyday world in the usual way, writing your report and grounding yourself.

Do this for seven days.

Meditation 5: The House of the Sun— Tiphareth

This meditation is in two parts. You might like to reread the descriptions in chapter 2 of *The Winged Bull* before this work.

Part 1

Follow Lilith across the bridge; the river scene fades as you find yourself again on the threshold. Contemplate the man, the woman, and the winged bull and step through the door. Find yourself in a place of great beauty, bigger inside than outside, a place of clean lines, of books, pictures, and statues; it feels like a meeting place between mundane life and the inner work of a temple space. Take the time to explore it thoroughly.

You realise that you are in the presence of the dark-haired woman who wears a long white robe and carries a lamp. She guides you to a room where you may sleep and rest. As you do so, you have many dreams and learn many things. Do not try to hold on to them, to rationalise or interpret them; maintain an awareness that these dreams are sorting the dissociated, frustrated parts of your psyche, joining and bringing them into harmony with the greater whole. By allowing, the work can happen.

Perform this meditation for seven days and note any progression or shift of feelings in your journal.

Part 2

Your usual walk across the bridge leads straight to your withdrawn sleeping place, where you wake from your sleep. Don a robe of cloth of gold, descend the stairs and find yourself in a circular golden room with an eternal light and a vase of sunflowers on the central altar. There are two thrones, one on either side. The dark-haired woman, now robed in green, sits in one, and you sit in the other. As you take your seat, you feel again the bull within you acquiring wings and purpose, and feel a current of power between you and the woman. She seems like the woods in spring, full of green life, and you feel within you the burning power of the sun. You hear a voice say, "Hekas, hekas, este be-beloi!" and you both rise and step forward to the altar as if obeying the same signal. You drink wine from the same cup, break bread and salt together, and then hold each other's wrists across the altar for a moment. You feel at one with her. This expands into an experience of the sun-power and the earth's green fire and the radiance of the rainbow.

Return in your usual way, withdrawing gently, and sit in stillness and contemplate the union of Ursula and Ted for a time. Then write your report and ground yourself.

Perform this meditation for seven days.

Meditation 6: The Desert Path— Tiphareth to Daath

Once again cross the bridge, to find yourself unlocking the outer door, observed by the winged bull in the niche, and walk up the stairs... Find yourself in the temple of Tiphareth (Brangwyn's house). You walk through the rooms looking for Ursula, but cannot find her. Out of the corner of your eye you seem to glimpse her in mirrors or pictures, but she is nowhere to be found. As you search the house you notice old, shadowy corners, disused rooms filled with junk, and you feel frustrated and disillusioned, helpless again. You come across an old cracked mirror leaning against a wall and look into the images in the fractured surface. Some express your longing for Ursula, the hidden priestess, but in others you see your rage and frustration, your pain and resentment.

You step into the mirror and find yourself in a confusing labyrinth of doors going from room to room, tableau to tableau, glimpsing Ursula in the distance but never finding her. Beside you is Hugo Astley whispering in your ear, trying to distract and pull you from your true search. You keep walking, eventually leaving him behind, and come to the threshold of a door, to find Ursula washing the doorstep.

Pause here and contemplate your journey, then let the images fade and sit with this in your heart. Return to your everyday state and contemplate the journey and the challenge before concluding in the usual way.

Do this for seven days.

Meditation 7: The Place beyond Duality— Daath

Note that although the Christ-energy has always been important to the Western Mystery Tradition, and the Christian story underpins much of the culture of the West, the image of the sacrificed god is key in many ancient cultures. So although Astley's original ritual intention in portraying the cross of crucifixion was specific and blasphemous to Christianity, we engage with it on a higher arc.

All the trappings become irrelevant to our connecting process of collaborating with the necessity for relevant sacrifice shown through all these ancient myths. To imagine ourselves in a cruciform position is to be at our most vulnerable and open—a state we rarely if ever reveal to anyone in the outside world, but a commitment to our wish for true authenticity in our inner state. With this in mind, we enact Ted's cathartic experiences to take us deep into the mystery of mediating and harmonising our fractured self.

After the preliminary exercises, cross the bridge and find yourself confronting Ursula on the doorstep, and feel overwhelming compassion as she kneels there.

You reach out to her but she vanishes, leaving behind the cloth and the bucket, and you squat down and clean the doorstep until all dirt is gone. As you scrub and scrub, feel all your residual frustration flowing into the water, moving through layers of resistance and resentment until all is gone. You wring out the cloth, hang it over the bucket neatly, and step inwards.

The house is a mirror of Brangwyn's house, but a shadow form. The pictures and books are distorted replicas of Brangwyns; pictures that disturb; books that conjure darkness. As you descend more deeply into the house, you come to the basement temple, with a table altar and a black cross.

Astley is waiting and binds you on the cross; there is a moment of dizziness and you descend into unconsciousness. When you emerge Ursula is lying on the table altar before you in a white robe and behind her are a throned billy goat and Astley robed in red and black and gold. There is incense and chanting and the invocation of the Bull without wings. Feel within you the anger and lust of the wingless bull seeking to push its way through. You feel the black cross holding you safely in place and the eyes of Ursula upon you. You hang there with the figures of the redeeming gods from all the ages with you; you are held upon the wheel, hung from the tree, tied upon the cross of matter.

The struggle within you builds to a crescendo until it changes and is released, as all is plunged into darkness. As you let go into that darkness, you feel the presence of Ursula releasing and leading you deeper inward, into a place of perfect stillness where you and she are one and safe. Focus on this place of safety; let it flood through you, relaxing and releasing, as the withdrawn priestess places her cloak around you, warming you.

Conclude as usual, coming back easily across the bridge to your everyday state of awareness: a relaxed, calm transition that allows time for recording the images, sensations, and feelings of witnessing and engaging with mystery. Ground yourself in the usual ways.

Meditation 8: Crowning

Cross the bridge and find yourself free and light, but still searching for Ursula, who once again cannot be found.

Travel the inner landscape of your life seeking the hidden Priestess, lightly and with your new sense of grace and the contained energy now freely available to you. You are drawn backwards in time and to the east, coming to an abandoned farmhouse broken down and decrepit. This is your time to spend repairing it, renewing it, placing within it the experiences of your quest. Tend the garden, clearing round the roses and planting primroses along the path.

And then, as you clear the ivy from the old walls, you find on either side of the door the images of a man and a woman, with a rainbow arch between them. At the keystone of the arch is the winged bull. You pass in through this door and find yourself in a large stone room with a fireplace and a great mirror. Lay and light the fire, clean the mirror, and wait: the priestess will come.

Return in the usual way, bringing back a profound sense of peace. Journal and ground yourself.

The Ritual of Tiphareth

Again, a simple ceremony that will not be overlong will take you deep within to complete this phase of the work. Through reaching down and beyond surface emotion, you connect to the spiritual source within, into the expansion of the contemplation of divine love and acceptance. Check that there will be no interruptions, having set aside time to prepare, work, journal, and gently return to the everyday world.

You Will Need:
- Space cleared in preparation and with awareness
- Comfortable seating
- A gold candle
- Low light in the room—sufficient to read easily
- A copy of *The Winged Bull*
- Optional: frankincense in a burner/a rose in a vase

Make yourself comfortable in a clear, clean space in front of the candle and with a token of the breath of love present—the scent of frankincense oil, a perfumed rose, or whatever seems right to you. Light the candle and sit with your spine straight, thinking of the middle sphere on the Tree of Life in your body: of how it joins and mediates between the higher and lower sephiroth, of how it connects the worlds of spirit and matter.

Summon the body of light so that it coincides with your physical body, formulate the intention to manifest Tiphareth, and around you sense a deep golden light, almost pulsating in its intensity, which spreads and surrounds you with an experience of loving awareness that transcends any physical emotion. Realise that, through consciously connecting to the source of love within, the veil has thinned, allowing you access to the house of the sun, and an understanding of the powerful and potent connectedness that goes beyond polarity and duality.

Keeping this awareness in your mind, gently browse the pages of *The Winged Bull.*

Remain aware of this imaginal space as you riffle through the pages. Read where you will as you pass through the book, with the winged bull present throughout and the characters travelling towards the joining of the animal, human, and spiritual aspects of themselves. Where have their lives and experiences touched yours? Allow that knowledge to blend into the heat of the golden light of beauty that suffuses your space.

Relax completely into the experience of magical reading, and as the scenes become more vivid, turn to the last chapter, and, behind you, build up the image of the man and woman sitting looking into the fire, at peace. Quietly read it aloud to yourself, an internal experience made more potent and real by your lips shaping the words.

As you finish reading, sink into silence with the characters, allowing the image of the winged bull to take flight effortlessly, dissolving your polarised attitudes and transmuting them into a loving acceptance of all that is. The evening sunshine through the windows and the glow of the fire combine to suffuse the room, surrounding you as you connect to both Ted and Ursula, and you feel the wings of spirit enabling your animal instincts and human intellect to soar into a realm of spiritual connection.

The three parts of your being connect, and behind you, the magical light of the room transmutes and you build an image of the rainbow and feel the winged bull soaring effortlessly. Let the presences radiate through you and bring the blessing of the winged bull to the world, for the benefit of all and for the evolutionary current.

As the feeling subsides, you feel the pull of the everyday world, and you return with the profound understanding of the power of beauty and love that connects all things. You allow the body of light to sink back into the physical body.

When you are ready, move on to contemplate Daath and the book *Moon Magic.*

─────20─────
Working with Daath
and *Moon Magic*

This is the culminating book and, in practical terms, the culmination of all our work. The mysterious sephirah Daath is the place where our personal lives touch cosmic life, and as we pursue these exercises we will find that we become more aware of the needs of the world and collective life and able to make the mystery tangible as a presence of catalytic transformation.

It is this tangible presence that the alchemists symbolised in the image of the philosopher's stone.[81] The practices of exploration and union we follow in this chapter open the possibility of creating the stone within us that, as we follow and trust its guiding light, extends its influence through our life and environment.

In this series of meditations we will work with the images of Rupert and Lilith, identifying with each in turn as we engage with the three sections of *Moon Magic*.

In the first section, "A Study in Telepathy," we will identify with Rupert, and in "The Moon Mistress" with Lilith; and in "The Door without a Key" we will address their union and move beyond them.

---

81. A catalytic alchemical substance that turns base metals to gold and confers immortality: it symbolises transformation through enlightenment.

In the meditations, the point of view changes frequently; you are often asked almost simultaneously to be, and also be with, the point-of-view character. This reflects the fluid nature of this story and encourages the freedom and flexibility needed to make new connections—vital to the continuing work.

As we began to sense in the earlier books, it is now clear that as we are reaching inwards, *so there is movement from the deeper, higher sephiroth,* reaching towards us in a two-way flow.

The preparatory meditations remain the same in terms of the relaxation exercises, the middle pillar, and the donning of the body of light, but the bridge meditation is replaced by this:

You find yourself walking along the London Embankment at night, through the mists, feeling the flowing life of the River Thames. As you walk, you become aware of the journey you have made through the paths and the spheres. Across the river you see Cleopatra's Needle and her sphinxes, and for a moment you feel the power of the obelisk and the presence of the Sphinx. You touch the hem of a great mystery and you find yourself before the bridge, crossing the river—not led, but choosing.

As you find yourself on the eastern bank, you are before the church door of Lilith's house. The door is open and just inside and to the left is Lilith with her broad-brimmed hat and black cloak; the cloak is drawn back and we see her rich robes beneath. She holds in her hand a cup shaped like a lotus. To your right on the other side of the door stands Rupert, in a black slouch hat and long black coat, open to reveal the white robe of an Egyptian priest. His hand rests on a bronze dagger thrust into a broad leather belt. Between and behind them is a great mirror, and within the mirror we see the form of a vast veiled goddess. Step onto the threshold of the door and commune with Lilith, Rupert, and the goddess.

This should be used as the entrance meditation for this sequence, and as you step across the threshold you will find yourself moving into each suggested exercise. This threshold meditation is carried out in your normal persona, while the continuing meditations require you to step into the forms of Rupert and Lilith.

Stage 1: A Study in Telepathy— The Journey of Rupert

Before performing the meditation, spend time contemplating the figure of Rupert. Visualise him, get to know him; find the parallels between his life and yours.

Meditation 1: Malkuth

Perform the preparatory exercises and the threshold meditation and then, as you step across the threshold, it is as if you are stepping into the persona of Rupert. Feel his power and achievement; feel his frustration and sense of stuckness. Notice parallels in your life. Contemplate his marriage, his lonely room and the relationship he has with his wife; feel the sense of duty that keeps him chained. Feel his trapped, pacing energy and the sickness of his wife and the union that is not a union. Consider the chains in your life and the things, people, and situations that you are fused with. Bring to mind the experiences of Hugh Paston, Wilfred Maxwell, and Ted Murchison you have already worked on. Let it all come together in this figure of Rupert, in the middle of his life, in the midst of his despair. As before, be aware that, simply with your engaged attention, change will begin to occur.

As the images fade, sit in the body of light and feel the energies and images embody within you, before returning fully and grounding yourself.

Perform this meditation for seven days.

Meditation 2: The Underworld Way, Part 1

Perform the preparatory exercises and the threshold meditation. As you step across the threshold, you are once again with Rupert and the

degree ceremony, feeling the weight of the academic robes that symbolise all of the outer achievements and the inner despair. Strip yourself of the robe, drop the identity, and walk out into the night; stand
on the embankment and contemplate the river, letting your awareness
flow with the river to the sea and surrendering to the deep. As you continue your walk, see the shadowy figure of a woman walking ahead. As
you do so, you bring to mind the dreams of the cloaked woman who
walks ahead of you through land and seascape and you quicken your
steps, but no matter how quickly you walk you cannot catch her up.
You return to your lodgings and look out across the river, where you
see a small church lit up as if for a service. You sleep and dream. Let the
images fade and sit in the body of light; feel the change of identity and
the opening up of the inner path, before returning fully, feeling expansive and relaxed. Do this for seven days.

Meditation 2: The Underworld Way, Part 2

After the preparatory meditations and the threshold meditation, find
yourself, as Rupert, following the woman along the embankment, able
this time to match her fluid speed. This time you follow her across
the bridge, seeing, as you are halfway across, the evening star shining
in the east. You follow her to the threshold of the church and seek to
step inside. She turns and shines her flashlight right into your eyes,
asking you why you have come and denying you entrance. Return to
your room and contemplate the experience. Let the images fade and sit
in the body of light, feeling the challenge of the woman and the sense
of threshold. Return feeling strengthened and grounded. Do this for
seven days.

Meditation 3: Yesod

The preparatory meditations and the threshold meditation lead you
to find yourself sitting in Rupert's room, making the journey now in
vision, walking alongside the plane trees and crossing the bridge. You
strongly visualise the door of Lilith's home, and with an effort of will

you step through, seeing for a moment a beautiful room with a great fire burning and the face of a woman with dark hair and brown eyes.

Let yourself be absorbed in the woman: give your attention and energy to her. After a little while you find yourself moving to another place; you are wandering in an Egyptian temple and find the steps that lead to an underground passage ... Go to the cave with the altar and the image of a vast woman hewn out of the living rock. Pray to her and be still in her presence. Then let the images fade, sit in the body of light, and feel the developing mastery of the inner ways and the sense of Lilith, the Priestess of the Dark Mother. Do this for seven days.

Meditation 4: The Alchemical Path

After the preparatory exercises and the threshold meditation, find yourself in Rupert's clinic room in the midst of outer affairs; feel the strain and struggle of outer life. See and feel the moment when Lilith walks into the room; feel the shock of the union of worlds and opposites and the journey to Lilith's home as she takes charge. Feel the ongoing communion between them and the entrance into the temple of Isis. As Rupert, you sit in an easy chair in front of the fire and allow every muscle in your body to slacken and relax in this enchanted place as you surrender in the place of the priestess.

Let the images fade and sit in the body of light, feeling the crossover of opposites and the exploration of the inner temple. Do this for seven days.

Stage 2: The Moon Mistress—
The Journey of Lilith

As you did with Rupert, spend time reading about Lilith and contemplating her. Feel your relationship with her and the parallels in your own life.

Meditation 1: Malkuth

Do the preparatory exercises and the threshold meditation, and as you step across the threshold, step into the persona of Lilith: become aware of her wish to create a temple and work with a priest in order to bring balance between the sexes and renew the mysteries of the Goddess. Feel her connection to the Dark Isis and her sense of the damage that has been caused by the denial of this great being. Remember with her the work done with Wilfred Maxwell, and bring to mind Ursula Brangwyn and Mona, seeing them as also linked to this deep work of renewal. With Lilith's wider awareness, contemplate Egypt and Atlantis and the work of the inner priesthood. Let her sit within your heart and sit within hers, and feel the deep weave of connection start to form. Let the images fade and sit in the body of light, letting the presence of Lilith and all the priestesses of the books be in your embodied experience.

Return as usual, grounding yourself. Do this for seven days.

Meditation 2: The Underworld Way

Do the preparatory exercises and the threshold meditation, and as you step into Lilith, find yourself driving east in her small black sports car in the dusk: notice the moment when she nearly collides with Rupert, the crossing of the paths, and accompany her to the finding of the church and Meatyard. Contemplate the creation of the church: be with Lilith and Meatyard as they renew it; involve yourself in the creation of the beauty of the living room, the bathroom, and the sleeping quarters.

Let the images fade, sitting in the body of light as you let the sense of the finding of the place of working resonate within you, before returning to the everyday world and writing your report. Do this for seven days.

Meditation 3: Yesod, Part 1

Do the preparatory meditations and the threshold meditation, crossing the threshold to become Lilith. Here, sit as Lilith, and with her, contemplate her dwelling: feel the sense of possibility, which is not yet becoming active. Walk with her in the evening along the wharf side by the dark, flowing water, and notice across the river the figure of Rupert Malcolm pacing in his room. Feel the connection and ignition that happens in the moment of connection, then return with her to the church and sit in meditation: notice the bowl and lilies, the golden fire in the water, and the mist rising, and relax into the presence of Isis.

Let the images fade, sit in the body of light, and feel the presence of Isis before returning fully. Do this for seven days.

Meditation 3: Yesod, Part 2

Do the preparatory meditations and the threshold meditation, crossing the threshold to become Lilith. As Lilith, find and create the eight-sided temple in the belfry. Contemplate the altar, the couch, the black pillar, the silver pillar, and the mirror. Pass through the mirror into the inner temple.

See the avenue of ram-headed sphinxes, and pass through the pylon into the temenos, the sacred enclosure, alongside the lotus pool and into the great hall, with its pillars and veiled Holy of Holies. Be aware of the eternal light hanging from the ceiling and the sarcophagus of Isis in the midst of the hall. Notice the small stairway to the underground temple, and follow it down into the deeps of the earth, coming into the small cave temple with the basalt image of the Dark Isis and the sacrificial altar. Contemplate the Dark Isis and dedicate yourself to her. From time to time you are aware of the astral presence of Rupert in the temple and the cave of the Dark Isis.

Let the images fade; sit in the body of light and feel the establishment of the inner temple and the beginning of the work of Rupert and Lilith. Do this for seven days.

Meditation 4: The Alchemical Path

Be aware of Lilith and accompany her as she travels to Rupert's clinic and confronts him; feel her steely determination and compassion, and notice the effect on both as they meet, after all their previous experiences. Travel with them back to Lilith's home and contemplate the unfolding relationship. Feel her sitting enthroned in the temple, reaching out to him. Be with her as she embraces the form of the lion-headed Sekhmet and creates the circle of fire around them both. Feel him projecting into the house and the inner temple and cave. Contemplate their connection. Consider in turn his presence in the temple, and her conscious projection into his world. Let the images fade; sit in the body of light and feel the process of alchemical fusion, wherein the energy is held safely and the work can continue.

Return to your grounded, everyday state and journal in the usual way.

Stage 3: The Door without a Key— The Joint Journey

Meditation: Tiphareth

Do the usual preparatory exercises and the threshold meditation, but as you step across the threshold, you will be aware of both Rupert and Lilith and this time your point of view will move between them.

In this process you are bringing together the archetypal masculine and feminine in your nature. Thus, find yourself in the upper temple with Rupert and Lilith; he lies on the altar-couch and she is behind him. They both face the mirror. Be aware of the central altar, the twin pillars, and the mirror. Be with Rupert as he sees Lilith in the mirror; be with Lilith as she holds his head. Move flexibly, lightly, and easily between the perspectives until you get a sense of their mutual gaze. As you look, the mirror clouds and the form of a veiled woman is seen in it: she steps through the mirror and gathers them both in her hands, blessing the work that is to come, and responds to the work they both bring before her. As the inner temple opens, we move through it, passing into the Holy of Holies. Old memory of desecration arises and is forgiven by the veiled goddess as Rupert is acknowledged as a servant of Isis. Feel the parallel in your own life, of any old sense of unworthiness falling away, as you pass through the curtain.

Let the images fade; sit in the body of light and let the feelings of the ritual embody within you. Do this for seven days.

Meditation: The Desert Way

Perform the preparatory exercises and the threshold meditation. Find yourself with Rupert and Lilith as they stand on either side of the altar. Feel the sense of the Goddess building up behind Lilith, and see her through Rupert's eyes. Feel and see the temple changing into a vast cave and hear the words of the Goddess: "I am the Veiled Isis of the shadows of the sanctuary. I am she that moveth as a shadow behind the tides of death and birth. I am she that cometh forth by night, and no man seeth my face. I am older than time and forgotten of the gods. No man may look upon my face and live, for in the hour he parteth my veil, he dieth." [82]

Kneel with Rupert and offer your life to the Goddess; sink down and down into the root of life, returning to the Mother, becoming her child. Enter into the stillness that is underneath all sound and motion: give all, receive all. Let the images fade and sit with the stillness and act of offering, before returning, renewed, in the usual gentle stages. Do this for seven days.

Meditation: Daath

Perform the preparatory exercises and the threshold meditation, as before, aligning with both of them and their deep connection with each other.

Find yourself in the temple with Rupert and Lilith, both robed in black: Rupert has a silver nemyss on his head and Lilith is crowned with the moon. Be with them as they stand side by side at the altar, looking between the pillars into the mirror. Feel the energy rise in Rupert as he raises his hands and invokes the Goddess. See the inner temple open in the mirror, and beyond the temple, the ancient cave.

As Lilith moves to stand with her back to the mirror, the Goddess steps into her. As Rupert, you speak for the division between the deep masculine and deep feminine in ourselves and in the world, and receive the blessing of the Goddess. Let the blessing flow through Lilith and Rupert to the whole world. Let the images fade; sit in the body

---

82. Fortune, *Moon Magic*, 145.

of light as the sense of the blessing sinks into your body and, through your body, into your world. Do this for seven days.

Meditation: Crowning Experience

Perform the preparatory exercises and the threshold exercise. Find yourself in the temple with Lilith and Rupert both robed in black and silver, facing each other across the altar. Be with Rupert as he raises his hands and calls up the power from below: descend with him into the deep earth and stand before the vast statue of the Black Isis. Offer yourself as a living sacrifice through which the deep life of the earth may rise. Let the earth-fire rise with you as you return to the temple, feeling rooted in earth and fire.

You raise your hand towards Lilith and project the earth-fire to her. There is a sound of bells and the surging of the sea, and it is as if the blackness of space and the silver fire of the stars flow to meet it. Rupert and Lilith clasp each other's hands, and with them you feel the pulsing of the pillars of the universe, becoming vast—both rooted in the deep sea and earth; both with heads in the stars becoming one, coeval, equal in the living flow of life, making the sacred marriage. They descend then back into the body, letting the power move through human levels, disentangling old distortion as the combined fire flows through the world and through all beings. The work sets in motion a new creation.

Let the images fade; sit in the body of light and feel Rupert and Lilith integrally within you. Feel the divine masculine and feminine finding a new balance within you. Feel the connection to all the priests and priestesses of this work all held within the field of the dark priest and priestess. Receive them into the deepest part of your heart and body and celebrate the marriage in all of your worlds. Feel the richness of understanding permeating your being.

Return slowly and gently, through the body of light and into the everyday world, to note your experiences.

The Ritual of Daath—
The Sacred Marriage

"There is a life behind the personality that uses personalities as masks. There are times when life puts off the mask and deep answers unto deep."[83]

Once again, and this time mediated through this most mysterious portal, you have the opportunity to sink into an appreciation of the sacred marriage within yourself. Allow the magical relationship of story and imagination to gently complete this cycle. As always, ensure that you will be free of interruptions, and allow time to prepare and to wind down afterwards, to make notes and gently return to the everyday world.

You Will Need:
- Space that you have cleared in preparation and with awareness
- Comfortable seating
- A silver candle
- Low light in the room—sufficient to read easily
- A copy of *Moon Magic*
- Lunar incense

Make yourself comfortable in a clear, clean space in front of the candle: light it and the lunar incense with intent and sit with your spine straight. As you focus on the candle, you become aware of a silver mist that gradually fills the room.

Rest in the mystery for a while, then pick up the book; see it as a repository of subtle energy, as are you. Through it runs the current of an esoteric teaching... Put it down gently and allow yourself to slip into a deeper meditative state.

---

83. Fortune, *The Goat-Foot God*, 304.

Behind you, sense the door of the church temple. Lilith and Rupert step forward and place their hands upon you in blessing and support; behind them, sense the mirror, the inner temple, the cave temple, and the Dark Isis.

Slowly and meditatively read the final two chapters of *Moon Magic*, pausing to feel the images and let them pass through you into the world.

Feel deeply the words of the penultimate paragraph, when Lilith and Rupert stand hand in hand, looking into the mirror ...

As you slowly read to the end, be the living threshold, the link between the worlds. Think of the current of Dion Fortune's work alive in the world; its connection to the best of the evolutionary impulse, still about its work of regeneration for society.

Feel all the priests and priestesses you have worked with, and, in a subtle sense, you have joined them, by right of your shared dedication and the work you have done. Feel them being joined by many more about the same work, in a convocation of light that sparks through the supporting silver web of mysterious connection as you hold up the silver candle and bless the world.

Sit with the energies for a timeless moment, and rest in the presence of the company.

Slowly you respond to the pull to return to the everyday, respecting the end of this process that has brought you so far. Give yourself time for reflection, for reviewing all your course notes if you wish. Allow space for the mystery to settle within before you ground yourself thoroughly, with movement, journaling, and walking in nature.

This concludes the course, remembering always ...

> No enunciation of the Truth will ever be complete, no method of
> training will ever be suitable for all temperaments, no one can do
> more than mark out the little plot of Infinity which he intends to
> cultivate, and thrust in the spade, trusting that the soil may even-
> tually be fruitful and free from weeds so far as the bounds he has
> set himself extend. [84]

A blessing on the work.

---

84. Fortune, *Esoteric Orders*, chap. 13.

Conclusion

The purpose of this book has been to examine a central and fundamental formula of Dion Fortune's work exploring the power of story, the Tree of Life. This was then applied in practical work by engaging our will, imagination, and body in an alchemical process of development. The Tree provides a mandala and framework that enables us to direct and deepen this inner process.

These are the fundamental steps of this process:

1. The experience of meeting a turning point in life and becoming available to the possibilities of change.

2. The descent into the body that establishes a connection between our inner and outer worlds: the experience of Malkuth.

3. This opens us to a conscious relationship with our inner world through which our centre of gravity starts to shift inwards: the underworld path.

4. This path takes us to the sphere of Yesod, the place of the foundation and the treasure house of images. Here we start to understand the power of archetypal story and make connection with our inner energies. As we become established in this sphere, we create the foundation for our subsequent inner work.

5. This then begins the journey between Yesod and Tiphareth, the alchemical path. This path involves working with the wheel of resistance called the veil of the temple, formed from the spinning wheel of thought, emotion, and memory that blocks our deeper understanding.

6. As we pierce the veil, we enter Tiphareth, the heart centre of our being, opening us to clarity, balance, and compassion.

7 This radiant presence draws us on to the desert path that leads to Daath, the gateway to the non-dual. This path, as the phrase implies, strips away our prior ways of knowing and being.

8. As we surrender into the path, we encounter Daath, a place of paradox and fusion of opposites that takes us into a new way of being.

9 The crowning experience completing the desert path leads us to Kether, the crown of the Tree. This crowning and integration leads us to touch on the deepest part of our nature. This part is sometimes referred to as *Ipsissimus*, meaning "our own very self."

The process leads us in a spiral back to the beginning, touching it all but on a higher, deeper arc. This is illustrated by the process of the four books, in that having completed the journey through *The Goat-Foot God*, we then begin it again in *The Sea Priestess*, and so on.

There is a great deal more in the books than has been described in this work, so having completed the workbook you will then be in a position to deepen your understanding and practice by returning to the novels. Many new insights will emerge; for example, in terms of further study, you can consider the way the four principal characters studied the path: Hugh Paston studies myth and story, Wilfred Maxwell communes with the moon, Ted Murchison invokes the gatekeeper of the gods, while Rupert Malcolm follows the inner priestess into the heart of the mystery.

Equally, there is much more that can be learned about the Tree of Life and the Qabalah, and if you are called to this, Dion Fortune's *The*

Mystical Qabalah will be of great benefit, as will the works of W. E. Butler.

Principally, the way forward will open step by step as you continue to practice the meditations and exercises and deepen your connection to your own soul.

This, if pursued, will lead you to the inner source of the teachings where, as W. E. Butler once said,

> Our next meeting will be in the lodge, where, beneath the soft radiance of the everburning flame above you, and with the light upon the altar casting its wavering radiance upon the symbols thereon, you will take the Oath of the Mysteries.... The gates stand open; enter into light. [85]

---

85. W. E. Butler, *Apprenticed to Magic*, 105.

Bibliography

Brodie-Innes, J. W. *The Devil's Mistress.* 1915. Reprint, Ramble House, 2009.

Butler, W. E. *Apprenticed to Magic.* 1962. Reprint, London: Aquarian Press, 1990.

———. *Lords of Light.* Rochester, VT: Destiny Books, 1990.

———. *Magic and the Qabalah.* London: Aquarian Press, 1964.

———. *Magic: Its Ritual, Power, and Purpose.* 1952. Reprint, London: Aquarian Press, 1967.

———. *The Magician: His Training and Work.* London: Aquarian Press, 1963.

Du Maurier, George. *Peter Ibbetson.* 1891. Reprint, London: The British Library, 2010.

Firth, Violet M. (Dion Fortune). *The Machinery of the Mind.* 1922. Reprint, York Beach, ME: Samuel Weiser, 1980.

Fortune, Dion. *Avalon of the Heart.* 1934. Reprint, New York: Samuel Weiser, 1971.

———. *The Demon Lover.* York Beach, ME: Samuel Weiser, 1980.

———. *Esoteric Orders and Their Work & The Training and Work of an Initiate.* London: Thorsons, 1987.

———. *The Goat-Foot God.* York Beach, ME: Samuel Weiser, 1999.

———. *The Magical Battle of Britain.* Bradford on Avon, UK: Golden Gates Press, 1993.

————. *Moon Magic.* York Beach, ME: Red Wheel/Weiser LLC, 2003.

————. *The Mystical Qabalah.* San Francisco, CA: Red Wheel/Weiser, 2000.

————. *Psychic Self-Defence.* London: SIL Trading Ltd., 1997.

————. *Sane Occultism.* Wellingborough: Aquarian Press, 1982.

————. *The Sea Priestess.* London: Society of the Inner Light, 1998.

————. *The Secrets of Doctor Taverner.* Wellingborough: Aquarian Press, 1989.

————. *The Winged Bull.* London: SIL Trading Ltd., 1998.

Huysmans, Joris-Karl. *Là-Bas.* 1891. Reprint, New York: Penguin Books, 2002.

Knight, Gareth. *Dion Fortune and the Three Fold Way.* London: SIL Trading Ltd., 2002.

Mason, A. E. W. *The Prisoner in the Opal.* London: Sphere Books, 1974.

Mitchison, Naomi. *The Corn King and the Spring Queen.* Edinburgh: Canongate Classics, 1998.

Parfitt, Will. *The New Kabbalah for Life.* Glastonbury: PS Avalon, 2014.

Regardie, Israel. *The Art of True Healing.* Cheltenham: Helios Book Service, 1964.

————. *The Middle Pillar.* St. Paul, MN: Llewellyn Worldwide, 1998.

Acknowledgments

Thanks, first and foremost, to Dion Fortune, the presiding genius of a magical current that continues to flow unabated and is still relevant today.

To the teachers of the late nineteenth and early twentieth centuries who informed the development of her ideas; to those who still work with the current; and to all personal influences on the path, especially teachers Robert King, W. E. Butler, and Tom Oloman.

To all writers of occult fiction who have introduced magic to their readers, particularly during those fertile decades a century ago, when scientific advances made a proper understanding of it seem so very possible.

And lastly, thanks to all at Llewellyn for their continued enthusiasm, professionalism, and support.

To Write to the Authors

If you wish to contact the authors or would like more information about this book, please write to the authors in care of Llewellyn Worldwide Ltd. and we will forward your request. Both the authors and the publisher appreciate hearing from you and learning of your enjoyment of this book and how it has helped you. Llewellyn Worldwide Ltd. cannot guarantee that every letter written to the authors can be answered, but all will be forwarded. Please write to:

Penny Billington and Ian Rees
⅍ Llewellyn Worldwide
2143 Wooddale Drive
Woodbury, MN 55125-2989

Please enclose a self-addressed stamped envelope for reply,
or $1.00 to cover costs. If outside the U.S.A., enclose
an international postal reply coupon.

Many of Llewellyn's authors have websites with additional information and resources. For more information, please visit our website at http://www.llewellyn.com

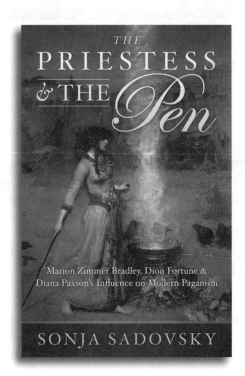

THE
PRIESTESS
& THE Pen

Marion Zimmer Bradley, Dion Fortune &
Diana Paxson's Influence on Modern Paganism

SONJA SADOVSKY

The Priestess & the Pen
Marion Zimmer Bradley, Dion Fortune & Diana Paxson's Influence on Modern Paganism
SONJA SADOVSKY

This important book by debut author Sonja Sadovsky shines new light on how three captivating minds shaped the course of history. The fantasy novels of Dion Fortune, Marion Zimmer Bradley, and Diana L. Paxson influenced the image of the priestess in Neopagan and Goddess-centered spirituality throughout the world. The *Priestess & the Pen* shows how their work changed the way women are depicted in literature, created space for women to reclaim their power, and energized the women's equality movement.

Presenting a reinterpretation of the Goddess as fourfold rather than threefold, *The Priestess & the Pen* adds dimension and relevance to the traditional Triple Goddess archetype in a way that has never before been considered with such compelling clarity. This book is poised to become a vital interpretation of the Pagan priestess.

978-0-7387-3800-0, 240 pp., 5 ³⁄₁₆ x 8   **$16.99**

To order, call 1-877-NEW-WRLD
Prices subject to change without notice
Order at Llewellyn.com 24 hours a day, 7 days a week!

Magical
Qabalah

For Beginners

A Comprehensive Guide to Occult Knowledge

FRATER BARRABBAS

Magical Qabalah for Beginners
A Comprehensive Guide to Occult Knowledge
Frater Barrabbas

Qabalah comes from the Hebrew root *QBL*, which means "to receive or accept instruction." In *Magical Qabalah for Beginners,* Frater Barrabbas instructs the ritual magician and occult student on the history and theory of Qabalah as well as its practical ritual use. Using a combination of Greek philosophy and Jewish occultism, Frater Barrabbas presents the Qabalah in five basic but essential parts, covering the ten sephiroth, the twenty-two paths, the four worlds, the three negative veils, and the Tree of Life.

With practical tools and exercises, Frater Barrabbas shows how to make the Qabalah an important part of any occultist's spiritual and magical practice. Discover the essential tools for systematically incorporating the Qabalah into practical use: tables of correspondence, numerology, acronyms and formula, sigils and ciphers, contemplation, and the theurgy of ascension.

978-0-7387-3244-2, 360 pp., 5³/₁₆ x 8   **$15.99**
